CW00450029

P
6497

The Shape of the New Europe

The European Union and European identity were until recently the objects of separate branches of scholarship and inquiry. With the entry of Central and Eastern European members into the EU, it has become clear that its future can no longer be considered in isolation from the future of European identity. Taking Jürgen Habermas's plea for a European constitution and a normative foundation for the EU as its starting point, this volume brings together the ideas of distinguished scholars in philosophy, political science, sociology, history, law and theology in order to address the shifting relationship between constitutionality, political culture, history and collective identity. The book argues that the future shape of Europe will not only result from external processes of globalisation but from the interaction between these social spheres within Europe.

RALF ROGOWSKI is Reader in Law in the School of Law at the University of Warwick. He is the co-author of *Labour Market Efficiency in the European Union* (1998) and editor of *The European Social Model and Transitional Labour Markets* (forthcoming), *Constitutional Courts in Comparison* (2002), *Civil Law* (1996) and *Challenges to European Legal Scholarship* (1996).

CHARLES TURNER is Senior Lecturer in Sociology in the Department of Sociology at the University of Warwick. He is the author of *Modernity and Politics in the Work of Max Weber* (1992) and co-editor with Robert Fine of *Social Theory after the Holocaust* (2000).

The Shape of the New Europe

Edited by

Ralf Rogowski and Charles Turner

CAMBRIDGE
UNIVERSITY PRESS

CAMBRIDGE UNIVERSITY PRESS
Cambridge, New York, Melbourne, Madrid, Cape Town, Singapore, São Paulo

Cambridge University Press
The Edinburgh Building, Cambridge CB2 2RU, UK

Published in the United States of America by Cambridge University Press,
New York

www.cambridge.org
Information on this title: www.cambridge.org/9780521601085

© Cambridge University Press 2006

This book is in copyright. Subject to statutory exception and to the
provisions of relevant collective licensing agreements, no reproduction of
any part may take place without the written permission of
Cambridge University Press.

First published 2006

Printed in the United Kingdom at the University Press, Cambridge

A catalogue record for this book is available from the British Library

Library of Congress Cataloging-in-Publication data

The Shape of the new Europe / edited by Ralf Rogowski and Charles Turner.
  p. cm.
Includes bibliographical references and index.
ISBN-13: 978-0-521-84128-3 (handback)
ISBN-13: 978-0-521-60108-5 (pbk.)
1. European federation. 2. European Union. 3. Political culture–Europe.
4. Europe–Politics and government–1989- 5. National characteristics,
European. I. Rogowski, Ralf. II. Turner, Charles, 1962- III. Title.

JN15.S4513 2006
341.242′2–dc22

                                              2006029770

ISBN-13 978-0-521-84128-3 hardback
ISBN-10 0-521-84128-3 hardback
ISBN-13 978-0-521-60108-5 paperback
ISBN-10 0-521-60108-8 paperback

Cambridge University Press has no responsibility for the persistence or
accuracy of URLs for external or third-party Internet websites referred to in
this book, and does not guarantee that any content on such websites is, or
will remain, accurate or appropriate.

Contents

Contributors

RALF DAHRENDORF is Research Professor of Social and Political Theory at the Social Science Research Center (WZB) Berlin and a member of the House of Lords.

GERARD DELANTY is Professor of Sociology in the University of Liverpool.

HEIDRUN FRIESE is a Fellow at the UMR CNRS Centre de Recherches Interdisciplinaires sur l'Allemagne, Paris.

JÜRGEN HABERMAS is Emeritus Professor of Philosophy in the Johann-Wolfang-Goethe Universität, Frankfurt.

JOHN A. HALL is James McGill Professor of Sociology at McGill University, Montreal.

RICHARD KEARNEY is Charles B. Seelig Professor in Philosophy at Boston College, Chestnut Hill, Massachusetts.

WILLIAM OUTHWAITE is Professor of Sociology in the University of Sussex.

RICHARD H. ROBERTS is Honary Professor in Residence in the Department of Religious Studies at the University of Stirling.

RALF ROGOWSKI is Reader in Law at Warwick University.

PHILIPPE C. SCHMITTER is Professorial Fellow in the Department of Political and Social Sciences at the European University Institute, Florence.

CHARLES TURNER is Senior Lecturer in Sociology at Warwick University.

PETER WAGNER is Professor of Political and Social Sciences at the European University Institute, Florence.

Acknowledgements

The idea for this book arose out of a conference organised by the editors and held at Warwick University in 2001. For help and support, both at the conference and in the subsequent completion of this project, we would like to thank Jim Beckford, Bernadette Boyle, Robert Fine, Frances Jones, Lisa Mann, Kai Miederer, Lesley Morris, Jiti Nichani, Paola Toninato and Rolando Vazquez.

1   Europe: Law, Politics, History, Culture

Ralf Rogowski and Charles Turner

The enlargement of the European Union (EU) to include ten new states prompted an immediate debate centring on such questions as migration, border controls, labour regulation, the common agricultural policy, the costs of regional subsidies and defence. Such debates are as important as they are inevitable. But enlargement also raised issues that go beyond the agenda of economic, monetary and political integration, issues that concern the limits and integrity of European culture as such. While the accession of Finland, Sweden and Austria during the 1990s increased the size of the EU, membership for the new states which joined in 2004 and for those seeking membership in the future raises questions more profound and far-reaching than those concerning the feasibility of the EU's current decision-making procedures. For most of those new states, membership of the EU is at the same time part of a 'return to Europe' in a broader sense. The fact that some of these states have Slavic populations, that some have immature democratic polities, or large peasant populations, or populations which have for centuries been within the orbit of orthodox Christianity or Islam, raises questions about Europe's internal cultural identity. Such questions have become more sharply focused as a result of the larger geo-political and cultural realignments of which Europe is a part.

To be sure, there is no logical reason why debate about European culture and identity should be dependent upon shifts in geopolitics. But the fact is that the attention of intellectuals has been drawn towards it precisely in times of geopolitical uncertainty. The period between the beginning of the First World War and the formation of the European Coal and Steel Community, for instance, produced many of the more important and profound philosophical and literary reflections on Europe.[1] By contrast, as long as the Cold War division of Europe persisted, little serious work on European identity appeared.[2] It was as though the economic and political barrier that was the Iron Curtain gave rise to a cultural and intellectual barrier of comparable proportions.

Not only did the thoughts of politicians and bureaucrats about the prosperity of Western Europe assume the immovability of this barrier with the East, Western scholars and intellectuals too were, throughout the Cold War, content to have the opportunity for travel, cultural exchange and general curiosity without taking it as much as they might have. The collapse of communism was a cultural as well as a political shock to them, inducing the realisation that they had some catching up to do; a task they were not always able to carry out without assuming that the book of Eastern European cultures had hitherto been closed to them by forces beyond their control.[3] According to this view, Soviet communism was a crude form of modernisation which in Russia had turned millions of peasants into *homo sovieticus* and which had actively suppressed the national traditions of its Eastern European satellite states. The irony of this position was that it overlooked one of the paradoxes of really existing socialism, namely that, as Marx himself would doubtless have observed, chronic economic failure meant that the forces that are most likely to destroy local, specific cultures and identities – rapid and successful economic and technological progress – were held in check. The factories, steelworks and tower block complexes which were strewn across postwar Eastern Europe did not replace but came to exist alongside indigenous art and architecture, religious beliefs and folk traditions. Added to which was an economy in which the individual's prospects of substantial material gain were limited. The consequence of this was that, in what were officially workers' states based upon a philosophy of historical materialism, non-material sources of personal identity – sources which have little to do with one's position in the division of labour or one's career – came to play a more prominent role in the individual's search for meaning or significance than they did and do in the prosperous Western democracies.[4] If it is true, as is often claimed by political sociologists, that Leninist approaches to political and economic conduct survived communism's demise, then it is also true that today in Eastern Europe questions of culture are, still, not as readily reducible to those of economics or politics as they are in the West.[5] This means that the difference between the historical regions of Europe is not merely one between, say, Protestant, Catholic and Orthodox cultures,[6] but between modes of conceptualising the relationship between economics, politics, law and culture. An illustration of this point was provided by the arguments about whether Christianity should be mentioned in a European constitution. These were not so much arguments between the religious and the secular as arguments between those who see the EU as a cultural entity with economic and political characteristics and those who see it as a technical and pragmatic entity with a cultural background. Indeed, one of the reasons why it makes sense to say that EU enlargement is also EU transformation is that the rationale for membership among some of its new members is qualitatively distinct from that of its founders. The original European Coal and Steel Community, later the European Economic Community (EEC), was a political and economic response to the ravages and horrors of war, designed to put an end to war in Europe through shared political goals and sustained economic growth. It was accompanied too by a measure of collective European guilt – German and Italian fascism could be seen as a European failure; the nihilistic consequence of an inflated Promethean ambition – and a willingness to accept a substantial American military and political presence on European soil. The economic success of the original EEC then defined the terms under which subsequent prospective members applied: the goal of greater economic prosperity could be had, with the sacrificing of a measure of sovereignty a price worth paying. By contrast, while it is undeniable that these possibilities play a role in the motivation of today's new members, the economic circumstances of the current EU are much less favourable to their being realised than was the case in the early 1970s or, arguably, the early 1980s.[7] More importantly, for the new EU members, alongside questions of prosperity and security lie those of cultural and geo-political identity. Membership of the EU, as much as that of NATO, is a means of putting behind them the legacy of Soviet imperialism and ensuring a 'return to Europe'. This is no mere symbolic gesture for these countries, but expresses a belief widely held in the former Eastern bloc that there is a basic civilisational distinction between the Russia under whose influence they suffered and the Europe to which they genuinely belong.[8]

It is for this reason that we combine in this volume considerations of a more technocratic or pragmatic type with those concerning European identity and culture. In order to do so it is necessary to specify just how that relationship is to be conceived, and to do so in such a way that the terms in which the volume is conceived make sense to a broad European audience. Such a project faces the difficulty that different versions of this relationship resonate differently in different parts of Europe, and that these differences become more not less palpable with the enlargement of the EU. As long as the Cold War persisted, so one might argue, the distinction between questions concerning the EEC (later the EU) and questions concerning European culture as such could be kept separate from one another in such a way that the relationship between them was, for better or worse, of little intellectual interest. Discussions of the future of the former could and did take place in isolation from discussions of the latter, so that the technocratic-pragmatic agenda of European policy making could remain distinct from that of cultural history. The enlargement of the EU marks a shift in this relationship, not in the sense that the geographical limits of the EU become the limits of the European world, but in the sense that the gap between the meaning of 'Europe' as a set of organisations and institutions and of 'Europe' as a political, civilisational and legal entity has narrowed. As a consequence, the idea that economics, politics and culture are simply branches of a complex division of intellectual labour is difficult to sustain. Sociologists of culture are right to be bored by books about the relationship between the European Commission and the Council of Ministers or comparative studies of social security in five European states, East and West. The suspicion of ignorance or irrelevance that political scientists and economists are prone to direct at books entitled *The Anthropology of Europe* is often justified.[9] If this volume contributes to anything, it will be to overcoming this mutual suspicion.

The reader will see that each of its contributors responds at some point to the ideas set down in Jürgen Habermas's arguments for a European constitution, and may be forgiven for thinking that Habermas's ideas are the focus of the book. But Habermas's writings on Europe raise so many questions and hint at so many agendas that the chapters are arranged in such a way that these ideas are addressed from a variety of angles, so that each section may be read as a way of refocusing the contributions in other sections.

Constitutionality and political participation

In 2003, much publicity was given to the activities of the European Convention and to its remit, the production of a draft EU constitution. The impression was created in some quarters that this marked a decisive new phase in the EU's development, a definitive move towards a single European state. In others it was seen as confirmation that a fully united Europe having the status of a polity was inherent in the European project from its start. This latter view is by no means a Eurosceptic one, for as Joseph Weiler has pointed out, what emerged following the Schuman Plan and the Treaty of Rome in the 1950s was already 'a constitutional legal order the constitutional theory of which has not been worked out, its long-term, transcendent values not sufficiently elaborated'.[10] On this view, Maastricht was shocking precisely because it announced what had always been the case. It was thus 'the beginning of the first truly Europe-wide public constitutional "hearkening" of an act to which the peoples of Europe and its member states had already said, in one way or another, "we will do":[11]

... more than any other concept of European integration, constitutionalism has been the meeting ground of the various disciplines, principally political science, international relations, political economy, law and more recently sociology, which engage, conceptualise, and theorise about, European integration. To understand the intellectual history of constitutionalisation is to understand a goodly chunk of integration studies as a cross-disciplinary endeavour.[12]

We do not aim to trace this intellectual history here; nor are the essays in this volume readily placed under the heading of 'integration studies'. But in responding in some way to Habermas's arguments in favour of a European constitution, they are responding to an essay that is itself positioned in the interdisciplinary meeting ground to which Weiler refers. To be sure, Habermas's arguments, as outlined in Chapter 2 in this volume, are directed towards the idea of a constitution in the American sense, rather than to the attribution of a constitutional status to an existing European Legal Order.[13] But it is worth remembering that his proposal for a constitution as the consolidation of a European legal order – in which human beings are ruled by laws rather than by other human beings – has changed into an account of the political culture of the EU, of its dominant modes of communication, and of its possible legitimacy, a legitimacy which is conceptualised not only according to political criteria such as democratic decision-making and transparency, but also according to social criteria derived from the already existing achievements of the postwar Western European states in welfare, legal rights and personal security.[14] Such achievements would be the basis, moreover, for a European political identity in which there would be no need to resort to the idea of Europe as an 'imagined community', or community of fate (*Schicksalsgemeinschaft*). This is the point of Habermas's repeated emphasis on the idea of a European public sphere and of 'constitutional patriotism', first developed in the context of intra-state affairs.[15]

Such a view is not without its critics. It may be asked, for instance, whether 'Europe' as a political entity can be theorised with tools developed for the purposes of mainstream political sociology. Philippe Schmitter (Chapter 3) argues that the EU is not comparable to a nation-state and that consequently questions of citizenship, representation and decision-making at the EU level require a different set of intellectual responses. First, to seek to constitutionalise an entity whose precise status – federation, confederation, something in between – is unclear may produce unexpected effects. Second, a European constitution cannot be the work of specialists, but may require lengthier processes of consultation than those that preceded the French and Dutch referenda of 2005. To this end Schmitter has set down a set of detailed proposals for a European-wide referendum, the establishment of two parallel constituent assemblies, and a subsequent referendum in which European citizens would be invited to choose between two alternative sets of arrangements. He suggests, therefore, a European polity with two constitutions, one for a core and one for a peripheral set of members, as a viable future arrangement.

Habermas's social theoretical rationale for a European constitution, and Schmitter's proposal for policy-makers, can be contrasted with Larry Siedentop's concerns of the consequences of EU enlargement for political culture in a broader sense. The argument in his *Democracy in Europe*[16] is that the future success of the EU is dependent on the mobilisation of consent and creation of European level legitimacy to an extent that was not the case at the time of the European Coal and Steel Community's inception. Furthermore, the prospects for such mobilisation are hampered by the influence on European policy-making of a French political elite whose instincts are more technocratic than constitutional. Drawing on the experience of federalism in the United States of America, Siedentop argues that there is an intrinsic connection between federalism, self-government and what he calls the 'constitutional sense'. The consequence of the lack of such a constitutional sense in Europe is that the much-vaunted subsidiarity may result less in regional self-government than in a parochial form of regionalism to which the civic traditions built up at the level of nation-states are irrelevant.[17]

Each of these arguments, concerning social legitimacy (Habermas), political democracy (Schmitter) and self-government (Siedentop), are in a way projections onto a larger canvas of arguments developed at the level of intra-state affairs. In one sense, such projections run up against the fact that the EU is, in political terms, a cipher. It has no military power and no tax-raising powers; it has indeed no government comparable to those of its nation-state members. Yet in another sense the key components of the transformation of the EEC into the EU have made such projections inevitable. With the introduction of a political union in 1992, a vision of Europe as a constitutional unity has come to prevail over one of Europe as a community of member states bound by treaties and counter-measures. In particular, the introduction of rights of citizens as a result of negotiations that led to the Maastricht Treaty[18] has helped spawn a discourse of European citizenship in which a language and tradition of thought geared for an understanding of the internal politics of nation-states is asked to make sense of a larger and different entity.

This has had two important consequences. The first is uncertainty about whether the EU can be described as a polity at all. As Philippe Schmitter has acerbically put it:

Try to imagine a polity that did not have the following: a single locus of clearly defined supreme authority; an established and relatively centralised hierarchy of public offices; a predefined and distinctive public sphere of competency within which it can make decisions binding on all; a fixed and contiguous territory over which it exercises authority; a unique recognition by other polities, membership in international organisations and exclusive capacity to conclude international treaties; an overarching identity and symbolic presence for its subjects/citizens, but did have the capability to take decisions, resolve conflicts, produce public goods, coordinate behaviour, generate revenue, incorporate new members, allocate expenditures ... and even declare and wage war![19]

Political science, for all the voluminous literature that it has produced on Europe, has struggled to find the tools with which to define this entity, which is neither purely intergovernmental and therefore not describable in the language of neo-realist international relations, nor yet a supra-national entity describable in the language of neo-functionalism.[20]

The second problem is that even if the EU can be described as a polity, it remains unclear whether it should have a postnational character or that of a nation-state writ large. Habermas's claims, for instance, to have identified a broad, postnational consciousness among the European peoples,[21] a consciousness which would form the core of a European political identity, should be set against Weiler's wariness about the consequences of introducing 'citizenship' into European discourse:

If indeed, the classical vocabulary of citizenship is the vocabulary of the state, the nation and peoplehood, its very introduction into the discourse of European integration is problematic, for it conflicts with one of Europe's articles of faith, encapsulated for decades in the preamble to the treaty of Rome. Mystery, mist and mirrors notwithstanding, one thing has always seemed clear: that the community and Union were about 'laying the foundations of an ever closer union of the peoples of Europe.' Not the creation of one people, but the union of many.[22]

These two questions – that of the character of a European polity and that of whether a European people is possible or desirable – may be treated separately. Yet they converge on a theme, which increasingly forms the (often unacknowledged) core of the current debate on Europe: legitimacy. There are a number of reasons for this: a growing

awareness that the EEC's original rationale – a technocratic and economic response to a political catastrophe – no longer has a hold on the
populations of Europe; the disintegration of Yugoslavia, in the face of
which the EU proved itself unable or unwilling to act; the internal
transformation of the EEC from a set of intergovernmental institutions
with a constitutional character into a union, which increasingly defines
itself explicitly as a legal and political entity; the addition of new
members for whom the cultural and civilisational motives for membership are as strong as economic-pragmatic ones; the decreased capacity
of the EU to meet the latter expectations in any case.

To be sure, among policy-makers in Brussels a technocratic agenda
persists, so much so that it may be argued that whatever normative
justification the EEC might once have had has given way in official
statements to the imperatives of a single currency, the stringencies of the
growth and stability pact, and a legal discourse that is not readily
digestible. The possible legitimacy deficit is implicitly, if comically,
illustrated by the design of the euro currency itself; with concessions to
member state identity being expressed in member-specific coinage
design, the notes proving more recalcitrant, and resort being had not to
the roster of writers and composers who once adorned national
currencies, but to the indeterminate, non-culture specific bridges and
viaducts of a child's architectural fantasy. Lest it be thought that such
remarks belong more to popular commentary than social theoretical
analysis, they illustrate a problem that besets discussions of Europe at all
levels, namely the tension – economic, political, legal, cultural –
between state-specific and supranational sources of identity and
legitimation. For some this is a source of intellectual and political
confusion, for others it implies that, regardless of moves towards
constitutionalisation and monetary union, the EU will remain an *a la
carte* affair, with a range of types of fit between directives and their
implementation, and between aspiration and achievement.

European polity and European civil society

Let us say, then, that we are dealing here with a polity which, while
it is neither a confederation nor a nation-state writ large, is a polity
nonetheless in search of the resources by which it might be legitimated
and justified. Let us say further that one of the most important of
such resources for any polity is its historiography, and with it the stories
it tells about itself. As Heidrun Friese and Peter Wagner point out in
their contribution to this volume (Chapter 4), the legitimation of the
European polity is hampered by the existence of at least three distinct

narratives of European political modernity: narratives of universal human rights, of the modern states system and of democracy. Existing contributions to the debate on European integration often combine an emphasis on two of these narratives with a neglect of the third. The political sociology alternative proposed here is to see existing political arrangements as compromises between different political theories that political science frequently keeps apart. For instance, the postwar Western European settlement was a temporary compromise between liberalism, nationalism and socialism. Taking up Habermas's suggestion about the artificial or constructed character of the European polity, Friese and Wagner push this further by arguing that European integration in the present be seen not as part of an evolutionary process but as requiring an act of foundation; central to which would be a reworking of three sources of justification: political and civil liberties, organised social solidarity and community. Though they hesitate to say so, their resort to the term 'political form' may also be read as a response to the thesis set down by Carl Schmitt, according to which European political modernity could be narrated precisely as a single story, one which would have as its last line the claim that a Europe whose intellectual and spiritual foundations were no longer Catholic was incapable of political form. As Schmitt put it:

Should economic thinking succeed in realising its utopian goal and in bringing about an absolutely unpolitical condition of human society, the Church would remain the only agency of political thinking and political form.[23]

Friese and Wagner's contribution reminds us that there are several varieties of modernity, and several attendant stories to be told, a plurality on which the Schmittian narrative runs aground. Much of the current debate over Europe revolves around the question of whether any act of foundation for Europe runs aground for the same reasons.

At the same time, the bases for the political legitimacy of a European polity – political and civil liberties, organised social solidarity and community – are themselves already of a social nature, and remind us of the importance of civil society as the arena in which legitimacy will be either maintained or challenged in the future. And William Outhwaite (Chapter 5) concludes from this that civil society may be as much a condition for European integration as something that grows out of it. Noting the relative absence of anything that can be described as a European cultural (as opposed to political) elite, and the absence of a corresponding European culture of *consensus*, he suggests that the future of European integration and ultimately the legitimacy of European political institutions may depend upon the manner in which *conflicts* between European-wide civil society organisations can emerge and be resolved.

European history and European culture

Yet the deepening and extension of political science and political sociology goes only so far. In one of the best essays on the future of Europe, Tony Judt has written:

> Just as an obsession with growth has left a moral vacuum at the heart of some modern nations, so the abstract, materialist quality of the idea of Europe is proving insufficient to legitimate its own institutions and retain popular confidence. The mere objective of unification is not enough to capture the imagination and allegiance of those left behind by change, the more so in that it is no longer accompanied by a convincing promise of indefinitely extended well-being.[24]

If debates among policy-makers and constitutional theorists need to be supplemented and sometimes regrounded by a political sociology of Europe, EU expansion invites the further supplementation of political sociology by historical/cultural sociology and civilisational analysis. To be sure, such a move cannot wholly dispel current anxieties about cultural stereotyping or combat a popular academic wariness towards substantive generalisations about how different societies hold together. The belief in common, shared elements of human culture across societies is the product of a healthy impulse, just as the invocation of cultural difference can be a ready tool in the hands of xenophobes. Yet it would be a bleak prospect if the search for European legitimation were to stop short at deracinated blueprints for human rights legislation, welfare arrangements and labour protection, important though these are, and if the voice of substantive European cultural achievement were to be wholly silenced.

The problem here is to specify cultural achievements, which could act as a source of legitimacy, while avoiding a language of aggressive self-assertion. Habermas and Weiler are understandably wary of any theory of Europe that conceptualises Europe as a community of fate. Yet as Judt suggests, a Europe that has lost some of its forward-looking vitality and whose current growth rates are low is bound to draw upon elements of its heritage for making sense of itself. This means that historical arguments about the legitimacy of a European polity may be pushed further than Habermas does, even in the face of the apparent shattering of everything worthy of the term 'European achievement' in two world wars.

Yet the undoubted success of the EEC and later EU, our historical distance from the wars from which it arose, the geographical expansion of the EU eastwards to encompass many more of the locations at which, at different times and for different purposes, Asia has been said to begin, the realisation or the assertion that Europe is the Westward extension of the Asian landmass,[25] and the increasing political pertinence of questions of cultural identity, make the need for reflection on specifically European cultural achievement hard to avoid. This is all the more so in view of the fact that, as Gerard Delanty points out (Chapter 7), should a further wave of enlargement take place, it will do so in the context of a civilisational encounter between the EU countries and the candidate countries, which will be if anything sharper than that which took place between the existing fifteen and the ten new members in 2004.

How far can a civilisational perspective be taken? The later contributions in this volume offer different answers. John A. Hall (Chapter 6), in tracing the history of the relationship between great imperial powers and small states, asks in his contribution to this volume the provocative question: 'given enlargement, can the EU become a successful Austro-Hungary?' He concludes that there are grounds for treating the EU as a different entity altogether, namely a capitalist state, and that this has serious implications for the prospects of 'ever closer union'. Hall's perspective is inspired by Gellnerian assumptions and so does not push civilisational analysis as far as some sociologists of culture might.

Gerard Delanty has fewer inhibitions, arguing that the enlargement of the EU transfigures the very character of European integration. In contrast to a nation-state centred approach and the vagueness of globalisation theory, he adopts a perspective drawn from the analysis of civilisations found in the writings of Weber, Elias and Eisenstadt. Distinguishing between three 'civilisational constellations', namely the Occidental Christian, the Byzantine-Slavic and the Ottoman Islamic, he argues that a confrontation between the fragments of these civilisations might lead to a European identity that is not trapped between instrumental systemic steering mechanisms and ethnic paricularism at the level of lifeworlds.

If such cultural analysis reframes historical sociology, then Richard Roberts (Chapter 8) offers an account of Europe's spiritual foundations, which takes the argument to another dimension altogether. Taking up the theme of 'the souls of Europe', he identifies a dialectic of aggression at the heart of most analyses of European modernity and a strategy of 'accommodation to modernity' in writings from

Troeltsch to Spengler. He concludes, however, that a reconfiguration of the 'European religious field', centred on neo-Pagan, New Age and Celticist movements, hints at a significant shift away from the dialectic of aggression and at a possible alternative vision of European legitimacy.

Richard Kearney (Chapter 9) offers a specific example of integration at work on a smaller scale. The 1998 Good Friday Agreement in Ireland is seen as a test case for the kinds of experiments that the sharing of sovereignty involves. The basis for a European citizenship must, Kearney argues, be a recognition that shared narratives and symbols are as important as a shared legal framework, and that culture and law be seen as mutually reinforcing. He illustrates this thesis with an account of the history of the relationship between the indigenous and settler populations on the island of Ireland, the link between this and changing conceptions of sovereignty, and seeks to show that both British and Irish national identity are dependent upon and grow directly out of this encounter, which moves both in the direction of a postnationalist identity.

The European cultural turn

In view of these ideas, what European cultural achievements could serve as a source of legitimation for a future European polity? The debates on the cultural foundations of European identity *per se*, which have rumbled along as an intellectual sideshow since well before the Second World War, are a tempting source of ideas. Take, for instance, one of the most neglected yet pregnant accounts, from a speech given by Max Scheler in Vienna in 1917:

In our federal form of political articulation, which for a long time has withdrawn from the individual state the property of sovereignty, we Germans and the Swiss have, constitutionally speaking, at least the beginnings of a great example showing how the genuine freedom of smaller historical regional and political units can in all things co-exist with the centralising technical necessities of modern industry and even of an overall imperial economy. Let us hope that this kind of community will become a model for Christian Europe in the coming age! For ... it is in the constitution of a federal state that the Christian idea of community is most present today.[26]

Thirty years later, in the aftermath of the Second World War, T. S. Eliot expressed a less overtly Christian vision but one which also accorded a foundational status to culture:

No political and economic organisation, however much goodwill it commands, can supply what cultural unity gives. If we dissipate or throw away our common patrimony of culture, then all the organisation and planning of the most ingenious minds will not help us, or bring us closer together.[27]

Today such boldness of formulation is rare, voices of this sort less prominent than they once were – Eliot's address ends, for instance, with an appeal to 'the men of letters of Europe' – and the hesitancy about what constitutes European cultural identity is manifest in the arguments surrounding the respective weight to be accorded to Christianity, classical culture, Roman law and the enlightenment in the preamble to the European Constitutional Treaty. European unity has become a dull topic, efforts to specify what it consists in constantly running up against their own parochialism. A source of European legitimacy seems even more elusive. It is here that the contribution of Ralf Dahrendorf (Chapter 10) becomes important. While he does not formulate the question of Europe directly in terms of legitimation processes, he makes it clear that the goal of European unity carries with it no clear normative weight of its own, and that it may even be achieved at the cost of a neglect of such questions. Hence his argument that Europe should seek to maintain and nurture its core achievement, what he calls 'openness', regardless of whether it is united.

In the concluding section we take up this theme of cultural achievements, and point, with caution, to one in particular – the separation of religion and politics – which has some affinities to Dahrendorf's idea of an open Europe. It has its origins in a specific cultural-civilisational complex but is general enough to be defensible as the basis for the delicate balance between freedom and security, which characterises the political culture that Europeans have come to understand and inhabit. Geopolitical conflict has recently been interpreted as a clash between the secular West (Europe and America) and societies in which religion plays a more prominent role in public life. But the truth about Europe is more complex. Within what was once Latin Christendom, for whatever reasons and through whatever concatenation of circumstance, there emerged a distinction between religious and secular authority, the subsequent further differentiation of a secular political authority capable of grounding itself, and a variety of forms of accommodation between church and state, and between religious denominations. A simple observation perhaps, but one that can be made central to an understanding of what it was that Eastern Europe freed itself from and what it has now embraced, an understanding which remains elusive when we frame our discussions through terms such as 'capitalist' and 'non-capitalist,' 'democratic' and 'non-democratic'.

Consider the claim that Western Europe had maintained its identity throughout the Cold War through a contrast with 'godless communism', or that communism was the result of pushing to its atheistic limits wholly secular principles of the European enlightenment. The claim is paradoxical because it has also been argued that communism in practice owed much to a specifically Russian Orthodox Caesaro-Papist tradition, in which the specifically Western (Catholic and post-Reformation) separation of secular and sacred authority had never gained a foothold. The godlessness of communism would then be the expression not so much of extreme European secularism (the enlightenment pushed to its limits) as of the unimaginability of a world in which religious belief and secular authority might co-exist, the consequence being that secular authority relied upon practices which were themselves rooted in existing religious traditions.[28]

This is important because it suggests that the opposition to communism in the Soviet Union's satellite states, and the desire to 'return to Europe' which accompanied it, was not simply something driven by a logic of 'freedom' for marginalised or suppressed activities and groups, a freedom conceptualised in universal terms, but was also a struggle to extricate oneself from the orbit of one civilisation and join, or rejoin, another. The struggle against communism was, for many Eastern European dissidents, an anti-colonial affair to be sure, but it was neither a struggle between national self-assertion and a metropolitan centre, nor between the universal principles of market economics and the universal principles of Leninism, but one between a clearly identifiable (and identifiable with) civilisation in which religious and secular were distinct, and a clearly identifiable civilisation in which they were not and in which it could not.[29]

It might be argued that much of this vision has been diluted or even lost since 1989, yet there is little point in championing the EU and its enlargement without some reference to the achievements that legitimate it. At the same time this needs to be done with caution. Switzerland and Norway are no less European for not having joined the EU, nor would the nation-states of Eastern Europe be less European had they decided that sustainable market economy and stable democracy were best pursued outside the EU for another five or ten years. Yet join it they have, and among the many meanings of their having done so is that of having set an organisational seal upon the separation of religion and politics, the rejection of theocracy or its modern ideological equivalent, and the endorsement of a culture of critical self-reflection and intellectual curiosity, which can only flourish under such conditions.[30] A productive balance between religion and politics within a secular state as a formula perhaps lacks elegance, but it describes reasonably accurately a general rationale for the type of societies which European societies have become.

Yet as the EU expands it will inevitably face the prospect of membership from countries with distinctly different traditions of practices. The most obvious cases are Russia and Turkey, the latter having been a secular state for most of the twentieth century but only at the expense of the society's domination by a military elite and a business oligarchy. It is not, then, for purely geographical reasons that commentators refer to 'the European parts' of both countries. Russia and Turkey are neither a threat to Europe nor culturally inferior to it. However, they are, because of the continuities of their traditions of practices, a civilisational challenge. And they will invite reflection on Europe's own cultural achievements, which take us beyond the question of secular political authority into more profound dimensions of cultural identity, towards the question of what it means to be European and what types of human being we expect the future inhabitants of Europe to be. Despite the tensions between Europe and the Islamic world, which have found their way into the media spotlight in recent years, Europe does not yet have to face up to the question of its core values; a European essence if you will. That time may well come, especially if those pragmatic historical achievements to which we have alluded prove weak under pressure. Bold accounts along these lines are rare today; rarer than they were in the interwar period.

One exception is the essay by Remi Brague, who has sought to define the core of the European tradition, and in so doing hinted at an alternative to, or modification of, the Habermas–Weiler image of core European values of rationality, human rights and democracy as sources of legitimacy. It is perhaps no surprise that, like his interwar predecessors, Brague is a Catholic, but the importance of his work is that, while it identifies Europe historically with Latin Christendom, it takes the account of European identity beyond both the image of a European enlightenment 'project' and that of 'Catholic Europe'. Brague's argument is that Latin Christendom is distinguished from Byzantine and Islamic culture by the fact that it has been defined from the outset by what he calls its eccentricity, by a readiness to derive the sources of its identity from outside itself. European culture is much less self-contained than we are inclined to assume, and has since Roman Christianity drawn upon the dual heritage of Jerusalem and Athens:

... unlike Byzantium, Europe has not been able to perdure through the continuity of a language that had been the support of a very great literature, in peaceable possession of a classical heritage that assured it the feeling of cultural superiority. Nor, like the Muslim world, has it been able to compensate for its initial dependence on exterior sources through the impression of ennobling or enlarging the knowledge it inherited in making it attain the language chosen by God for His ultimately unadulterated message and by diffusing it over the territory His definitive religion covered. Europe, therefore, had to confront a consciousness of having borrowed, without hope of restitution, from a source that it could neither regain nor surpass.[31]

In contrast to the image of a series of 'breakthroughs' to the modern world via reformation, enlightenment or renaissance, or through the industrial and scientific revolutions, Brague argues that the germs of such developments were already contained within Latin Christendom itself, an eccentric culture that distinguished itself through its awareness of and dependence upon what it was not. The details of his account are less important than the conclusion he draws about the distinction between Islamic and European cultural identity, namely that:

...Islamic civilisation, in contrast to Europe, has hardly dreamed of using its knowledge of the foreign as an instrument that would permit it, through comparison and distancing in relation to itself, to understand itself by becoming conscious of the non-obvious character of its cultural practices.[32]

'The non-obvious character of its cultural practices'. If one were searching for a brief formula for the distinctive cultural achievement that might legitimate the cultural background of a European polity, act as a pole of attraction for the 'return to Europe' and define the core values of Europe's future, it would be hard to imagine anything more felicitous. For what Brague points to is something that might take the debate over Europe beyond the alternatives of universalist rationalism and cultural relativism, enlightenment and romanticism, *Gesellschaft* and *Gemeinschaft*, towards an idea of Europe as a set of attitudes and procedures, which are characterised by their irreducibility to any essence, of a series of intellectual and political processes premised upon the refusal of self-evidence, upon contingency and endless self-reflection. Beyond the gradual emergence of secular states in which the relationship between religion and politics has scope for considerable variation, it is precisely Europe's endless critical reflection upon itself that lies at the heart of European identity.[33] Moreover, it is the manner in which Europeans have reflected upon their identity which has continued to confirm them as members of an eccentric culture. Nowhere is this more starkly reflected than in the relationship between Europe and its classical heritage, a heritage which Europeans allude to as somehow their own yet which is external to them:

> As the sources of European culture are not 'us', nothing invites us to restrain their study to the occidentals that we are. Thus, the distance between us and the ancient Greeks is not, in principle, less than that which separates them from other modern cultures. For the modern European to appropriate them to himself he would require a disappropriation of himself that is fundamentally just as great as it would be for an African or Chinese. In this way, to study the classics is in no way to Occidentalise oneself.[34]

> I will say therefore to Europeans: 'You don't exist!' There are no Europeans. Europe is a culture. Now, culture is a work on oneself by oneself, an effort to assimilate what goes beyond the individual. In consequence, it cannot be inherited. On the contrary, it must be conquered in each. One cannot be born European, but one can work to become one.[35]

Culture as a work on oneself by oneself; this working on oneself as a distinctively European characteristic. If Brague is right, it suggests an image of Europeanness in which the voices of Max Weber, Hans Blumenberg, Michel Foucault and Richard Rorty exist alongside that of Habermas, one in which working on oneself takes place not for the sake of an identifiable-but-unfinished project but in the name of the infinite, never-ending task of self-questioning. Alongside the written constitution that Europeans may or may not ratify, Europe possesses, if it cares to reflect upon itself, the virtue of the continually renewable act of self-constitution.[36]

It goes without saying that EU commissioners and officials perhaps do not see themselves in quite these terms, and that the expression 'ever closer union' appears to imply a process with an end. We have also been reminded by Joseph Weiler that 'what Europe needs ... is not a constitution but an ethos and a *telos* to justify, if they can, the constitutional order it has already embraced'.[37] Yet many argue that the EU is an order *sui generis* whose final form is, as Schmitter has pointed out, uncertain enough to make talk of a final form premature, that there is no European people, no European *demos*, no European identity save that which is non-obvious and provisional. Might we not say, then, that for all the criticism levelled at it – its democratic deficit, faceless bureaucracy and waste – the EU embodies a quintessentially European principle as readily as any of its member states, working on itself to fashion something that defies our efforts to grasp it through familiar categories or to see it as something self-evident? Democracy, parliament, separation of powers, fiscal policy, defence policy, a constitution, the familiar apparatus of both popular and scholarly literature on the politics of modern states, are after all rendered non-obvious by the manner in which the EU conducts its business.

It may even be that the EU's notorious democratic deficit is a strength as well as a weakness. For as long as there is no European *demos* there is no constitutive power that grants familiar democratic authority to decision-making at a European level. Therefore, to strengthen the powers of the European parliament would be to strengthen the powers of an entity that lacks the legitimacy that would be claimed for it. As things stand, while the democratic deficit remains, political communication at the European level, while it does not meet the standards of the argumentative redemption of validity claims or the force of the better argument, does manage to preserve some of the features of an older European tradition: diplomacy, tact, ritual, compromise, negotiation and, yes, deals done behind closed doors. Yet together, as Weiler points out, they have been the accoutrements of a world of contingent and provisional but positive outcomes:

Constitutional actors in the member states accept the European constitutional discipline not because as a matter of legal doctrine ... They accept it as an autonomous voluntary act, endlessly renewed on each occasion ... When acceptance and subordination is voluntary, and repeatedly so, it constitutes an act of liberty and emancipation from the collective self-arrogance and constitutional fetishism: a high expression of constitutional tolerance.[38]

As a description of the ethos of the EU, this could hardly be bettered.

Notes

1 See for instance, Coudenhove-Kalergi 1943; Dawson 1932; Eliot 1947; Husserl 1970; Scheler 1960.
2 The majority of philosophical-cultural reflection in the 1980s, for instance, was directed specifically towards the concept of Central Europe. See Garton Ash 1989; Kundera 1984.
3 An implicit admission of this failure is contained in Enno Rudolph's astonishing claim that: 'We [in 2001] are witnessing an encounter of traditions, world views, religious and linguistic contexts, which hitherto knew nothing of each other or indeed stood in hostile competition to one another. Europe has to be seen to be European...' in Cerutti and Rudolph 2001, pp. 2–3.
4 As soon as one poses the question of resources for individual identity construction, the well-known 'convergence' thesis of Clark Kerr and the industrial society theorists of the 1950s becomes irrelevant. For however true it is that the economies of both Western and Eastern Europe were industrial, and that central to both was the management of enterprises,

the relationship between economic and non-economic conduct remained very different. One index of this was that, in their descriptions of the West, both party ideologues and dissident intellectual opponents made use of a category more at home in the rhetoric of nineteenth-century cultural conservatives: 'decadence'. When communism collapsed, the moral, anti-political critique characteristic of Vaclav Havel directed at the old regime became readily transferable to the starker features of the commercialism which replaced it in Eastern Europe's capital cities.

5 For a stark illustration of this, compare the tone and feel of the Polish Ministry of Culture website (http://www.mk.gov.pl) with that of the British Department of Culture, Media and Sport (http://www.culture.gov.uk). See also the numerous Western European, and especially British, publications now devoted to the intertwining of culture and economics, to the new cultural economy, and so on.

6 See Szücs 1988.

7 See Judt 1997, ch. 3.

8 This idea of a 'return to Europe', which emerged in Central Europe in the 1980s, is driven by a politics of recognition, according to which Soviet communism was a parenthetic phase which distorted a properly European cultural and political trajectory. For a forceful version of this thesis, see Vajda 1988. For a subtle and nuanced account of European and Russian identity see Milosz 1968. The idea of a 'return to Europe' differs profoundly from the slip of the tongue common among Western European commentators, in which the enlargement of the EU becomes the 'expansion of Europe'.

9 See Goddard et al. 1994.

10 Weiler 1999, p. 8.

11 Ibid.

12 Ibid., p. 224.

13 The difference is made obvious by the size of the respective documents.

14 Habermas 1998, in particular p. 119; and Habermas 2001, in particular p. 101.

15 On the public sphere see Habermas 1989. On constitutional patriotism see Habermas 1998, pp. 118–19 and Habermas 1996, pp. 465–6, 499–500, 507. For a critique of the application of constitutional patriotism to European affairs see Turner 2004.

16 Siedentop 2000.

17 Ibid., in particular ch. 5.

18 'Citizenship of the Union is hereby established. Every person holding the nationality of a Member state shall be a citizen of the Union.' Art. 8 (1) (now Art 17 (1)) EC Treaty.

19 Schmitter 1996, p. 131.

20 Schmitter himself has shown (ibid, pp. 133–6) how, with the help of some simple but judicious variables – in this case two: the arrangements between what he calls the EU's territorial constituencies and its functional constituencies – one can generate four ideal typical forms of polity, depending on whether or not the territorial integrity of states is maintained and whether or not functional interests are represented via national or

transnational bodies. He gives Latin names to each arrangement: *confederatio, federatio, consortio* and *condominio*. The important point here is that the EU is the evolving product of contingent negotiation and policy-making in a way in which no nation-state is, and that therefore it may develop in any one of these directions. But Schmitter's point is that the social sciences generally remain ill-equipped to deal conceptually with large-scale social processes of this sort. In the case of the EU a particular temptation is to seek to overcome the descriptive difficulty by simply adopting the terminology of Euro-speak employed by the technocrats and negotiators in Brussels, on the grounds that this language, however abstruse, is real in its effects. For a classic critique of this way of doing political science, see Voegelin 1952.

21 Habermas 1996, pp. 119–20.

22 Weiler 1998, p. 327.

23 Schmitt 1996, p. 25.

24 Judt 1997, pp. 117–18. In his more recent book (Judt 2005) he implies in the last chapter a connection between this lack of a sense of infinite growth and the emergence of a culture of commemoration. The unhealthy obsession with the past exacerbates the difficulty of grasping the future.

25 See especially Pocock 1997, pp. 297–317.

26 Scheler 1960, p. 386.

27 Eliot 1947, p. 123. Eliot's essay, 'The Unity of European Culture' was first delivered as three radio talks in German and published separately in German in 1946 as *Die Einheit der europäischen Kultur*.

28 See Kharkhordin 1999.

29 On Leninism as a civilisation see Jowitt 1992.

30 In the light of recent disputes over freedom of religious expression in Germany, France and Britain that may appear premature. In terms of the analysis set down here, these three states, though they have very different arrangements between religion and the state, do belong to the same non-theocratic civilisation. Hence the presence of an established national church in England does not preclude a national government's open endorsement of 'faith' schools, just as secular French republicanism does not preclude the proper upkeep of its cathedrals as part of national heritage. Though it should be added that official resistance to religious symbolism in French schools has brought to the fore what might be called secular theocratic attitudes within the ranks of French republicans.

31 Brague 2002, p. 99.

32 Ibid, p. 112.

33 In this sense Derrida's 'deconstruction' of the 'idea of the European idea' forms a necessary part of Europe's process of self-identification and critical reflection upon its own identity. See Derrida 1992.

34 Brague 2002, p. 142.

35 Ibid., pp. 148–9.

36 See Plessner 1987.

37 Weiler 1996, p. 106.

38 Weiler 2001, p. 53.

References

Brague, Remi, [1992] 2002, *Eccentric Culture. A Theory of Western Civilisation.* South Bend, IN: St Augustine's Press.

Cerutti, Furio and Enno Rudolph (eds.), 2001, *A Soul for Europe.* 2 vols. Leuven: Peeters.

Coudenhove-Kalergi, Richard Nicolaus Graf von, 1943, *Crusade for Pan-Europe. Autobiography of a Man and a Movement.* New York: Putnam.

Dawson, Christopher, 1932, *The Making of Europe.* London: Sheed and Ward.

Derrida, Jacques, 1992, *The Other Heading. Reflections on Today's Europe.* Bloomington, IN: Indiana University Press.

Eliot, T. S., 1946, *Die Einheit der europäischen Kultur.* Berlin: Habel Verlagsbuchhandlung.

1947, 'The Unity of European Culture', in *Notes Towards a Definition of Culture.* London: Faber.

Garton Ash, Timothy, 1989, 'Does Central Europe Exist?', in Timothy Garton Ash, *The Uses of Adversity.* Cambridge: Granta pp. 161–91.

Goddard, Victoria A., Josep R. Llobera, and Chris Shore (eds.), 1994, *The Anthropology of Europe.* Oxford: Berg.

Habermas, Jürgen, [1962] 1989, *The Structural Transformation of the Public Sphere. An Inquiry into a Category of Bourgeois Society.* Cambridge, MA: MIT Press.

[1992] 1996, *Between Facts and Norms. Contributions to a Discourse Theory of Law and Democracy.* Cambridge, MA: MIT Press.

[1996] 1998, *The Inclusion of the Other.* Cambridge, MA: MIT Press

[1998] 2001, *The Postnational Constellation.* Cambridge, MA: MIT Press.

Husserl, Edmund, [1938] 1970, *The Crisis of the European Sciences and Transcendental Philosophy.* Evanston, IL: Northwestern University Press.

Jowitt, Kenneth, 1992, *New World Disorder.* Berkeley, CA: University of California Press.

Kundera, Milan, 1984, 'The Tragedy of Central Europe', *New York Review of Books,* 26 April, 33–8.

Kharkhordin, Oleg, 1999, *The Collective and the Individual in Russia: A Study of Practices.* Berkeley, CA: University of California Press.

Judt, Tony, 1997, *A Grand Illusion.* London: Penguin.

2005, *Postwar. A History of Europe since 1945.* London: Heinemann.

Miłosz, Czesław, 1968, *Native Realm.* New York: Doubleday.

Plessner, Helmuth, 1987, 'Macht und menschliche Natur', in Helmuth Plessner, *Gesammelte Schriften V.* Frankfurt: Suhrkamp, pp. 135–234.

Pocock, J. G. A., 1997, 'Deconstructing Europe', in Peter Gowan and Perry Anderson (eds.), *The Question of Europe,* London: Verso, pp. 297–317.

Scheler, Max, 1960, *On the Eternal in Man.* London: S.C.M. Press.

Schmitt, Carl, [1923] 1996, *Roman Catholicism and Political Form.* London: Greenwood Press.

Schmitter, Philippe, 1996, 'Imagining the Future of the Euro-Polity', in Gary Marks, Fritz Scharpf, Philippe Schmitter and Wolfgang Streeck, *Governance in the European Union,* London: SAGE, pp. 121–50.

Siedentop, Larry, 2000, *Democracy in Europe*. London: Allen Lane.

Szűcs, Jenő, 1988, 'The Three Historical Regions of Europe', in John Keane (ed.), *Civil Society and the State*. London: Verso, 291–332.

Turner, Charles, 2004, 'Jürgen Habermas: European or German?', *European Journal of Political Theory*, Vol. **3** (3), pp. 293–314.

Vajda, Mihaly, 1988, 'East-Central European Perspectives', in John Keane (ed.), *Civil Society and the State*. London: Verso, pp. 333–60.

Voegelin, Eric, 1952, *The New Science of Politics*. Chicago, IL: University of Chicago Press.

Weiler, Joseph, 1999, *A Constitution for Europe*. Cambridge: Cambridge University Press.

1996, 'European Neo-constitutionalism: in Search of Foundations for the European Constitutional Order', *Political Studies*, Vol. **44**, pp. 517–33.

1999, *A Constitution for Europe*. Cambridge: Cambridge University Press.

2001, 'European Democracy and the Principle of Toleration: The Soul of Europe', in Furio Cerutti and Enno Rudolph (eds.), *A Soul for Europe*, Vol. I. Leuven: Peeters, pp. 33–54.

Part I

Constitutionality and Political Participation

2   Why Europe Needs a Constitution

Jürgen Habermas

There is a remarkable contrast between the expectations and demands of those who pushed for European unification immediately after the Second World War, and those who contemplate the continuation of this project today — at the very least, a striking difference in rhetoric and ostensible aim. While the first generation advocates of European integration did not hesitate to speak of the project they had in mind as a 'United States of Europe', evoking the example of the USA, current discussion has moved away from the model of a federal state, avoiding even the term 'federation'.[1] Larry Siedentop's recent book *Democracy in Europe* expresses a more cautious mood:

[A] great constitutional debate need not involve a prior commitment to federalism as the most desirable outcome in Europe. It may reveal that Europe is in the process of inventing a new political form, something more than a confederation but less than a federation — an association of sovereign states which pool their sovereignty only in very restricted areas to varying degrees, an association which does not seek to have the coercive power to act directly on individuals in the fashion of nation states.[2]

Does this shift in climate reflect a sound realism, born of a learning-process of over four decades, or is it rather the sign of a mood of hesitance, if not outright defeatism?

Siedentop misses the mark when he complains of the lack of any profound or inspired *constitutional* debate on the fate of Europe, capable of seizing the imagination of its peoples. For our situation today is not comparable to that of either the Federalists or the delegates to the Assemblée Nationale. At the end of the eighteenth century, in Philadelphia and Paris, the Founding Fathers and the French Revolutionaries were engaged in an extraordinary undertaking, without historical precedent. More than two hundred years later, we are not merely heirs to a long-established practice of constitution-making; in a sense, the constitutional question does not provide the key to the main problem we have to solve. For the challenge before us is not to *invent* anything but to *conserve* the great democratic achievements of the

25

European nation-state, beyond its own limits. These achievements include not only formal guarantees of civil rights, but levels of social welfare, education and leisure that are the precondition of both an effective private autonomy and of democratic citizenship. This means that constitutional debates over the future of Europe are now increasingly the province of highly specialised discourses among economists, sociologists and political scientists, rather than the domain of constitutional lawyers and political philosophers. On the other hand, we should not underestimate the symbolic weight of the sheer fact that a constitutional debate is now publicly under way. As a political collectivity, Europe cannot take hold in the consciousness of its citizens simply in the shape of a common currency. The intergovernmental arrangement at Maastricht lacks that power of symbolic crystallisation which only a political act of foundation can give.

An Ever-closer Union?

Let us then start from the question: why should we pursue the project of an 'ever-closer Union' any further at all? Recent calls from Rau, Schroeder and Fischer – the German President, Chancellor and Foreign Minister – to move ahead with a European constitution have met sceptical reactions in the UK, France and most of the other member states. But even if we were to accept this as an urgent and desirable project, a second and more troubling question arises. Would the European Union (EU) in its present state meet the most fundamental preconditions for acquiring the constitutional shape of any kind of federation – that is, a community of nation-states that itself assumes some qualities of a state?

Why should we pursue the project of a constitution for Europe? Let me address this question from two angles: (1) immediate political goals; and (2) dilemmas stemming from virtually irreversible decisions of the past. If we consider the first, it is clear that while the original political aims of European integration have lost much of their relevance, they have since been replaced by an even more ambitious political agenda. The first generation of dedicated Euro-federalists set the process in train after the Second World War with two immediate purposes in mind: to put an end to the bloody history of warfare between European nations, and to contain the potentially threatening power of a recovering post-fascist Germany. Though everybody believes that the first goal has already been achieved the relevance of peace-keeping issues survives in a different context. In the course of the Kosovo war, its participants became aware of subtle yet important differences in the way that the USA and the UK, on the one hand, and the continental nations of Europe on the other, justified this humanitarian intervention – the former resorting to maxims of traditional power politics, the latter appealing to more principled reasons for transforming classical international law into some sort of cosmopolitan order. This is a difference that exemplifies the rationale for developing an EU capable of speaking with one voice in matters of foreign and security policy, and bringing a stronger influence of its own to bear on NATO operations and United Nations (UN) decisions.

The second goal, the containment of a potentially dangerous Germany, may have lost its salience with the growing stability of democratic institutions and spread of liberal outlooks in the Federal Republic, even if the unification of the country has revived fears of some return to the self-assertive traditions of the German Reich. I need not pursue this question here, since neither of the two original motives for integration could be regarded as a sufficient justification for pushing the European project any further. The 'Carolingian' background of the founding fathers – Schuman, De Gasperi, Adenauer – with its explicit appeal to the Christian West, has vanished.

Of course, there was always a third strand in European integration – the straightforward economic argument that a unified Europe was the surest path to growth and welfare. Since the Coal and Steel Community of 1951, and the subsequent formation of Euratom and the European Community of 1958, more and more countries have become gradually integrated through the free exchange of people, goods, services and capital among them – a process now completed by the single market and single currency. The EU frames an ever denser network of trade-relations, 'foreign' direct investment, financial transactions and so forth. Alongside the USA and Japan, Europe has gained a rather strong position within the so-called Triad. Thus the rational expectation of mutual benefits within Europe and of differential competitive advantages on world markets could, to date, provide a legitimation 'through outcomes' for an ever-closer Union. But even making allowances for the consciousness-raising impact of the euro, it seems clear that henceforward economic achievements can at best stabilise the status quo. Economic expectations alone can hardly mobilise political support for the much riskier and more far-reaching project of a *political union* – one that deserves the name.

Beyond a 'Mere Market'

This further goal requires the legitimation of shared values.[3] There is always a trade-off between the efficiency and legitimacy of an administration. But great political innovations, such as an unprecedented design for a state of nation-states, demand political mobilisation for normative goals. Constitution-making has hitherto been a response to situations of crisis. Where is such a challenge, we might ask, in today's rather wealthy and peaceful societies of Western Europe? In Central and Eastern Europe, by contrast, transitional societies striving for inclusion and recognition within the EU do face a peculiar crisis of rapid modernisation – but their response to it has been a pronounced return to the nation-state, without much enthusiasm for a transfer of parts of their recently regained national sovereignty to Brussels. The current lack of motivation for political union, in either zone, makes the insufficiency of bare economic calculations all the more obvious. Economic justifications must at the very least be combined with ideas of a different kind – let us say, an interest in and affective attachment to a particular ethos: in other words, the attraction of a specific way of life. During the third quarter of the past century, Eric Hobsbawm's 'Golden Age', the citizens of Western Europe were fortunate enough to develop a distinctive form of life based on, but not exhausted by, a glistening material infrastructure. Today, against perceived threats from globalisation, they are prepared to defend the core of a welfare state that is the backbone of a society still oriented towards social, political and cultural inclusion. This is the orientation that is capable of embedding economic arguments for an ever-closer union into a much broader vision. Of course, rapid economic growth was the basis for a welfare state that provided the framework for the regeneration of postwar European societies. But the most important outcome of this regeneration has been the production of ways of life that have allowed the wealth and national diversity of a multi-secular culture to become attractively renewed.

The economic advantages of European unification are valid as arguments for further construction of the EU only if they can appeal to a cultural power of attraction extending far beyond material gains alone. Threats to this form of life, and the desire to preserve it, are spurs to a vision of a Europe capable of responding inventively to current challenges. In his magnificent speech of 28 May 2001, the French Prime Minister spoke of this 'European way of life' as the content of a political project:

> Up until recently, the primary focus of the European endeavour was on setting up the economic and monetary Union. ... But now we must broaden our perspective if we want Europe to be more than just one more market in a sea of globalisation. Europe is, after all, more than a market. It bears within it a societal model, the result of its history, which is taking shape in the ever closer ties being forged among European peoples.[4]

Globalisation and Social Solidarity

Economic globalisation, whether we interpret it as no more than an intensification of long-range trends or as an abrupt shift towards a new transnational configuration of capitalism, shares with all processes of accelerated modernisation some disquieting features. Rapid structural change distributes social costs more unequally, and increases status gaps between winners and losers, generally inflicting heavier burdens in the short run, and greater benefits only in the long term.[5] The last wave of economic globalisation did not stem from any inherent evolution of the system: it was the product in large measure of successive General Agreement on Tariffs and Trade (GATT) rounds – that is, of conscious political action. Democratic governments should therefore also have the chance, at least in principle, to counter the undesired social consequences of globalisation by complementary social and infrastructure policies. Such policies have to cope with the needs of two different groups.

Their purpose must be to bridge the time-gap for short-run losers by investing in human capital and temporary transfer payments, and to offer permanent compensation to long-run losers in – for example – the form of a basic income scheme or negative income tax. Since neither group is any longer in a strong veto position, the implementation of such designs is a difficult task. For the decision on whether or not to maintain an appropriate level of *general* social welfare largely depends on the degree of support for notions of distributive justice. But normative orientations move majorities of voters only to the extent that they can make a straightforward appeal to 'strong' traditions inscribed in established political cultures. In Western Europe, or at any rate its continental nations, this assumption is not quite unfounded. Here the political tradition of the workers' movement, the salience of Christian social doctrines and even a certain normative core of social liberalism still provide a formative background for social solidarity. In their public self representations, Social and Christian Democratic parties in particular support inclusive systems of social security and a substantive conception of citizenship, which stresses what John Rawls calls 'the fair value' of equally distributed rights. In terms of a comparative cultural analysis, we might speak of the unique European combination of public collectivisms and private individualism. As Göran Therborn remarks:

> The European road to and through modernity has also left a certain legacy of social norms, reflecting European experiences of class and gender. ... Collective bargaining, trade unions, public social services, the rights of women and children are all held more legitimate in Europe than in the rest of the contemporary world. They are expressed in social documents of the EU and of the Council of Europe.[6]

But if we grant this assumption, there remains the question of why national governments should not be in a better position to pursue countervailing policies more effectively than a heavy-handed EU bureaucracy. At issue here is the extent to which intensified global competition affects the scope of action of national governments. In a recent book I argued that there has been a shift towards a 'postnational constellation'.[7] Some counter-considerations have been adduced since then.[8] No linear relation exists, it is observed, between economic globalisation and the decreasing autonomy of the national state; nor is there always an inverse relation between levels of social welfare and employment. Independently of growing global pressures from without, the state has anyway had to learn to play a less dominant role within national arenas, in its interactions with powerful social agents.[9] National governments may be compelled to lower taxes on capital under the pressure of national competition, but they still seem to enjoy a range of options in policy areas that have an immediate impact on interdependent rates of unemployment and levels of social welfare.[10]

Normative Appeals

Such arguments do not undermine, however, the general thesis that national governments, whatever their internal profiles, are increasingly entangled in transnational networks, and thereby become ever more dependent on asymmetrically negotiated outcomes. Whatever social policies they choose, they must adapt to constraints imposed by deregulated markets, in particular global financial markets. That means lower taxes and fiscal limits, which compel them to accept increasing inequalities in the distribution of the gross national product (GDP).[11] The question therefore is: can any of our small or medium, entangled and accommodating nation-states preserve a separate capacity to escape enforced assimilation to the social model now imposed by the predominant global economic regime? This model is informed by an anthropological image of 'man' as rational chooser and entrepreneur, exploiting his or her own labour-power; by a moral view of society that accepts growing cleavages and exclusions; and by a political doctrine that trades a shrinking scope of democracy for freedoms of the market. These are the building blocks of a neo-liberal vision that does not sit well with the kind of normative self-understanding so far prevalent across Europe as a whole.

This diagnosis suggests a normatively loaded, perhaps a 'social-democratic', reading of the economic justification for the European project. It might be objected that any such partisan view must divide the political spectrum along ideological lines. But in the absence of a stronger motivation, this may be necessary to mobilise public debate. As a strategy, it is innocent insofar as its success would at best be a procedural outcome – the creation of a more encompassing political framework. A European constitution would enhance the capacity of the member states of the EU to act jointly, without prejudicing the particular course and content of what policies it might adopt. It would constitute a necessary, not a sufficient, condition for the kind of policies some of us are inclined to advocate. To the extent that European nations seek a certain re-regulation of the global economy, to counterbalance its undesired economic, social and cultural consequences, they have a reason for building a stronger EU with greater international influence. Mario Telò and Paul Magnette express the hope that:

Europe will develop an open regionalism that strikes an innovative balance between protectionism and free trade, social regulation and openness. The European Union is now being challenged to develop a better balance between deregulation and re-regulation than national rules have been able to achieve. ... The Union may be seen as a laboratory in which Europeans are striving to implement the values of justice and solidarity in the context of an increasing global economy.[12]

With a view to the future of a highly stratified world society, we Europeans have a legitimate interest in getting our voice heard in an international concert that is at present dominated by a vision quite different from ours.

This would be a way of giving a normative appeal to the European project for those who take a critical view of the impact of economic globalisation on nation-states. But even neo-liberals opposed to political goals of this kind must heed other considerations. For further reasons to move European integration forward lie in the uneasy effects of previous decisions that are now irreversible. There is first the need for a reform of EU institutions imposed by the contradiction between the limited capacity of the European Council to reach agreements among diverging member states, and the political decision to admit several new and even less homogeneous members. The enlargement of the EU increases the complexity of interests in need of coordination, which requires further integration or 'deepening' of the EU. The EU set schedules for enlargement that placed it under a self-imposed pressure for reform. However, enlargement has failed to act as a lever for the solution of the more severe structural problems that emerge (1) from an asymmetry between a rather dense horizontal integration through markets and the rather loose vertical integration of competing national governments, and (2) from a corresponding deficit in the democratic legitimation of EU decisions.

Positive Coordination

So far national governments have retained most of their competencies for cultural, economic and social policies, while they have transferred their monetary sovereignty to an independent and supposedly non-political institution, the European Central Bank. They have thereby renounced an important means of state intervention. As monetary union completes the process of economic integration, the need for harmonisation of major public policies increases. National governments, resting as they do on different schemes of taxation, social-policy regimes, neo-corporatist arrangements, remain entrenched in distinct legal and political traditions. They therefore tend to respond differently to the same stimuli, and the interactive effects of their disparate policies can produce mutually counterproductive backlashes. National governments still compete with one another in pursuit of the most promising adaptation of their welfare regimes to fiscal constraints imposed by the 'evaluation' of global financial markets. At the same time they face the challenge to agree on minimal social standards – steps in the direction of a 'social union', as envisaged by Delors, to promote a European-wide convergence in levels of provision and benefit.

Yet these discrepancies between an advanced economic and a retarded political integration could be overcome by the construction of higher-order political agencies, capable of 'catching up' with the pressures of deregulated markets. From this perspective, the European project can be seen as a common attempt by the national governments to recover in Brussels something of the capacity for intervention that they have lost at home. This is at any rate the view of those who called for common economic management of the euro-zone, and in the long run harmonisation of corporation taxes within it. Such a move would also meet another well-known problem. The so-called 'democratic deficit' of European authorities, in particular of the Commission, is a source of growing dissatisfaction within the broader population – not only of the smaller states such as Ireland or Denmark, or countries that have temporarily rejected entry into the EU such as Norway or Switzerland. So far, the Commission has mainly pushed market-enhancement policies that require only 'negative coordination', which means that national governments are expected to refrain from doing things. Beyond this threshold, the present kind of indirect legitimation through national governments is no longer sufficient.

Regulatory policies with a widely perceived redistributive effect would require 'positive coordination' on both the output-side (that is, implementation) and the input-side (that is, legitimation) of a quite different kind. At present, legitimacy flows more or less through the channels of democratic institutions and procedures within each nation-state. This level of legitimation is appropriate for inter-governmental negotiations and treaties. But it falls short of what is needed for the kind of supranational and transnational decision-making that has long since developed within the institutional framework of the EU and its huge network of committees. It is estimated that European directives already affect up to 70 per cent of the regulations of national agencies. But they lack any serious exposure to a timely and careful public opinion or will-formation in those national arenas that are today alone accessible to holders of a European passport.

The opacity of decision-making processes at the European level, and the lack of opportunity for any participation in them, cause mutual distrust among citizens. Claus Offe has described the issues that stir fears within, and arouse rivalries between, different nations – concerns over fiscal redistribution, over immigration from and investment-flows to other states, over the social and economic consequences of intensified competition between countries with different levels of productivity, and so forth. Though himself a sceptical observer, Offe suggests 'state-building' as the solution – a European state-building which does not reproduce the template of the nation-state – and remarks that:

the agency that will eventually realize a regime of 'organized civility' governing the entire European space ... will have to conform to two criteria that all

European states have now come to take as the standards of acceptable political rule: legitimacy and efficacy.[13]

Civic Nations

So much for the reasons why we should support and promote the project of a European constitution in the first place. But does Europe in its present shape meet the conditions necessary for the realisation of such a design – that is: for the establishment, not simply of a confederation, but a federation of nation-states? We may address first the familiar objections of the Eurosceptics, and then deal more specifically with some of the prerequisites for an EU that would assume at least some qualities of a state.

Eurosceptics reject a shift in the basis of legitimation of the EU from international treaties to a European constitution with the argument, 'there is as yet no European people'.[14] According to this view, what is missing is the very subject of a constituent process, the collective singular of 'a people' capable of defining itself as a democratic nation. I have criticised this 'no demos' thesis on both conceptual and empirical grounds.[15] A nation of citizens must not be confused with a community of fate shaped by common descent, language and history. This confusion fails to capture the voluntaristic character of a civic nation, the collective identity of which exists neither independent of nor prior to the democratic process from which it springs. Such a civic, as opposed to ethnic, conception of 'the nation' reflects both the actual historical trajectory of the European nation-states and the fact that democratic citizenship establishes an abstract, legally mediated solidarity between strangers.

Historically, national consciousness as the first modern form of social integration was fostered by new forms of communication, the development of which was indeed facilitated by the stabilising contexts of traditional communities. The fact that modern democracy and the nation-state have developed in tandem, however, does not indicate a priority of the latter over the former. It rather reveals a circular process in the course of which democracy and the nation-state stabilised each other. Both have jointly produced the striking innovation of a civic solidarity that provides the cement of national societies. National consciousness emerged as much from the mass communication of formally educated readers as from the mobilisation of enfranchised voters and drafted soldiers. It has been shaped as much by the intellectual construction of national histories as by the discourse of competing parties, struggling for political power.

There are two lessons to be learnt from the history of the European nation-states. If the emergence of national consciousness involved a painful process of abstraction, leading from local and dynastic identities to national and democratic ones, why, first, should this generation of a highly artificial kind of civic solidarity − a 'solidarity among strangers' − be doomed to come to a final halt just at the borders of our classical nation-states? And second, the artificial conditions in which national consciousness came into existence recall the empirical circumstances necessary for an extension of that process of identity-formation beyond national boundaries. These are: the emergence of a European civil society; the construction of a European-wide public sphere; and the shaping of a political culture that can be shared by all European citizens.

A Catalytic Constitution

These functional prerequisites of a democratically constituted EU project points of convergence between rather complex processes. We should not forget, however, that this convergence in turn depends on the catalytic effect of a constitution. This would have to begin with a single European referendum, arousing a Europe-wide constitutional debate, which would in itself represent a unique opportunity for transnational communication, and which would have the potential for a self-fulfilling prophecy. Europe has to apply to itself, as a whole, 'the logic of the circular creation of state and society that shaped the modern history of European countries'.[16]

The European constitution not only makes manifest the shift in powers that has already taken place. It can also release and foster further shifts. Once the EU gains financial autonomy, the Commission assumes the functions of a government and the Council becomes something like a second chamber, the European Parliament can attract more attention for the better-staged and more visible exercise of competencies, which are already remarkable. Full budgetary powers would not be necessary in the beginning. The focus of politics would move to some extent from national capitals to the European centres, not just through the activities of lobbyists and business organisations which have quite a strong presence in Brussels already, but through those of political parties, labour unions, civic or cultural associations, public interest groups, social movements and 'pressure from the street' − protests no longer merely by farmers or lorry drivers, but arising from the initiatives of citizens at large. Relevant interests formed along lines of political ideology, economic sector, occupational position, social class, religion, ethnicity and gender would moreover fuse across national boundaries.[17] The perceived transnational overlap of parallel interests would give rise to cross-boundary networks and a properly European party system, displacing territorial by functional principles of organisation.

Creating a Public Sphere

There will be no remedy for the legitimation deficit, however, without a European-wide public sphere – a network that gives citizens of all member states an equal opportunity to take part in an encompassing process of focused political communication. Democratic legitimation requires mutual contact between, on the one hand, institutionalised deliberation and decision-making within parliaments, courts and administrative bodies and, on the other, an inclusive process of informal mass communication. The function of the communicational infrastructure of a democratic public sphere is to turn relevant societal problems into topics of concern, and to allow the general public to relate, at the same time, to the same topics, by taking an affirmative or negative stand on news and opinions. Over time, these implicit attitudes coagulate to constitute public opinion, even though most citizens do not send public messages beyond voting or non-voting. So far, however, the necessary infrastructure for a wide-ranging generation of diverse public opinions exists only within the confines of nation-states.

A European-wide public sphere must not be imagined as the projection of a familiar design from the national onto the European level. It will rather emerge from the mutual opening of existing national universes to one another, yielding to an interpenetration of mutually translated national communications. There is no need for a stratified public communication, each layer of which would correspond, one by one, to a different 'floor' of the multilevel political system. The agenda of European institutions will be included in each of a plurality of national publics, if these are interrelated in the right way.

The pressing question 'Can the European Union become a sphere of publics?'[18] is often answered from a supranational rather than a transnational perspective. If we look for monolingual (usually English-speaking) media with multinational audiences penetrating national borders we find a business elite reading the *Financial Times* and *The Economist*, or a political elite reading the *International Herald Tribune* with a digest of the *Frankfurter Allgemeine Zeitung* – which means: nothing specifically European. This is not a promising model for the audiovisual communications of a general public, even for cross-boundary communication via print media. In the audiovisual sector, the bilingual, French–German television channel *Arte* is already more plausible, though still aimed at a notionally supranational public. A real advance would be for national media to cover the substance of relevant controversies in the other countries, so that all the national public opinions converged on the same range of contributions to the same set of issues, regardless of their origin. This is what happens temporarily – if only for a few days – before and after the summits of the European Council, when the heads of the member states come together and deal with issues of equal perceived relevance for citizens across Europe. The fact that these multiple, horizontal flows of communication have to pass through the filters of translation does not reduce their essential significance.

The mere number of officially recognised languages constitutes at first glance an embarrassing obstacle to the formation of a shared polity for all. The official multilingualism of EU institutions is necessary for the mutual recognition of the equal worth and integrity of all national cultures. However, under the veil of this legal guarantee it becomes all the easier to use English as a working language at face-to-face level, wherever the parties lack another common idiom.[19] This is in fact what now happens anyway, in ever-wider circles. Small countries like the Netherlands, Denmark, Norway or Sweden provide good examples of the capacity of formal education in schools to spread English as a second 'first' language, across their whole populations.[20]

Sharing a Political Culture

The generation of a European public opinion depends on the vital inputs of actors within a European civil society. At the same time, a European-wide public sphere needs to be embedded in a political culture shared by all. This widely perceived requirement has stimulated a troubled discourse among intellectuals, since it has been difficult to separate the question 'What is Europe?' from the fact that the achievements of European culture – which did not, in fact, seriously reflect upon its own nature and origin until the eighteenth or nineteenth centuries – have been diffused across the globe.[21] The main religion in Europe, Christianity, obeyed its missionary imperative and expanded all over the world. The global spread of modern science and technology, of Roman law and the Napoleonic Code, of human rights, democracy and the nation-state started from Europe as well. Let me therefore mention two more specific experiences of our countries that resonate still in the rather remarkable responses they have evoked. For Europe has, more than any other culture, faced and overcome structural conflicts, sharp confrontations and lasting tensions, in the social as well as in the temporal dimension.

In the social dimension, modern Europe has developed institutional arrangements for the productive resolution of intellectual, social and political conflicts. In the course of painful, if not fatal struggles, it has learnt how to cope with deep cleavages, schisms and rivalries between secular and ecclesiastical powers, city and countryside, faith and knowledge, and how to get along with endemic conflicts between militant religious confessions and belligerent states. In the temporal dimension, modern Europe has institutionalised a comprehensive spectrum of competing conservative, liberal and socialist interpretations of capitalist modernisation, in an ideological system of political parties. In the course of a heroic intellectual appropriation of a rich Jewish and Greek, Roman and Christian heritage, Europe has thus learnt a sensitive attitude and a balanced response, both to the deplorable losses incurred by the disintegration of a traditional past and to the promise of future benefits from the 'creative destruction' of present productivity.

These are dispositions that act as a spur to critical reflection on our own blind spots, and to a de-centring of selective perspectives. They are not in contradiction with the well-taken − and only too deserved − critique of our aggressive colonial and Eurocratic past; the critique of Eurocentrism itself emerges from a continuing self-criticism. The secularisation of the egalitarian and individualist universalism that informs our normative self-understanding is not the least among the achievements of modern Europe.

The fact that the death penalty is still practised elsewhere − even in the USA − reminds us of some specific features of our heritage: the Council of Europe with the European Convention of Human Rights, and its European Social Charter, have transformed Europe into an area of human rights, more specific and more binding than in any other area of the world. The clear and general European support for the International Criminal Court, again in contrast to US fears, is also in the same line.[22]

What forms the common core of a European identity is the character of the painful learning process it has gone through, as much as its results. It is the lasting memory of nationalist excess and moral abyss that lends to our present commitments the quality of a peculiar achievement. This historical background should ease the transition

to a postnational democracy based on the mutual recognition
of the differences between strong and proud national cultures.
Neither 'assimilation' nor 'coexistence' – in the sense of a pale *modus
vivendi* – are appropriate terms for our history of learning how
to construct new and ever more sophisticated forms of a 'solidarity
among strangers'. Today, moreover, the European nation-states are
being brought together by the challenges that they all face equally.
All are in the process of becoming countries of immigration and
multicultural societies. All are exposed to an economic and cultural
globalisation that awakes memories of a shared history of conflict and
reconciliation – and of a comparatively low threshold of tolerance
towards exclusion.

This new awareness of what Europeans have in common has
found an admirable expression in the EU Charter of Fundamental
Rights. The members of the 'Convention', as it is called, reached
agreement on this document within a remarkably short space of time.
Even though the European Council in Nice only 'proclaimed' and did
not adopt in binding fashion its catalogue of basic rights, the Charter
will exert a decisive influence on the European Court of Justice. Thus
far the Court has been primarily concerned with the implications
of the 'four freedoms' of market participation – free movement
of persons, goods, services and capital. The Charter goes beyond
this limited view, articulating a social vision of the European project.[23]
It also shows what Europeans link together normatively. Responding
to recent developments in biotechnology, Article 3 specifies each
person's right to his or her physical and mental integrity, and
prohibits any practice of positive eugenics or the reproductive cloning
of human organisms.

Designing a Framework

Taking it as a premise that a European constitution is both feasible
and desirable, let me finish with a few remarks on some problems to do
with its design. According to the former foreign minister of Germany,
Joschka Fischer, we face the task of finding the right combination of
a 'Europe of nation-states' with a 'Europe of citizens'.[24] He offers
some more or less conventional alternatives for strengthening the
European Parliament, establishing an effective and legitimate executive, and creating a democratically accountable Court of Justice.[25]
These proposals do not exhaust the range of imaginative options, but
Fischer rightly focuses on the core problem of a federation of nation-
states that need to preserve their integrity by occupying a much more

influential position than the constituent elements of a federal state normally do.[26] The intergovernmental element of negotiation between former nation-states will remain strong. Compared with the presidential regime of the USA, an EU of nation-states would have to display the following general features:

- a Parliament that would resemble the Congress in *some* respects (a similar division of powers and, compared with the European parliamentary systems, relatively weak political parties);
- a legislative 'chamber of nations' that would have more competences than the American Senate, and a Commission that would be much less powerful than the White House (thus splitting the classical functions of a strong presidency between the two);
- a European Court that would be as influential as the Supreme Court for similar reasons (the regulatory complexity of an enlarged and socially diversified EU would require detailed interpretation of a principled constitution, cutting through the jungle of existing treaties).[27]

The political substance of a European constitution should consist of a definite answer to the issue of the territorial boundaries of the EU, and a not-too-definite answer to the question of how competences are to be distributed between federal and national institutions. It is important to settle the thorny problem of which countries will finally belong to, and which are to be excluded from, the EU; the determination of frontiers is compatible with a 'variable geometry' that would facilitate the process. For the time being, we might differentiate between a centre and a periphery, depending on the pace and degree of integration. The issue of a 'Europe of different speeds' touches on the problem of a provisional regulation of competences which leaves some room for experiments. The delimitation of what is to be reserved for federal authorities, what is up for co-legislation and what remains in the competence of national legislatures must certainly be settled in broad outline from the beginning. But this part of the organisational nucleus of the constitution should be kept open for revisions at fixed dates, so that we can learn from unanticipated consequences within a stable framework. Such a temporalisation of essential clauses squares with the idea of a democratic constitution as an ever more exhaustive realisation of a system of basic rights under changing historical circumstances.[28]

'Subsidiarity' is the functional principle that meets the needs of the diverse and territorially distinct units of a federation. But the wider the differences — in size of territory and population, economic weight and level of development, political power and cultural form of life or collective identity – between these constituent units, the greater the danger that majority decisions at the higher instances will violate the principles of equal protection and mutual recognition of diversity. Structural minorities limit the range of valid majority decisions. In such situations, legitimacy can only be secured on the condition that some areas are reserved for consensual negotiations. As we know from countries like Switzerland or the Netherlands, however, consensual procedures suffer from a lack of transparency. Here European-wide referenda would give citizens broader opportunities and more effective means to participate in the shaping of policies.[29]

Some minor suggestions are worth consideration. It would help to overcome the legitimation deficit, and to strengthen the connections between the federal legislature and national arenas, either if certain members of the European Parliament at the same time held seats in their respective national parliaments, or if the largely neglected Conference of Community and European Affairs Committees of Parliaments of the European Union (COSAC) (which has met twice a year since 1989) could reanimate horizontal debate between national parliaments and so help to prompt a re-parliamentarisation of European politics.[30] Are there alternative modes of legitimation too? The approach labelled 'comitology' attributes legitimating merits to the deliberative politics of the great number of committees working in support of the Commission.[31] But here there is a deficit on the output as well as input side, since federal legislation is implemented only through national, regional and local authorities. To meet this problem, Ingo Pernice has suggested transforming the present Committee of Regions into a chamber that would give sub-national state actors a stronger influence on EU policies, and thereby facilitate the enforcement of European law on the ground.[32]

The Politics of Unification

For European unification to move forward, however, there still remains a vacant space which would have to be filled by the political will of competent actors. The overwhelming majority of the population that is currently resistant or hesitant can only be won for Europe if the project is extricated from the pallid abstraction of administrative measures and technical discourse: in other words, is politicised. Intellectuals have not picked up this ball. Still less have politicians wanted to burn their fingers with such an unpopular topic. But no reform of procedures and institutions can succeed before the content of the political project behind it becomes dearer.

The markedly national orientation of the current Bush Administration can be regarded as an opportunity for the EU to define a more distinctive foreign and security policy towards the conflicts in the Middle East and the Balkans, and relations with Russia and China. Differences that are coming more into the open in environmental, military and juridical fields contribute to a soundless strengthening of European identity. Still more important is the question of what role Europe wishes to play in the Security Council and, above all, in world economic institutions. Contrasting justifications of humanitarian intervention, not to speak of basic economic outlooks, divide the founder states of the EU from the UK and Scandinavia. But it is better to bring these smouldering conflicts out into the open than to let the EU splinter over dilemmas that remain unresolved. In any case, a Europe of two or three speeds is preferable to one that breaks up or crumbles away.

Notes

1 Niess 2000.
2 Siedentop 2000, p. 1.
3 Fossum 2000.
4 Jospin 2001.
5 Vobruba 2000.
6 Therborn 2000, p. 51.
7 Habermas 2000.
8 Grande and Risse 2000.
9 Esser 1999.
10 Scharpf 2000.
11 Hauser and Becker 1999.
12 Telò and Magnette 2001, p. 51.
13 Offe 2002, p. 84.
14 Böckenförde 1997.
15 See Habermas 1998.
16 Offe 2002, p. 84.
17 Schmitter 1996.
18 This is the title of an informative empirical analysis by Philip Schlesinger and Deirdre Kevin. See Schlesinger and Kevin 2000.
19 Kraus 2000a and 2000b.
20 Kraus (2000b) cites a poll finding that even a majority of the German-speaking Swiss prefer English to the two other national languages for communication across linguistic borders.
21 Boer 1998.
22 Therborn 2001.
23 Däubler 2000.

24 Fischer 2000.
25 Fischer offers an option between the models of the US Senate and the German Bundesrat for the second chamber, and a choice between two constructions, one developed from the European Council of Ministers, and the other resembling the present Council, but with a directly elected president, for the executive.
26 In this respect Article 3 of the new Swiss Constitution is interesting, in that it applies the principle of subsidiarity to yield a rather strong position to the constitutive units: 'The cantons are sovereign, so long as their sovereignty suffers no restriction from federal constitution; they exercise all rights that are not transferred to the confederation'.
27 See the proposal for reorganisation of the treaties: European University Institute, *A Basic Treaty for the European Union*, May 2000.
28 See my argument in Habermas 1996, ch. 9.
29 Grande 1996 and 2000.
30 Blichner 2000.
31 Joerges and Everson 2000.
32 Pernice 1999. For another conception, see Rousseau 2000.

References

Blichner, Lars, 2000, 'Interparliamentary Discourse and the Quest for Legitimacy', in Erik Oddvar Eriksen and John Erik Fossum (eds.), *Democracy in the European Union*. London: Routledge, pp. 140–63.

Böckenförde, Ernst-Wolfgang, 1997, *Welchen Weg geht Europa?* Munich: Carl Friedrich von Siemens Stiftung.

Boer, Pim den, 1998, 'Europe as an Idea', *European Review*, Vol. 6, October, 395–402.

Däubler, Wolfgang, 2000, 'In bester Verfassung', *Blätter für deutsche und internationale Politik*, Vol. 11, 1315–21.

Esser, Josef, 1999, 'Der kooperative Nationalstaat im Zeitalter der "Globalisierung"', in Diether Döring (ed.), *Sozialstaat in der Globalisierung*. Frankfurt: Suhrkamp, pp. 117–44.

European University Institute, 2000, *A Basic Treaty for the European Union*, May.

Fischer, Joschka, 2000, 'From Confederacy to Federation: Thoughts on the Finality of European Integration'. Speech at the Humboldt University in Berlin, 12 May 2000. Available at: http://www.jeanmonnetprogram.org/papers/00/joschka_fischer_en.rtf

Fossum, John, 2000, 'Constitution-making in the European Union', in Erik Oddvar Eriksen and John Erik Fossum (eds.), *Democracy in the European Union: Integration through Deliberation?* London: Routledge, pp. 111–63.

Grande, Edgar, 1996, 'Demokratische Legitimation und europäische Integration', *Leviathan*, Vol. 24, 339–60.

Grande, Edgar, 2000, 'Postnational Democracy in Europe', in Michael Greven and Louis Pauly (eds.), *Democracy beyond the State?* Oxford: Rowman & Littlefield, pp. 115–38.

Grande, Edgar and Thomas Risse, 2000, 'Bridging the Gap', *Zeitschrift für internationale Beziehungen*, Vol. 7(2), 235–66.

Habermas, Jürgen, 1996, *Between Facts and Norms*. Cambridge, MA: MIT Press.

1998, 'On the Relation between the Nation, Rule of Law and Democracy', in Jürgen Habermas, *The Inclusion of the Other*. Cambridge, MA: Polity, pp. 129–54.

2000, *The Postnational Constellation*. Cambridge, MA: MIT Press.

Hauser, Richard and Irene Becker, 1999, 'Wird unsere Einkommensverteilung immer ungleicher? Einige Forschungsergebnisse', in Diether Döring (ed.), *Sozialstaat in der Globalisierung*. Frankfurt: Suhrkamp, pp. 40–87.

Joerges, Christian and Michelle Everson, 2000, 'Challenging the Bureaucratic Challenge', in Erik Oddvar Eriksen and John Erik Fossum (eds.), *Democracy in the European Union*. London: Routledge, pp. 164–88.

Jospin Lionel, 2001, 'On the Future of an Enlarged Europe'. Speech of the French Prime Minister to the Foreign Press Association, Paris, 28 May 2001. Available at: http://europa.eu.int/constitution/futurum/documents/speech/sp280501_en.htm

Kraus, Peter, 2000a, 'Von Westfalen nach Kosmopolis. Die Proglematik kultureller Identität in der Europäischen Politik', *Berliner Journal für Soziologie*, Vol. **2**, 203–18.

2000b, 'Political Unity and Linguistic Diversity in Europe', *Archives Européennes de Sociologie*, Vol. **41**, 138–63.

Niess, Frank, 2000, 'Das "F-Wort"', *Blätter fur deutsche und internationale Politik*, Vol. **9**, 1105–15.

Offe, Claus, 2002, 'Is There, or Can There Be, a "European Society"?', in Ines Katenhusen and Wolfram Lamping (eds.), *Demokratie in Europa*. Opladen: Leske & Budrich, pp. 71–90.

Pernice, Ingolf, 1999, 'Which Institutions for What Kind of Europe? Proposals for the Reform of the European Union in the Year 2000'. WHI Working Paper 2/99, Walter Hallstein-Institute for European Constitutional Law at the Humboldt University, Berlin.

Rousseau, Dominique, 2000, 'Pour une constitution européenne', *Le Debat*, Vol. **108**, 54–73.

Scharpf, Fritz, 2000, 'The Viability of Advanced Welfare States in the International Economy', *Journal of European Public Policy*, Vol. 7, 190–228.

Schlesinger, Philip and Deirdre Kevin, 2000, 'Can the European Union Become a Sphere of Publics?', in Erik Oddvar Eriksen and John Erik Fossum (eds.), *Democracy in the European Union: Integration through Deliberation?* London: Routledge, pp. 206–29.

Schmitter, Philippe, 1996, 'Imagining the Future of the Euro-Polity', in Gary Marks, Fritz Scharpf, Philippe Schmitter and Wolfgang Streeck, *Governance in the European Union*. London: SAGE, pp. 121–50.

Siedentop, Larry, 2000, *Democracy in Europe*. London: Routledge.

Telò, Mario and Paul Magnette, 2001, 'Social Justice and Solidarity', in Furio Cerutti and Enno Rudolph (eds.), *A Soul for Europe*, Vol. I. Leuven: Peeters, pp. 73–89.

Therborn, Göran, 2001, 'Europe's Breaks with Itself. The European Economy and the History, Modernity and World Future of Europe', in Furio Cerutti and Enno Rudolph (eds.), *A Soul for Europe*, Vol. II. Leuven: Peeters, pp. 73–94.

Vobruba, Georg, 2000, 'Actors in Processes of Inclusion and Exclusion', *Social Policy and Administration*, December, 603–13.

3   Why Constitutionalise the European Union?

Philippe C. Schmitter

The question of whether and, if so, when to constitutionalise the European Union (EU) entered serious public debate with the speech of Joschka Fischer at Humboldt University in 2000. In virtually all member states, prominent politicians subsequently felt compelled to express their opinion on this issue. Not surprisingly, they came up with very different versions of what such a European constitution should contain. Some wanted it in order to limit any further expansion of the competences of the EU; others wanted it in order to provide the EU with sufficient authority to cope with a wider agenda and a large number of members. But on two things there seemed to be general agreement: (1) the EU could not continue solely on the basis of treaties that have to be revised periodically and ratified by each member state – if only because this had already become much more difficult to do with fifteen members and even more so with twenty-five; and (2) this change in the fundamental institutional basis of European integration should happen sooner rather than later.

I remain convinced that both of these assumptions were (and still are) wrong. The EU does not need a constitution, not only because it has not done badly with a quasi-constitution based on successive treaties, but also because the flexibility provided by the lack of an agreed distribution of competences between it and its member states and, especially, the absence of a common definition of its political end-state (the so-called *finalité politique*) are precisely what the EU will need in the coming years when it will have to face the dual challenges of governing the effects of monetary unification and coping with the dislocations generated by enlargement.

Moreover, history suggests that the EU is not ready for a full-scale constitutionalisation of its polity. In the absence of revolution, *coup d'état*, liberation from foreign occupation, defeat or victory in international war, armed conflict between domestic opponents, sustained mobilisation of urban populations against the *ancien régime* and/or

46

major economic collapse, virtually none of its member states have been able to find the 'political opportunity space' for major overhauls of their ruling institutions.[1] The fact that they all (with one exception) have written constitutions and that this is a presumptive *sine qua non* for enduring democracy indicates that at some time in the future this issue will have to be tackled − if the EU is ever to democratise itself definitively. But the effort to tackle it 'sooner rather than later' (in 2003−2004) was definitely premature. Many different drafts of a potential European constitution have been produced, circulated and promoted over the past decades with little or no effect. The reason that these previous efforts had so little effect may be due less to the quality of the political and legal talent that went into assembling these impressive documents than to the way in which they were drafted and discussed. But in some respects something similar may be said of the draft constitution that was finally arrived at in 2004. It was indelibly tainted by the process that produced it.[2]

For the reigning assumption throughout has been that anything as important as constitutionalising Europe must be treated as a momentous and concentrated event, and not as a gradual and fitful process. Above all, that it must be accomplished by experts (constitutional lawyers, for the most part) and protected from the pleading of special interests and the scrutiny of mass publics.[3] Only these specialists, so it has been assumed, can be trusted to produce a coherent and consistent draft that will not reflect the self-serving aims of politicians and their surrounding clienteles.[4]

In my view, this *au-dessus de la mêlée* strategy may have worked relatively well in past circumstances when some sort of national emergency or founding moment provided the context for deliberation and choice. It will not produce the same beneficial result in the case of the EU for the simple reason that there is no foreseeable emergency and the founding moment has already occurred − half a century ago![5] What was needed, in my opinion, was an entirely new strategy that would adopt a much longer timeframe and seek deliberately to involve special interests and mass publics at various stages of the process. Only by deliberately politicising the issues involved at the level of Europe as a whole and by gradually building up expectations concerning a more definitive set of rules with regard to citizenship, representation and decision-making can one imagine a successful constitutionalisation of the EU.[6] Admittedly, this is not the way the member states went about accomplishing this task when it faced them, but the EU is not a mere repetition of previous nation, state and regime-building processes and it may well be leading to an outcome that is unprecedented.[7]

The starting point should have been the open acknowledgement that it is by no means clear whether the EU should be constitutionalised now or, if it is, how this should be accomplished. Constitutional lawyers and 'federalists' obviously are trained to think that such a 'signed, sealed and ratified' document is essential for the promotion of an orderly political process. But the EU had not been functioning so badly with its *pastiche* of treaties which itself had already converted into a quasi-constitution.[8] Moreover, before agreement on the current text was reached, each relevant actor – politicians and constitutional experts – had his or her preferred format based on perceptions of previous performance at the national level in Europe and North America. These range from a loosely linked confederation to a tightly co-ordinated federation and include all the intermediate points along this continuum.

However, the most serious problem is one of design. Even with a constitution in place and agreed upon by all members, they would have no reason to be confident that it will have the same (presumably beneficial) impact when applied to the supranational level. Because, contrary to the views of various Eurosceptics or plain anti-Europeans, the EU is still *un objet politique non-identifié* and not yet a state, contitutionalising it as a confederation or a federation or something in between may have quite unexpected effects. The massive shift in scale, the greater heterogeneity of interests, the solidly entrenched national (and sub-national) identities of its citizens, the wider range of development levels and, most of all, the unprecedented nature of its gradual and voluntary formation, all conspire to make the outcome of a constitutionalised European polity much less predictable than the earlier national efforts.

An Initial Referendum

Had the intrinsic uncertainty and unpredictability involved in the effort to constitutionalise the EU been properly acknowledged, the answer should have been obvious: turn to the citizens of Europe in their collective wisdom and try to ascertain what their expectations and assumptions may be. Such a proposal would not be a populist appeal that presumes that 'the people' (there is no such thing in Europe) are united, know what they want and can be counted upon to produce their own constitution by some process of widespread, mass deliberation. It is simply a prudential observation that, especially when experts manifestly do not know what their clients want or what to do in order to satisfy those desires, it makes good political sense not to move too far ahead of them and to initiate a gradual effort aimed at getting European citizens to think about the meta-rules that should eventually govern the accountability of their rulers — and to do so before a crisis emerges that will force them to act more hurriedly and less reflexively. Doubtless, the first returns from such a popular consultation will be confused and vary considerably from one country or region to another, but considered as a process that might take twelve to fifteen years the effort may well be worth the while. Moreover, were it done in a specifically 'open-ended' fashion, the information gathered would be invaluable in crafting a flexible and asymmetric institutional format that should fit the emerging European polity much better than the more classic federal or confederal ones.

In what follows I sketch the outline of a set of consultative democratic processes that might be organised, not merely as an adjunct to constitutionalisation, but as the central defining element of it. The fact that nothing like this has actually been tried is, in my view, less a testament to its lack of realism or to a democratic deficit at the heart of the EU than to a prevailing lack of political imagination. As long as the peculiar entity that is the EU is not recognised for what it is, this lacuna will continue to characterise the EU's deliberations at the highest level. As the process that has been put in train with the finalisation of a constitutional treaty appears to have run into the sand as a result of the referenda in France and the Netherlands that resulted in a 'no' vote, an opportunity arises for haphazardness to be replaced by something more orderly.

Imagine, initially, that a referendum had been attached to one of the regular elections to the European Parliament. Imagine, furthermore, that, contrary to the widespread popular understanding of what a referendum is — a simple alternative between 'yes' and 'no' to a question formulated by politicians for whom 'yes' is the only acceptable answer — voters be asked the following question:[9]

Should the deputies chosen on … (not the present but the forthcoming) election to the European Parliament form a constituent assembly to draft a democratic constitution for the European Union?
Choose one from the three alternatives below:

[1] No, the existing institutions of the EU should only be modified by treaties that have been negotiated and ratified unanimously by its sovereign member states.

[2] Yes, but the constituent assembly should devote its primary effort to limiting the powers of the EU and to ensuring the continued sovereignty of its member states.

[3] Yes, and the constituent assembly should produce a draft designed to make
the institutions of the EU capable of acting effectively in the interests of
Europe as a whole, even if that means reducing the sovereignty of its
member states.

The wording is a bit rough, but the reader will have grasped the
intent. EU citizens would be offered what could be described as a meta-
policy choice the outcome of which, as far as I can judge, would be
quite uncertain. It might even have to be repeated several times before a
clear majority preferred the latter two, positive options. Until such
a relative consensus exists in the public at large, however, I am
convinced that all efforts at constitutionalisation by select groups
of politicians or experts will be fruitless. What is especially important
is that EU citizens be made aware sufficiently in advance (i.e. five
years before its convocation) that such a possibility exists and that it
be made clear to them that the constitutionalising process will be
a genuinely open and competitive one. Despite the relative success
of anti-EU parties in the European elections of June 2004,
there remains an intrinsic bias in such elections to produce an assembly
whose preferences are considerably more 'federal' than those of the
population at large. Admittedly the low (and declining) turnout for
European elections does present a problem of self-selectivity; nevertheless, one could legitimately expect that the prospect of a constituent
assembly based on rival conceptions of the future Euro polity would
be a sufficient incentive to convince Eurosceptics and even Europhobes
to participate in, rather than seek to undermine, its deliberations.
The result should be an assembly of representatives that better reflects
the full range of citizen preferences – and, incidentally, might have
contributed significantly to the creation of a distinctive 'European
Public Sphere' in the course of its convocation. It is worth recalling here
that such a public sphere in its classical Habermasian sense exists
only in the most fledgling of forms.

The decision rule in response to this non-binding referendum
would naturally have to be complex and layered and would have to
be clarified in advance, but it should include at least the following:
(1) no official activity involving the drafting of a European constitution would take place until a substantial proportion of the voting
electorate in a majority of member states approved either alternative 2
or 3; (2) if, as seems likely, the voting public turns out to be divided
between a 'confederal' option limiting EU powers and a 'federal' option
expanding them, then the subsequent drafting process would have
to involve two parallel constituent assemblies – both obviously in
contact with each other and sharing substantial portions of the text

(for example on issues of basic rights), but intending to produce alternative texts; (3) the elected deputies would be expected but not compelled to follow initially the expressed 'mandate' of their respective national or regional constituency,[10] i.e. they would participate in either the confederal or the federal deliberative process depending on how the vote went (presumably the deputies from constituencies that chose the first option would initially abstain from participation in either assembly); (4) however, once the drafting process had started and deputies had gained a better understanding of the issues at stake, they would be permitted to 'cross the aisle', but would be individually responsible for doing so and for justifying their behaviour to their constituents (deputies from 'no' constituencies could likewise change their minds and join one of the drafting parties); (5) leaving aside the marginal possibility that the two rival assemblies might converge upon a single text, the intermediate product of this, no doubt, lengthy and contentious process would be two versions of a European constitution for subsequent debate and eventual ratification; (6) the Council of Ministers would have to agree unanimously to go ahead with the rival texts – without necessarily indicating its preference for one or the other;[11] and (7) national (and, in some countries, sub-national) parliaments would be called upon to discuss the respective texts and to approve their submission without amendment to the citizenry for definitive ratification.[12]

The mere existence of a constitutional treaty – 230 pages of it – is only the first step in a process which is likely to be protracted in any case and whose outcome is uncertain. And it reminds us that the history of the European Economic Community (EEC)/European Community (EC)/EU has never been one of *fait accompli*. We can go further and suggest that for a genuine 'constitutionalising process' to occur it would be necessary to sustain, over a considerable period of time, an exchange with the European citizenry. A model for this that would be well worth studying is the recent experience of South Africa. Its constituent assembly met over an entire year in a particularly open and public fashion. Extensive hearings were held; individuals and groups were invited to contact the drafting group by electronic means; a regular newsletter was published and widely circulated; the entire proceedings were extensively covered in the mass media; the ensuing draft was made available (in more than a dozen languages) to all citizens; special efforts were made to use language intelligible to the average person; the final version was ratified only after an intensive process of public justification and debate.

The fact that in the South African case these deliberations emerged from a history of social and political trauma is beside the point.

If it followed a comparable set of procedures, the EU would have an additional advantage. In the high likelihood that two rival versions of the European constitution were drafted simultaneously within the same constituent assembly, the flow of information and, hence, interest in the debate should be enhanced. Citizens and their parties, associations and movements would be offered competitive projects with which they could identify, as a result of which they would be more likely to feel that their efforts were making a difference.

A Second Referendum

The definitive ratification of the European constitution would involve a second Europe-wide referendum – to be held simultaneously and identically in all member states – at which European citizens would be asked to choose between the two texts, or to reject both.

At this point, a very complex situation could arise and it is precisely this prospect that may encourage greater co-operation (not to say, collusion) among the drafters. The European electorate could reject both the confederal and federal texts, although this seems unlikely given both the previous consultation at the initiation of the process and the symbolic investment subsequently involved. A clear majority of the citizenry in virtually all member states would most probably approve one or the other of the texts. What does not seem likely to me – barring some unforeseeable convergence of opinion among national and sub-national publics that have, so far, expressed quite divergent preferences with regard to EU institutions – is that they would approve the same text. So, we are led to the (tentative) conclusion that the 'confederal' version will prevail in some countries and the 'federal' one in others – perhaps, with some even opting for no constitution at all. Confusing as it may sound, such an outcome would be an accurate reflection of the 'diversity in unity' that is such a major element in Europe's political reality as well as being a central plank of much Europhile rhetoric. And taking it on board might also obviate the need for the language of stark choices – either one is a full partner or no partner at all – which can dominate EU discussion at the level of national politics.

The question, of course, is what to do 'constitutionally' in the face of this divided outcome. Giving up altogether would make a mockery of all the preceding effort; going ahead by installing the version that gathered the most support would override a (presumably) sizeable minority.[13] The unorthodox, but nonetheless appropriate response might well be to go ahead with both. No doubt this is a horrifying thought to juridical purists, but perhaps it would be a viable concession to the diversity embedded in European society. Suppose for a minute that both constitutions shared two elements: (1) a joint definition of account-ability in terms of basic democratic principles; and (2) a minimum common denominator in terms of substantive policies. These would constitute a dual *acquis communautaire* that all present and future members of the EU agree to respect. They would then be free to differ primarily along the following lines:

> *Irrevocability.* The 'federal' version in order to be credible would have to commit its member states (and their sub-units) to a permanent arrangement without foreseeable dissolution, whereas, the 'confederal' charter is likely to contain the explicit right to independent withdrawal.
>
> *Competences.* In the weaker document, the subsidiary powers of the central government would be explicitly limited to a pre-determined list and all remaining powers would be exclusively assigned to the member states or their sub-units; in the stronger version, not only would the list of exclusive federal competences be more extensive, but it would also be easier to extend it should the functional necessity arise. Both documents might contain provisions for so-called 'shared' or 'overlapping' powers, as well as for the establish-ment of independent regulatory commissions. The former is more characteristic of 'co-operative federalism'; the latter of a more centralised version.
>
> *Decision rules.* Presumably, the federal version would rely more extensively on weighted or simple majority principles; the confederal one would stress the need for higher thresholds, even for unanimity on certain issues. Needless to say, the respective roles of the Council of Ministers, the Commission and the Parliament (or their successors) could be expected to differ considerably − although both versions would involve more-or-less the same institutions and rules for admission to them. Both are also likely to share an emphasis on the participation of governments of member states (as in Germany and Switzerland) rather than individual citizens grouped according to territorial constituencies (as in the USA).
>
> *Asymmetries.* Should the stronger draft follow the classic federalist formula, the emphasis would be on the uniformity of rights and obligations for all participating individuals

and collectivities; the weaker version might well include provisions for differential (as well as deferred) forms of participation.

These do not seem to me to be radically divergent principles and they should be compatible within the same polity. One subset of members – those in which the confederal alternative prevailed – would be bound by a different, less constraining, set of rules than would those whose citizenries had chosen the federal one. Europe would find itself with a 'core area' that was prepared to move ahead further and faster toward political integration and a 'periphery' that accepted a common *acquis communautaire*, but was unwilling to extend for the foreseeable future.[14] Needless to say, the latter countries would have the right – once they had experienced the consequences of peripheral status – to join the former – but only once had they gone through all the formalities of inter-governmental negotiation and ratification via popular referendum. Those countries (and their populations) that initially chose the federal option could, however, change their political status only under quite exceptional conditions.

I admit that designing a polity whose members would be subject to two different constitutions (even if the one were to be firmly embedded within the other) does not sound like an ideal state of affairs. Some parallels do exist (e.g. the status of self-governing Native American tribes within the USA, that of the so-called 'historical regions' in Spain or that claimed by Quebec within the Canadian Federation) and both systems would be inserted within the same overriding judicial procedure for resolving eventual conflicts (presuming the comprehensive justiciability of the European Court of Justice [ECJ]). Nevertheless, the best one could claim is that such a flexible formula does correspond to the reality of contemporary Europe (and even more to an EU that has expanded to more than twenty members) and that it might just prove to be a temporary expedient.

Notes

1 I can only think of one clear case: Switzerland in the early 1870s. It would be interesting to explore this exception, although the fact that this country had a 'one party dominant system' (*Freisinnige/Radical*) at the time must have been an important factor – and, not one that can be repeated at the EU-level.

2 One has to admit that the 'Convention' mode was innovative and a considerable improvement over past efforts. Deliberate attempts were made

to reach out to organisations in civil society and a wide range of professional expertise. The fact that, with the exception of a few specialised groups, the process failed to attract the attention of wider publics I interpret as a confirmation of my observation above that its timing was wrong. Virtually no one, with the obvious exception of its participants, the 'Conventionnels', was convinced of its imperative necessity.

3 As mentioned, the Convention did break new ground in terms of openness – although when the deadline approached, the drafting process receded into a small executive group.

4 The fact that several of these constitutional drafts have come out of the European Parliament and that one of their most manifest objectives was to increase the powers of that very same institution suggests that 'institutional' – if not 'personal' – self-interest cannot be ruled out of the process.

5 Should they occur, the various and sundry 'crises' that are likely to be generated by Eastern enlargement, as well as by politicisation at the national level in response to monetary unification and implementation deficits in other policy areas, are better addressed by episodic inter-governmental negotiations.

6 Agreement among the EU heads of government about a constitution, the ratification of which faces considerable obstacles, is a very different thing from a successfully constitutionalised EU.

7 Something that I have argued previously in Schmitter 1996.

8 On the 'quasi-constitutional' status of the EEC/EC/EU treaties, see Weiler 1996.

9 A minor problem involved the fact that one country, the UK, continued until recently to use a first-past-the-post, simple majoritarian system for electing its European deputies. Nothing could be less appropriate for a constituent assembly where it is especially important that the widest possible range of political preferences be included in the deliberations. The ideal system would be proportional representation based on closed lists (to improve the prospects for intraparty discipline) for sub-national constituencies – at least, in the larger countries and in those with significant regional disparities or identities.

10 One possible objection to this 'assignment principle' could well be that the results across constituencies within the same country will tend to differ within and not just between existing political parties. Indeed, given the internal divisions that can be observed over much less significant issues, one can imagine that European deputies are quite likely to be elected under the same party label by voters who have revealed their preference for quite different types of European polity – or even for no constitutionalised European polity at all. Much as this might make national party politicians wary of offering their followers such a potentially divisive opportunity, it does offer a splendid opportunity for the structuring of a genuinely European party system. The two drafting committees – the 'confederals' and the 'federals' – could well be the prototypes of future bi-polarised competition at the supra-national level.

11 Presumably with this power to put a halt to the entire process, the Council would be in a position to influence the deliberations of the European

56   *Philippe C. Schmitter* / Constitutionality and Political Participation

Parliament's two drafting assemblies and this should contribute to a more even-handed treatment of institutional checks and balances than if it were left exclusively in the hands of parliamentarians.

12 Presumably, individual deputies and parties would use this occasion to promote one or the other version – or to convince their followers to reject both.

13 As the example of the Basque response to the 1975 Spanish constitution demonstrates, even a minority within a minority region can use its rejection of a constitution that was otherwise massively approved by the electorate to question the legitimacy of the document and even to justify armed resistance to the regime it empowers.

14 The viability of such a 'dual' polity would depend to some degree on where and not just whether such a centre–periphery split developed. Hopefully, the federalists would be concentrated in a contiguous core area – more-or-less coincident with the original Six – and the confederalists would find themselves on the Northern, Southern and Eastern frontiers. Gradually and voluntarily, the outer layers could be expected to join the core (with the likely exception of Switzerland which, for the foreseeable future, will retain its status as 'the hole in the European doughnut').

References

Baubock, R. and J. Melchior (eds.), 1997, 'Grundrechte in der Europäischen Union. Ein Konferenzbericht'. Wien: Institut für Höhere Studien/Reihe Politikwissenschaft No. 44.
Bellamy, R. and D. Castiglione, 1996, 'Costituzionalismo e democrazia in una prospettiva europea', *Teoria Politica*, Vol. **12**(3), 47–70.
Bribosia, H., 1998, *Rapporteur. Quelle charte constitutionnelle pour l'Union européenne? Stratégies et options pour renforcer le caractère constitutionnel des traités*. Florence: Robert Schuman Centre, European University Institute.
Castiglione, D., 1995, 'Contracts and Constitutions', in R. Bellamy, V. Bufacchi and D. Castiglione (eds.), *Democracy and Constitutional Culture in the Union of Europe*. London: Lothian Foundation Press, pp. 59–79.
Cruz Vilaça, J.L. da, F. Herman, G. Howe, *et al.*, 1996, *Does Europe Need a Constitution?* Brussels: The Philippe Morris Institute for Public Policy Research.
Curtin, D., 1995, 'The Shaping of a European Constitution and the 1996 IGC: "Flexibility" as a Key Paradigm?', *Aussenwirtschaft*, Vol. **50**(1), 237–56.
Dehousse, R., 1995, 'Constitutional Reform in the European Community. Are there Alternatives to the Majority Avenue?', *West European Politics*, Vol. **18**(3), 118–36.
Diez-Picazo, L.-M., 1995, 'Reflexiones sobre la idea de constitución europea', *Revista de Instituciones Europeas*, Vol. **20**(2), 533–59.
The Economist, 2000, 'Our Constitution for Europe', 26 October, pp. 11–12, 21–8.

Frosini, T. E., 1996, 'Luci ed ombre di una futura costituzione europea', *Studi Parliamentari e di Politica Costituzionale*, Vol. **111**, 67–78.

Mancini, F. G., 1991, 'The Making of a Constitution for Europe' in R. Keohane and S. Hoffman (eds.), 1994, *The New European Community*. Boulder, CO: Westview Press, pp. 177–94.

Padoa-Schioppa, A., 1995, 'Towards a European Constitution', *Federalist*, Vol. **37**(1), 8–25.

Pernice, I., 1999, 'Multilevel Constitutionalism and the Treaty of Amsterdam: European Constitution-making Revisited?', *Common Market Law Review*, Vol. **36**(4), 703–50.

2000, 'Der europäische Verfassungsverbund auf dem Wege der Konsolidierung', *Jahrbuch des Öffentlichen Rechts der Gegenwart*, Vol. **48**, 205–32.

Preuss, U. K., 1994, 'Europäische Einigung und die integrative Kraft von Verfassungen', in J. Gebhardt and R. Schmalz-Bruns (eds.), *Demokratie, Verfassung und Nation. Die politische Integration moderner Gesellschaften*. Baden-Baden: Nomos, pp. 271–87.

Ransome, P. (ed.), 1991, *Towards the United States of Europe – Studies on the Making of the European Constitution*. London: Lothian Foundation Press.

Reich, N., 1997, 'A European Constitution for Citizens: Reflections on the Rethinking of Union and Community Law', *European Law Journal*, Vol. **3**(2), 131–64.

Rousseau, D., 2000, 'Pour une Constitution européenne', *Le Débat*, Vol. **108**(5), 54–73.

Rupp, H.-H., 1995, 'Europäische "Verfassung" und demokratische Legitimation', *Archiv des Öffentlichen Rechts*, Vol. **120**(2), 269–81.

Rusconi, G. E., 1997, 'Quale "democrazia costituzionale"? La corte federale nella politica tedesca e il problema della costituzione europea', *Rivista Italiana di Scienza Politica*, Vol. **27**(2), 273–306.

Schmitter, Philippe, 1996, 'Imagining the Future of the Euro-Polity', in Gary Marks, Fritz Scharpf, Philippe Schmitter and Wolfgang Streeck, *Governance in the European Union*, London: SAGE, pp. 121–50.

Seidel, M., 1995, 'Basic Aspects of a European Constitution', *Aussenwirtschaft*, Vol. **50**(1), 221–36.

Seurin, J.-L., 1994, 'Towards a European Constitution? Problems of Political Integration', *Public Law*, Vol. **38**, 625–36.

Shaw, J., 1999, 'Postnational Constitutionalism in the European Union', *Journal of European Public Policy*, Vol. **6**(4), 579–97.

2000, 'Relating Constitutionalism and Flexibility in the European Union', in G. de Búrca and J. Scott (eds.), *Constitutional Change in the EU. From Uniformity to Flexibility?* Oxford: Hart, pp. 337–58.

Velo, D., 1999, 'Costituzione europea, occupazione e sviluppo', *Nord e Sud*, Vol. **46**(5), 36–44.

Walker, N., 1999, 'Flexibility within a Metaconstitutional Frame. Reflections on the Future of Legal Authority in Europe', Harvard Jean Monnet Working Paper 12/99. Cambridge, MA: Harvard Law School.

Weiler, J.H.H., 1991, 'The Transformation of Europe', *Yale Law Journal*, Vol. **100**, 2403–83.

1995, 'Does Europe Need a Constititution? *Demos, Telos* and the German Maastricht Decision', *European Law Journal*, Vol. **1**(3), 219–58.

1996, 'European Neo-constitutionalism. In Search of Foundations for the European Constitutional Order', *Political Studies*, Vol. **44**, 517–33.

Part II

European Polity and European Civil Society

4   European Political Modernity

Heidrun Friese and Peter Wagner

After having discussed the need for 'normative impulses' for effective social and political integration in Europe, impulses that can only come about 'through overlapping projects for a common political culture', Jürgen Habermas, in the title essay to *The Postnational Constellation*, immediately reassures his readers that such projects 'can be constructed in the common historical horizon that the citizens of Europe already find themselves in'. And a moment later he indeed identifies an already existing 'normative self-understanding of European modernity'.[1] What, though, is this self-understanding of European modernity, and what is its specificity?

Some have objected to Habermas, or to all those who try to identify normative underpinnings for European political integration, that such European self-understanding is either entirely indistinct from the general self-understanding of the West, i.e. a commitment to human rights and liberal democracy, or highly problematic, because it makes overly 'thick' presuppositions, which are untenable against the background of European cultural diversity, and risks reviving non-liberal European political traditions.[2] The proposition made in the following attempt to reconstruct the normative self-understanding of European political modernity is different. It suggests, on the one hand, that the general, universalist commitment to liberal democracy is insufficient to understand Western polities. The commitment to political modernity does not lead unequivocally to a certain institutional form of the polity. It is open to interpretation, and the existing polities that share this commitment are indeed based on a variety of such interpretations.[3] And while, on the other hand, a certain lack of such commitment is both possible and likely even in the West, there is not a single scale of 'political modernisation', on which the USA, and possibly the UK, always appear at the top, and continental European polities lag behind. A closer analysis not only needs to be open to a large variety of interpretations of political modernity, it also needs to accept ambivalences in that very commitment, ambivalences which can never be resolved once and for all.

In other words, our starting point is the assumption that, while such normative self-understandings may contain general and universal elements, they are always specific and situated in the time and space of the social life to which they refer. And in this chapter we retrieve them through a brief history of political ideas in Europe and a history of European socio-political forms. Such retrieval aims at identifying the specificity of the European self-understanding of political modernity. At the same time, it will need to address a theoretical question: individualist liberalism is often considered to be the pivotal philosophy of political modernity, and a review of the European historical experience can help understand why this is so.[4] However, individualist liberalism is also insufficient and unsatisfactory as the guiding political philosophy of modernity, and an analysis of the struggles about European political modernity can show how the self-understanding of a modern polity can point beyond individualist liberalism.[5]

Three Narratives of Political Europe: Liberty, Statehood and Democracy

Before our own reconstruction starts, we may recall familiar ways of telling the story of political Europe. First, there is the *liberal* story, the story of the gradual extension of civic rights. It normally starts with the Magna Carta (1215) and then the Habeas Corpus Act (1679) as early indications of the recognition that the reign of rulers over the inhabitants of their territory could be formally limited. Even though the position of these two bills remains supreme in the textbook version of the liberal story, historical research has found many more instances of the recognition of such rights in Europe. Often, though, these rights were themselves limited to certain groups of human beings on a territory, or to rather small and narrowly confined polities, such as the merchant cities around the Baltic Sea and the North Sea or the city republics on the Northern rim of the Mediterranean Sea.

This story then makes a leap to the *Déclaration des droits de l'homme et du citoyen* in revolutionary France in 1789. It is a leap in several respects: the declaration applies to a large European polity, and it even has explicit universal leanings. Furthermore, it clearly refers to the singular human being, and it does not make the rights it contains dependent on any qualities of this being, beyond being human. The history of Europe in the one and a half centuries succeeding this declaration can nevertheless only with difficulties be read as the gradual realisation of the aims of that declaration. It needed the United Nations Universal Declaration of Human Rights in 1948, after the end of Nazism and the Second World War, to add a further chapter to the liberal story. But from this moment on, the narration appears to proceed smoothly again. It then turns into a story of local European origins, some limited and partial institutionalisation in this local context, then a giant step towards universalisation of the normative claims, followed by a long and difficult process of globalisation, that is, the actual spreading of the claims around the world.

The second story of political Europe has at first sight very little relation to the first one; it is the story of the development of the modern state system. It has two clear starting points. In intellectual history, it starts with the elaboration of the concept of sovereignty, first in Jean Bodin, then in Thomas Hobbes; in political history, it starts with the Treaty of Westphalia (1648) that marks the end of the Thirty Years War. The former establishes the idea that a state should have full control over its territory and its population; the latter applies this idea to end the religious wars in Europe. From now on, to idealise the story considerably, religious unity and its connection to state authority should secure domestic peace, whereas the establishment of clear territorial boundaries together with the principle of non-interference should secure peaceful relations between states.

Clearly, though, the principle of sovereignty was a suitable means to domestic peace at best, since the principle of non-interference was hardly accepted, and the new state system is better characterised by inter-state anarchy, that is, the absence of any regulatory principle.[6] Ways of establishing 'perpetual peace' kept preoccupying political thinkers, and the gradual elaboration of international law was seen as the most promising route, intended ultimately to lead to a cosmopolitan political order. This last chapter turns the story of state development, like the liberal story, into a narrative about gradual globalisation. Unlike the liberal story, though, it stalls at a certain point. While a cosmopolitan political order is currently often seen as desirable, many observers regard it is unrealistic at the same time. The formation of the European Union (EU) can then be seen as a step in that direction, turning interstate relations into lawful ones and even transforming them halfway into domestic relations. At the same time, this political Europe remains territorially confined, with 'anarchic' relations to other parts of the world.

The third story about European political modernity is the narrative of the rise of democracy. It has the longest roots, but also the largest gaps.

It starts in the Greek *polis*, with the moment of the simultaneous invention of politics and philosophy, as some theorists put it,[7] then undergoes significant transformations in the Roman Republic and, much later, the Florentine and Venetian republics, without though entirely subsiding. Its full reassertion, however, is an event of the eighteenth century: in the history of ideas, with the transformation of the concept of state sovereignty into the one of popular sovereignty, most clearly by Jean-Jacques Rousseau; and in political history, with the American and the French Revolutions, marking the age of the 'democratic revolution'.[8]

As with the related moment in the liberal story, the chapter on the late eighteenth century did not really mark a breakthrough from whence the story could unfold smoothly. Perceptive observers, like Alexis de Tocqueville, recognised early on that there would be no final halt before universal suffrage had established the concept of the 'unit citizen', and the late nineteenth century witnessed gradual extensions of the suffrage in many European states. However, the Old Regime proved to be persistent, and it was only the end of the First World War that brought about what one would now call a first wave of transitions to democracy. And one would need to wait for the end of the Second World War to witness the consolidation of some of these democracies, and for the closing decades of the twentieth century to observe further waves of democratisation in Southern and Eastern Europe.

Connections and Tensions

All of these stories have a certain plausibility and persuasiveness. At least at first sight they are quite different stories, and it is not evident how they are, or could be, systematically connected. Both the relations and the tensions need to be explored, before a more comprehensive narrative can be developed.

Let us first look at the parallels between them. First of all, these stories are European stories in the sense of pointing to the European origins of the political developments they emphasise. But none of them remains confined to the territory of Europe. In some cases, the principal location in which the story unfolds seems to shift in the course of time, mostly to North America, and Europe has to re-enter the narrative at a later point. In the case of the first and the third story there certainly is a universal prospect and promise, even though it is not globally accepted at all times. Thus, these are essentially linear stories, even though it remains to be seen whether they will keep unfolding. As to the second story, its precise continuation is even in normative doubt. Even committed cosmopolitans have most often constructed their global utopia as a confederation of free republics rather than as one global polity. There are reasons to argue, then, that this story will or should be stopped before its theoretical culmination.

The second story is also central in this account as it is the focus of tension between the narratives. The first and the second story, namely, can be easily connected in a narrative of the 'rise of liberal institutions and customs', as it is sometimes put nowadays.[9] The basic political theory adopted here is individualist liberalism, fully compatible with the first narrative, and the modern state is then nothing but the 'container' that holds free individuals together and gives their freedom a legal form. One can just as easily connect the third story to the second one, but then the emphasis would shift to the commitment to collective self-determination.[10] This would essentially be the democratic story, but once again with a sense of the 'container' in which social life and political action unfolds. While in both cases, the story of state development appears to provide nothing but an empty shell, the importance of this question – the question of political form – should not be underestimated. The meaning of this form changes considerably when one connects it to the third story instead of the first one.

This is not to say, though, that the first story and the third story are unconnected. The Declaration of Human Rights in France, and in the form of the Bill of Rights in the USA, emerges with the democratic revolutions at the end of the eighteenth century. And the re-emergence of the former after the dark middle of the twentieth century appears to be historically connected to the late-twentieth-century waves of democratisation. It seems difficult to sever the right to individual self-determination from the right to collective self-determination. Nevertheless, an overemphasis on individual self-determination has often concerned political theorists, at least from Edmund Burke onwards, who worried about the viability of the polity when individual liberty asserts itself too strongly. Conversely, an overemphasis on collective self-determination brought the commitment to democracy in the vicinity of totalitarianism, or at least to the possibility of the 'tyranny of the majority' (De Tocqueville).[11] Thus, it is striking to see the absence of a serious concern for political form in the heydays of both movements for freedom. It is as if personal freedom and democracy are self-evident and uncontroversial if one only believes in them. In the recent past, only some, so to say, republican critics of totalitarianism, such as

Hannah Arendt or Claude Lefort, were able to see that there was
a version of the connection of (bourgeois) liberalism with (nationalist)
democracy that was more destructive of freedom than any other
political regime of modernity, and that the neglect of political form
was crucial for this destruction of freedom.[12]

European Integration – the End of which Story?

This is not just a historical reflection on the times before the
consolidation of democracy. The tension between the three narratives
is at the core of political modernity. It is alive and well in much of the
current reasoning about the political theory of European integration.
There are two main ways of thinking politically about contemporary
Europe and these are precisely selective combinations of the three
narratives above.

First, European integration is often referred to as a combination
of the liberal story and the story of state development. In this account,
the existing European polities, the nation-states, have provided
a viable combination of liberty and democracy, but this combination
is challenged by the socio-economic transformations of our time,
mostly known by the short-hand of globalisation. The solution to the
current problem, in this view, is to extend the reach of state action
while safeguarding the guarantees for civic liberty. The actual process
of European integration is then seen as following this maxim. For
instance, of the two truly European institutions, one, the European
Court of Justice (ECJ), serves to protect 'civic' liberties; the other
one, the European Central Bank, expands the reach of state action
where it was most crucially needed, namely in guiding the economy
by its most basic parameter, the money supply. In addition, the
European Commission fulfils its work best, in this view, when it
accepts the fact that it is not democratically legitimised and
concentrates its efforts exclusively on enhancing the efficiency of state
action.[13] This account, thus, combines a commitment to 'civic'
liberty with one of state efficiency at the expense of collective self-
determination.

In contrast, other contributors to the debate on European political
integration combine the third story with the second one at the expense
of the first. In this case, the European nation-state has provided a combination of democracy, trust and solidarity that is unlikely to be
improved upon. The nation-state is the form in which large-scale societies have developed the ability to act upon themselves. In this respect,
it stands out positively in comparison both to 'traditional' societies

marked by illegitimate forms of hierarchy and to any future postnational society.[14] This reasoning provides the background to all versions of Euroscepticism. Normatively, it prefers to halt political Europeanisation sooner rather than later, but it also maintains a distance from any liberal multi-culturalism within the existing nation-states, since the undermining of historically constituted relations of trust and solidarity is seen as an ever-present danger.

The normative standpoints of these two positions are opposed to one another. Nevertheless, these positions share an important background assumption about the current political condition, namely that it is marked by a rather strong pressure towards continuation of the liberal story, as indicated by the increase of the free movement of people, goods, services and capital, often referred to as the economic and social dimensions of globalisation. At the same time, such continuation of the liberal story is often seen as requiring a continuation of the story of state development beyond the point where it was halted, since it is states and their attempts at boundary control that are impediments to further increase of individual liberties. Such continuation of the state story in the direction of a cosmopolitan order, in turn, appears difficult without interrupting, or at least considerably re-telling, the story of the rise of democracy.

All this means that political modernity needs to be conceptualised in terms of persistent tensions between different exigencies, rather than in terms of a yet to be achieved solution. While not at all averse to the idea of a political narrative, political theory and political science have mostly devoted their energy to the further refinement of the separate stories of liberty, sovereign statehood and democracy, often as linear, even though temporarily interrupted accounts of evolutionary progress. The underlying assumption was that the three stories unfold unproblematically in parallel, or even that they converge over time until full political modernity is achieved. The observation, though, that a given political condition can more fruitfully be seen as a compromise reached in balancing the tensions between the exigencies of liberty, statehood and democracy leads us to look in more detail at a historical variety of such conditions as chapters in a more comprehensive story which contains elements of some or even all of the three separate narratives.

Re-narrating European Political Modernity

Our narrative of European political modernity falls into seven stages.

*From Greece to Christian Rome, or the particular soul and the
universal individual*

A mention of Greek democracy is *de rigueur* in accounts of European
political modernity, but it is most often accompanied by remarks
about the highly different kind of polity and conception of politics which
make the Greek understanding of democracy untenable for contemporary purposes. This is true, but only in a narrowly constructed story of
the rise of democracy. In a broader view, there are other political issues
at stake in the ancient heritage of European politics. We may indicate
some of its contents.

The Greek *polis* at its apex created a strong relation between the idea
of democracy and the concern for the self such that the care for the
soul inspires the rules of the polity and guides political behaviour.[15]
One of the consequences of this view was the limitation of political
action to free men. Such restriction certainly had to be lifted under
conditions of political modernity, as we now understand it. Once all
members of a polity participate in it freely and equally, however,
any strong substantive relation between the individual member of
the polity and the participation in the fate of the polity would also
often be incompatible with political modernity, on grounds namely of
the – 'negative', as it should later be called – freedom of the individual,
which entails the possibility of choosing a self and 'soul' that is largely
unrelated to the polity. This, at least, is the reasoning that stands
behind individualist liberalism, which emerges much later in European
history, after devastating experiences with strong commitments of
the political self to substantive issues, e.g. in terms of religious or ethnic
forms of collective identity.

Nevertheless, the question of the relationship between self and
polity, which was cast in specific terms in the Greek polity could never
entirely disappear from the agenda of political modernity. In a transformed version, European romanticism, too, had a strong view of the
self and linked it to the cultural-linguistic conception of the polity that
stood in the background of (at least, some version of) the European
nation-state. In contemporary debate, the attempt at reviving 'civic
republicanism' and a concept of *virtù*, in explicit contrast to individualist liberalism, reiterates the same theme in different form. Despite all
differences, thus, the Greek polity contained a tension that has stayed
with the European polities to the present day.

The emergence of the Roman Republic, and then Empire, displaced Greek political power, but not before appropriating elements
of its politico-philosophical orientations. The Christian religion

emerged out of an encounter of Judaism and Greek thought; and there was a fusion of some of these elements – all while being transformed – in Christian Rome. It has often been argued that this Roman fusion marks indeed 'the birth of Europe in the present sense of the word'.[16] Politico-philosophically, it contains ideas of the person, of law, of universalism,[17] all the while being unstable as a polity and much more uncertain of the ground on which it stands than any of its religious or political components had been on their own. Rémi Brague has even argued that this is the specificity of Europe: that it is secondary culturally towards ancient Greece and religiously towards Judaism, that it has an eccentric identity.[18]

From the Holy Roman Empire to the Westphalian State System: Progress or Disintegration?

The decline of the Holy Roman Empire and the emergence of the European states system after the Thirty Years War are often interpreted in terms of the difficulty of holding large empires together because of both their size and their diversity. The creation of a well-ordered system of smaller and more homogeneous states is then seen as political progress. However, the long-term transformation of the European polities from the universalistically inclined, yet weakly integrated Roman Empire into the plurality of religiously homogeneous, sovereign states seems to spell in at least two respects a chapter of decline in political modernity. First, although the background to the Westphalian agreement was a search for stable peace, there was less of a common orientation in the relations between rulers than before, the principle of non-interference being the only firm ground to stand on. Second, the commitment of the new polity was less universalist than that of the Empire. The principle of *cuius regio eius religio* allowed the ruler to decide about the value commitments of his/her subjects in the name of domestic peace.[19]

Despite this character of an imposition, the latter feature of the polity is sometimes seen as the first 'modern' version of the idea that there needs to be considerable value commonality between members of a polity, an idea that was constitutive for the later cultural-linguistic idea of the polity and that has acquired generalised form under the heading of 'communitarianism'. The complexity of the political situation makes this argument difficult to sustain. The inhabitants of the post-Westphalian states remained subjects of rulers and did not become citizens participating in the definition of the polity. For this reason, multi-religious and multi-lingual empires did not face any particular legitimacy problems during this period, whose novelty consisted in the form of the state rather than its substantive underpinnings. To avoid ambiguities in matters political, the state should have firm boundaries to the outside and be internally sovereign.[20] As such, and increasingly based on a formal bureaucracy, often for fiscal purposes, this emerging modern state, although not liberal at all, could become the container in which claims to liberty could unfold.[21] In other words, the experience of that period underlines the relationship between formal sovereign statehood and rights-based individual liberty. The fragmentation of Europe into several neatly divided polities, in contrast, is often overlooked when the accomplishment of sovereignty is underlined.

From the Religious Wars to the Revolution, or from State Sovereignty to Popular Sovereignty

Furthermore, the 'early modern' configuration of state and society is often regarded merely as an interim between the feudal order and modern society, as it was to emerge after the democratic and industrial revolutions. The state is seen as having already reached its modern form, while still lacking democratic legitimacy. Thus, the remaining obstacle on the way to political modernity is the tension between sovereign statehood and democracy. And the solution to it is the move from state sovereignty to popular sovereignty, or in terms of the history of political thought, the move from Bodin via Hobbes to Locke and Rousseau. Once that solution is reached, liberty, sovereignty and democracy are connected and full political modernity is accomplished.

This interpretation, though, strikes us immediately as one that focuses exclusively on domestic issues, whereas interstate issues had hitherto been at least as central in political thought. Since Enlightenment cosmopolitanism stands at the threshold from the Old Regime to the revolutions, a look at its way of dealing with these issues can elucidate this problem. Enlightenment political thought, most clearly exemplified by Kant, recognised not one, but two main problems in the old order, namely internal restrictions to liberty and interstate anarchy. The answer to these problems was equally clear. The internal restrictions were to be overcome by the combined commitment of the polity to liberty and equality; and interstate anarchy would be overcome by a cosmopolitan order composed of democratic republics. Furthermore, these two solutions could be regarded as connected: democratic republics would be less inclined to warfare than autocratic regimes, and civic liberties could thrive better under conditions of peace.

While the *problématique* was well recognised, the requirements for a solution were higher than Enlightenment theorists expected. The move to popular sovereignty went along with a stronger understanding of membership in a polity than the 'early modern state' had known. As long as it was the state that was sovereign over a territory and a population, it mattered very little to the rulers who the members – more precisely: subjects – were over whom they ruled. When, however, the people themselves were to exercise sovereignty, the idea of an unproblematically emerging *volonté générale* soon ceased to have plausibility. Because democracy introduced a closer connection between those who govern and those who are governed, membership became an important issue. The French revolutionaries were still optimistic and aimed at granting membership to everybody who adhered to republican ideas. Very soon after, and not least due to the failure of the Revolution to spread across Europe and establish a European republic or federation of republics, the cultural-linguistic theory of the polity gained ground, offering itself as the solution to the problem of value diversity under conditions of democracy.

For these reasons, then, the empires also started to lose legitimacy from the democratic revolutions onwards. It is insufficient to regard them as just another form of Old Regime, which could not withstand the calls for liberty and democracy. If that had been the only issue, then something like a Habsburg or Ottoman revolution should have been as conceivable as a French revolution, whereas in historical fact it was not. Unlike in the French case, the viability of the form of the state was as much in question as the form of government, and the reason for this was found at the time in the diversity of the population, containing several cultural-linguistic entities rather than one. One may speculate whether the Habsburg Empire, had it been able to liberalise and democratise before the call for national self-determination arose, could have become a model for European integration. Or one can ask whether a democratically deficient EU does not resemble the Habsburg Empire during its enlightened period, governing relatively efficiently and granting some degree of autonomy to its constituent nations.[22]

From National-liberalism and Social Solidarity to Totalitarianism

Enlightenment and romanticism were founding inspirations for political philosophy during the emergence of political modernity, that is, the era around the French Revolution that was to shape European political history for the following one and a half centuries. The opposition between them is often exaggerated, both as general philosophies and as political philosophies. The national-liberalism of the first half of the nineteenth century and the ideological support of the movements for collective self-determination, combined rather well the exigencies of both democracy and liberty with the quest for republican statehood. As such a compromise, it accepted and expressed 'the difficulty that the modern ideology has in providing a sufficient image of social life'.[23] Subsequently, though, the struggles during much of the nineteenth century can only be discussed in terms of the increasing inability to live politically with the ambiguity that this founding tension created.

From the middle of the nineteenth century onwards, it was increasingly recognised that there was a second founding tension at the heart of European political modernity. With its commitment to fraternity, beyond liberty and equality, the French Revolution laid the basis for what was later to be either called class struggle or the social question.[24] In France, this issue was discussed early on as a biased interpretation of the revolutionary commitment, namely one that overemphasised (individual) liberty and equality of civic rights at the expense of collective organisation for the achievement of substantive equality by means of social solidarity.[25] The relationship between social and liberal commitments was increasingly ridden with tension. In many countries, the social question was repressed rather than solved; and in response, the collective movements for solidarity accepted the limitation of individual liberties as a precondition for a satisfactory answer to it.

In this constellation, towards the end of the nineteenth century, cultural-linguistic or socio-economic theories of the polity were increasingly regarded as alternatives to, rather than complements of, an individualist-liberal theory of the polity. As liberalism was widely seen in deep crisis, economically because of recurring depressions and the inability to deal with poverty and misery, and politically because of the advent of 'mass society' and large-scale social organisation, both of these alternatives found increasing plausibility and support. Since their modes of reasoning, though sharing the critique of individualism, were also opposed to one another and their support came mostly from different groups in society, nationalism and socialism, and later communism as well, were often seen to oppose 'liberal society' from different directions. The resort to these political theories thus opened the space for increasingly aggressive nationalism, on the one hand, and for almost equally intransigent class struggle, on the other. It is important to add, though, that these theories remained committed to a form of democracy, of collective self-determination.[26] Unlike liberal theories, however, they made strong presuppositions as to the nature of the *demos*.

These tensions exploded with the First World War and its aftermath. The interwar period was marked by a loss of political language and by desperate, mostly ill-fated, attempts to regain such language or to recreate one. Nazism and Stalinism remain insufficiently understood as long as their attraction for large groups in society, and for intellectuals, is merely denounced without being addressed.[27] The intellectual outcome has been a bifurcation of social and political thought, which emerged in direct response to totalitarianism, and which persists to this day. In political philosophy proper, the advent of totalitarianism was interpreted by thinkers from the European continent, such as Isaiah Berlin, Karl Popper and Jacob Talmon, as demonstrating the inescapability of some form of individualist liberalism as the founding philosophy of modern societies with a commitment to human rights and values. The most famous statement in this respect is certainly Isaiah Berlin's plea for negative liberty to be given preference over positive liberty.[28] It is important to note that many of these thinkers, Berlin and Talmon in particular, had affinities to more substantively rich alternatives of political philosophy and that they did not abandon those alternatives lightly. Historical experience had demonstrated though, in their view, that all more substantive political philosophies, once they served as the underpinning for political orders, were prone to produce catastrophic results. The next generation of political theorists, with John Rawls as the towering figure, accepted those findings, but lacked the historical experience and the awareness of the questions that were still raised in the middle of the twentieth century. For them, rights-based individualist liberalism was the only ground to stand on.

In philosophy and critical theory, conclusions drawn from the experiences of the first half of the twentieth century took a more radical shape. They tended to refer to the attempted annihilation of European Jewry in particular, rather than to totalitarianism more generally. And from this specific event in human history it drew conclusions about the availability – or non-availability – of a language of representation. This is Adorno's intellectual trajectory from his first remarks on the status of poetry after Auschwitz to his *Negative Dialectics*, and Lyotard's from his early writing about Auschwitz to the rejection of all narratives of emancipation. Writers such as Paul Celan, Primo Levi and Sarah Kofman have struggled with the question of the possibility of language and representation after this experience for all of their lives, and this question, though it can be temporarily repressed, is bound to stay with us.[29] In political terms, doubt about the possibility of representation led directly to scepticism with regard to grasping that which human beings may have in common – and thus the very possibility of politics. For fear of hypostatising or essentialising community, as pre-totalitarian critical thinkers tended to do in the face of the damage inflicted by individualism, recent post-totalitarian political thinkers see community as 'inoperative'[30] and justice and democracy as always yet 'to come'.[31]

Les Trente Glorieuses, or the Post-disaster Compromise

Such debates had little influence on the reconstitution of polities in post-Second World War Europe.[32] Certainly, political reconstruction was marked by a stronger emphasis on civic liberty and the rule of law than during the first half of the twentieth century. However, the relatively stable West European political orders of the 'thirty glorious years'[33] were not based on the pure proceduralism of rights-based individualist liberalism. Domestically, as liberal-democratic nation-states with increasingly developed welfare policies, they showed signs of a compromise between liberal justifications and those of a linguistic-cultural and a social nature. In this way they combined the three political theories that were rather strongly pitted against each other during the first half of the century – liberalism, nationalism and socialism – into a viable arrangement. This was not theoretically consistent, but was seen as satisfactory by a large majority of the population, as increasing 'mass loyalty'[34] seemed to demonstrate until the late 1960s.

At the same time, in many respects this compromise fell short of normative requirements of political modernity. For instance, based on its 'cultural' component, it often justified gender inequality in law and limited the right to cultural expression for 'minorities'. Furthermore, as illustrated by divorce and abortion, it made moral standards compulsory that are in fact contested, so that their inscription into law can be seen as violating the right of the individual. The context of the Cold War was used as a justification for restrictions to political expression, in particular to socialist/communist groups. This compromise tied those justifications together by recourse to an empirical science of politics and society, which was to guide the way on a path of wealth and loyalty and the employment of which was never free of technocratic undertones.

The liberal-democratic welfarist nation-state in Europe, in the shape which it had acquired by around 1970, should be seen, then, less as the hitherto highest accomplishment of human history than as a temporary compromise between different requirements. This form of the West European polity, with all differences that existed between the nation-states, had achieved a quite inclusive democracy within a bounded state, which derived the justification for its boundary from a cultural-linguistic theory of the polity and used the limited membership as a basis for thick relations of trust and solidarity as well as of comprehensively safe-guarded, although culturally heavily circumscribed, liberty.[35] It certainly was relatively successful in balancing the tension between those exigencies; as a compromise without firm and consistent solutions, however, it was bound to be only temporarily stable and to be challenged by future developments.

Liberal Challenges, Democratic Misconceptions, or from '1968' to '1989'

From the 1960s onwards, this polity was shaken not only by what is now referred to as processes of globalisation, but also by internal critique and demands for liberation from the constraints imposed by that socio-institutional configuration. In this sense, '1968' in Western Europe and, under significantly different conditions, '1989', first in Central and Eastern Europe and then in all of Europe, mark the most recent period of struggle over the foundations of the European polities. Both of these observations are significant for rethinking European political philosophy. First, it is erroneous to see 'globalisation' as an external shock to which an accomplished political modernity needs to react and in the face of which it tries to safeguard its achievements. Globalisation in both its economic and its cultural meaning emanates from inside the European societies − as well as others, of course − and is thus part of their modernity. If its effect is to unbalance the existing institutional arrangements, this demonstrates the temporary nature of what we have described as a compromise. Second, this compromise was not only unstable in the long run, it lacked a normative basis. The complex processes that led to the fall of Soviet socialism, even if they meant many other things as well, were also about liberation from constraints, as were the social and political activities often described by referring to the date 1968, or better: 'les années 68'. This struggle for freedom can be described, as Jürgen Habermas would put it, as expanding normative horizons, and as an integral part of a struggle about political modernity.

A political analysis of this recent past, though, cannot stop at this point. Both 1968 and 1989 fit rather easily into a narrative about (individual) liberty. The question whether they fit into a narrative about democracy is more difficult to answer. The year 1989 is commonly analysed by political scientists as one of the recent waves of democratisation. At the same time, though, it was also connected to terms such as 'anti-politics' by its own proponents, and collective self-determination, while it figured strongly as an objective of the protest movements, proved elusive when the initial protest coalitions fell apart after the existing institutions had been successfully challenged.[36] In this respect, there is a striking similarity between 1989 and 1968. The latter clearly had an initial view of a new collective subject that was announcing its arrival in the streets of Paris, Berlin and elsewhere; a new quality of collective self-determination and democracy was at stake. However, this project also fell apart into two quite diverse components, one that focused on the liberty of individual expression and another one that emphasised collectivism without much regard for the actual collectivity it was addressing.

The ambivalent nature of the democratic commitment of the West and the East European protest movements can be better understood by introducing the third basic partial narrative about political modernity: statehood. Both 'liberating' movements included some component of collective self-determination in their ambitions, even though the existing limits to individual self-determination may have been the most important driving motive. However, they can be taken to have implicitly assumed that collective self-determination, i.e. democracy, is a natural consequence of individual self-determination.[37] In other words, they underestimated the importance of a viable political form; and neglected the question of statehood.[38] As a result, both movements were highly successful as unsettling experiences, but less so in their efforts to reconstruct the political.

The Nascent European Polity as the Compromise of Our Era

In the light of the experience of extended internal and external warfare, the post-Second World War period brought with it the construction of a temporary stable compromise between liberal-democratic, cultural-linguistic and socio-economic foundations of the polity, institutionally expressed in the form of democratic-capitalist welfare states in Western Europe. One additional part of that compromise was the association of West European nation-states in what is now called the EU. Although being created as a direct response to the experience of intra-European warfare, for many years this association was not understood as a political form proper. Another dimension of that compromise was the political division of Europe, a division that arose out of different answers to the question of organised social solidarity, namely the socialist and Christian responses on one side, and the communist one on the other. If the last three decades effectively challenged that arrangement, with the fall of Soviet socialism finally bringing it down, it is notable that the construction of a truly European polity experienced an upsurge at the very moment of the final collapse of the Cold-War order. The question we need to return to, thus, is the question of whether and in which sense the construction of a European polity can be seen as the contemporary response to the perennial problem of interpreting and institutionalising political modernity.

The current institutional and intellectual restructurings entail the reopening of the question of the form of political modernity in Europe. This question was temporarily closed as an effect of the stability of the postwar and Cold-War institutional compromise.[39] It can safely be asserted that a novel answer to this political *problématique* needs to be found, an answer that restabilises a version of the old compromise or more likely introduces additional elements into it. It seems equally safe to state that no 'pure' answer will be found. Even so, a conceptual perspective on the task can be indicated. The current process of European integration needs to be analysed in terms of the resources available to actors and in terms of the current (global) political constellation. European integration has no self-propelled tendency, but is a constructive process.

Therefore, first, European integration needs to be regarded as that historically rare event, the deliberate founding of a polity, a founding, however, that is aware of its own impossibility, a foundation as rupture. This conceptual move has two implications. It requires, first, a shift from the conventional social and political sciences to the register of political theory and political philosophy. This move, second, changes the place of empirical socio-historical knowledge in the analysis. Neither is it to be relegated to a secondary position as in mainstream political theory nor can socio-historical features be taken to determine the outcome of a founding process. Rather, an analysis of the socio-historical background of the founding process serves to identify the situation in which this process takes place and the resources available to the actors in the present and thus permits the assessment of the conditions of possibility for particular forms of polity to emerge from the process of foundation.

Second, even while the search for an answer to the contemporary *problématique* means the search for a new compromise in the knowledge that this compromise is again temporary, this answer needs to respond appropriately to the contemporary situation. It seems safe to say that the emerging European polity needs to be placed in global context, with reference to the other major variety of Western modernity, the USA.[40]

Such repositioning, third, based on the emergence of a 'self-critical relation to national memory',[41] makes possible a selective retrieval of the resources developed across the history of European political modernity. Several layers of political commitment can be drawn upon. The period after the Second World War, and in particular the last three decades, have underlined the European commitment to civic and political liberties, and indeed opened the way towards further expansion of liberties, as happened in the post-1968 and post-1989 periods. Furthermore, a broad consensus prevails in Europe with regard to the commitment to organised social solidarity, given particular significance in a global context strongly marked by neo-liberal arguments against such commitment. Finally, the current restructuring demands a reconceptualisation of the 'communitarian' component of European political modernity. It makes no sense to talk about European political modernity if there is not some common commitment that is specific to Europe. Otherwise, we would return to the straight narrative of Western modernity as the gradual realisation of universal political values, without internal tensions and diversity, from which this chapter aimed to gain critical distance at the outset.

For some decades, the construction of European political institutions has been accompanied by a discussion about a 'European identity', first mentioned in 1973 and expressed formally in the Charter of Fundamental Rights in 2000.[42] This discussion is marked by ambivalence. On the one hand, there is a broad understanding of the need to avoid any strong commitment to a cultural heritage with the concomitant risk of exclusion and restrictive cultural determinism. The long-debated decision not to mention Christianity in the preamble to the Charter was one outcome of this. On the other hand, the whole debate is motivated by precisely the need to speak about 'common values' (preamble) which might guide orientations for action in a future in which those values may be at risk.

It is tempting to see these debates as attempts to square the circle or to arrive at rhetorical, 'superstructural' formulae needed to hold together an instrumental institutional construction for everybody's benefit. Such interpretations, though, would already look at the process from a distant outside, through some kind of hermeneutics of suspicion. In turn, what seems at stake in these processes is precisely the description of a *hermeneutic relation*, of a form of engagement with others and with the world, that is a common European value, and that as such a value goes beyond an instrumental relation to others and the world.

Conclusion: European Political Philosophy Beyond Liberalism

This is where the core of the question about a European political modernity seems to lie. We could have chosen to write the narrative of political Europe in terms of the European experience with liberty, rather than as that oscillation between three partial accounts that we have offered. Had we done so, a story of persistent, but also rather slow struggle would have emerged. There would have been no lack of commitment to liberty, but also disastrous, and sometimes widespread and long-lasting violations of the claim to freedom. The European experience would often have looked rather deficient, in terms of insights arrived at in Europe itself early in its modern history, and also in terms of political experiences elsewhere, in the USA, and at the fringes of Europe, in England.

Today, the extent of the European commitment to liberty is beyond question, and it is accompanied by a markedly self-critical relation to its own history. Under these circumstances, a different story of European political modernity may be told to balance the narrative of deficient liberty. In this story, European political modernity is marked by an often only half-conscious, often also ill-directed, but nevertheless viable and necessary resistance to individualist liberalism as the bottom-line and only firm ground of a politics of freedom.

There has long been a sense in Europe that an exclusive focus on individual liberty as the basic commitment of a polity is insufficient. Individualist liberalism is insufficient in theoretical terms, because it lacks criteria for determining what members of the polity have in common. In the face of that absence it tends to resort to a concept of reason, which in turn tends to be interpreted as instrumental rationality. In terms of political experience, furthermore, individualist liberalism tends to combine two potentially dangerous effects. Given that the protection of negative liberty is all the polity is about, it tends to withdraw energy from the effort of determining what members of a polity have in common. The dedication to private affairs, which it in turn encourages, is not problematic in itself, but under conditions of extended market relations it may be steadily transforming the world, thus increasing the worldlessness that further undermines action in common.[43]

Throughout its recent history, individualist liberalism has been opposed in Europe, to varying degrees, by discourses that insist on some need for substantive rooting of the polity, beyond the rational individual. Such grounding could be located either in prior common-alities among the members of the polity, not least commonalities of language and culture, or in the systematic consideration of sub-stantive concerns of needs and social interest in its institutional rules. In both cases, these discourses needed more than a formal under-standing of the collectivity they were referring to, such as a particular nation, and some understanding of collective self-determination that went beyond the agreement of the individual to enter into a social contract. It is in this sense that accounts of statehood and democracy needed to be an integral part of a narrative of liberty.

Undeniably, many of those discourses and the political activities that were inspired by them were often profoundly flawed. But once the legitimate questions that motivated them have been retrieved, the history of European political modernity can be re-read in terms of the political projects that were formulated and embarked on at various points in time, the dead ends that some of these projects ended in, and the transformation of political possibilities that the sequence of these projects resulted in. It was to such a retrieval and re-reading that this chapter has sought to contribute.

The hope – dim as it may be – that political possibilities may be better grasped in the future can ground itself on two observations: first, that political construction today is a European project with wider horizons than the earlier national ones with their particular restrictions and exclusions; and second, that this construction is already broadly inspired by a critical reassessment of the European experience of liberty and of its violations. In this sense, most optimistically, the current steps towards a political Europe could be both an explication of the European resistance to individualist liberalism and the creation of an institutional setting for the realisation of a fuller understanding of freedom.

Notes

1 Habermas 2001, p. 103.
2 The two views are not clear alternatives; they can be held together. See for instance Offe (1998). Similar views can be found in Siedentop, who provides a sophisticated version of British Euroscepticism: 'The history of Europe, the formation of these nation-states, survives in their distinctive political

cultures. The attempt to change these cultures too rapidly...would risk destroying the different forms of civic spirit which exist in Europe today' (Siedentop 2001, p. 231). Such sceptical views also resonate more generally with discussions of the 'democratic deficit' of the EU.

3 For a general reasoning along these lines, see Wagner (2001a, ch. 2); for an attempt to identify the varieties of moral-political philosophies in France and the USA, see most recently Lamont and Thévenot (2000).

4 For a critical history of (individualist) liberalism, see Manent (1995).

5 We suggest that individualist liberalism is insufficient both in terms of a normative guidance for a polity and for an empirical-analytical assessment of the European polity or of the nation-states of which the former is composed. More generally, we argue that normative underpinnings are always present in the basic institutional rules of a polity and that, therefore, the standard separation between normative political philosophy and empirical political science needs to be overcome.

6 See Bottici (2002) for a discussion of the tension between domestic and interstate relations in the post-Westphalian order.

7 See Arendt (1958) and Castoriadis (1990), as well as historians such as Meier (1990).

8 Palmer 1959.

9 Rorty 1989, p. 63.

10 We may add that this connection provides a context for the story of the decline of empires, which is an important part of the story of European political modernity. The quest for individual liberty was in principle reconcilable with the political form of empire, but the idea of collective self-determination was not, at least not for actors in the nineteenth and early twentieth century. We will come back to this question below.

11 De Tocqueville 1994, Vol. I, chs. 15 and 16. And one could argue that Carl Schmitt (1985) combined these two concerns in his view that liberalism and democracy are incompatible.

12 See Arendt 1958 and Lefort 1999.

13 For such a view, which is often − but to our mind unjustly − presented as the empirical-analytically most appropriate, 'realist' view, see Scharpf (1999) and Majone (1996); for a more detailed discussion of it, Friese and Wagner (2002).

14 For the most sophisticated version of this view, see Offe (1998).

15 Patočka 1983; see also Patočka (1996, pp. 81−2).

16 Patočka (1996, p. 109; see also p. 83): 'The Western Christian holy empire then gives rise to a much broader community than the Roman-Mediterranean had been while at the same time disciplining inner humanity and giving it greater depth. The care for the soul is thus what gave rise to Europe'. See also Meier (2002, ch. 3), for an assessment of the significance of Athens and Rome for the European *Sonderweg*.

17 On the idea of 'universal empire' in the Roman Republic see Cacciari (2002, pp. 25−7).

18 Brague 2002. Despite the subtlety of his reasoning, Brague's 'eccentricity' thesis makes Europe 'Western Christian' in religious terms and 'Roman' in political terms. A history of European political modernity – not Brague's project, certainly – would need to say more about the presence of orthodox Christianity (for a recent attempt, see Kristeva [2000]), Judaism and Islam in Europe. Marramao (2003) has convincingly argued that Europe's 'roots' are to be found in Jerusalem, Alexandria, Athens, Rome and Byzantium.

19 See, for instance, Galli 2002, pp. 47–8.

20 In his broad account of shifting philosophies of science as ways of understanding the world, Toulmin (1990) emphasised the reduction of ambiguity in the period after the religious wars.

21 As observed by authors as different as Gerhard Oestreich and Michel Foucault, indeed as a double process of disciplinisation and individualisa- tion. Oestreich, for instance, underlines the spreading of 'contractual thinking' and the emergence of 'genuine national rights' distinct from the feudal 'regionally secured liberty' (Oestreich 1982, pp. 266, 264, 268). For a view that insists on removing all ambivalence, see Siedentop (2001, p. 19): 'The process of state formation was, especially on the continent, essentially a despotic one'.

22 An early analysis of the dissolution of the Empire (Jászi 1971/1929) argues that the 'real outstanding and fundamental question...was not even perceived or formulated', the question, namely, 'how to satisfy the different national and cultural claims of the various nationalities in such a way as to give them ample possibilities to develop their historical individuality and consciousness but at the same time to build up a supernational conscious- ness of a state solidarity among them' (p. 433). See also the chapter by Hall in this volume.

23 Dumont 1983, pp. 130–1, our translation.

24 The term fraternity furthermore suggested that it is free and equal brothers that inhabit the republic, and thus that the sisters of these men were neither free nor equal to their brothers. The term fraternity was replaced by solidarity towards the end of the nineteenth century, thus eliminating the gender asymmetry conceptually, but often not in practice.

25 Sewell 1980, Donzelot 1984. At this point, the coincidence – in rough historical terms – of the 'democratic revolution' and the 'market revolution' would need to be discussed both in terms of its origins and its impact – another chapter yet unwritten, for some ideas see Wagner (2001b). For an analysis of the notion 'solidarity' in the French and German context, see Fiegle (2003).

26 See Manent 1995, p. 117.

27 Lefort 1999.

28 Berlin 1969.

29 Friese 2000 and 2004.

30 Nancy 1991.

31 Derrida 1997, p. 104; for Europe, see Friese 2002 and 2003.

32 As we shall argue later, it is only now that the republican-democratic failure of the nation-state at mid-century moves into the centre of attention in the

debate about European integration. At the end of war and Nazism, it had rather been the liberal failure and the failure of the state-system to preserve peace that inspired the rebuilding of the polities.

33 Fourastié 1979.

34 As the critical notion of the time had it. See Narr and Offe (1975).

35 For a more detailed historical reconstruction, see Wagner (1994, chs. 5–7).

36 In rejection of the politics of the regimes, this term broadly referred to the possibility of handling matters in common by 'civil society' alone, without its conceptual counter-part, the state. Reviewing intellectual involvement in politics in Central Europe at the end of the 1990s, Bozoki speaks of a 'period of lost illusions' (Bozoki 1999, p. 7).

37 Unlike 1968, 1989 was arguably also about liberation from imperial domination. The main reason for such a relative neglect may therefore lie in the fact that the collectivity of self-determination (the nation) and its political form (states pre-existing the period of domination, at least during the interwar period, but in many cases with a much longer historical trajectory) were taken for granted, just like the national-liberal movements took it for granted during the nineteenth century.

38 For a more detailed assessment of '1968' in such terms, see Wagner (2002).

39 It may have been a throwaway remark when Derrida recorded that it was suggested to him that the Russian term *perestrojka* should be translated as deconstruction (Derrida 1994, p. 89). But the connection that is created here between a political restructuring and an intellectual proposal captures indeed the linkage between a *problématique* and a situation that defines the urgency of a socio-philosophical quest.

40 Following the revolutions in France and North America, the history of 'Western' modernity is no longer identical to that of European modernity. Among the few works that demonstrate full awareness of this situation are Henningsen (1974) and Hardt and Negri (2000). However, further analysis is necessary both in terms of the difference in 'normative self-understandings' of modernity and the variety of modern political forms. For a beginning, see Wagner (1999).

41 Ferry 2000; François and Schulze 2001.

42 On the debate about European identity see Stråth (2000).

43 For more detail on this argument, see Wagner (2001b).

References

Adorno, Theodor W., 1973, *Negative Dialectics*. London: Routledge and Kegan Paul.

Arendt, Hannah, 1958, *The Human Condition*. Chicago, IL: The University of Chicago Press.

Berlin, Isaiah, 1969, 'Two Concepts of Liberty', in Isaiah Berlin, *Four Essays on Liberty*. Oxford: Oxford University Press, pp. 118–72.

Bottici, Chiara, 2002, *Globalisation. Sovereignty or Anarchy beyond Modernity?* Florence: European University Institute.

Bozoki, Andras, 1999, 'Introduction', in Andras Bozoki (ed.), *Intellectuals and Politics in Central Europe*. New York: Central European University Press, pp. 1–15.

Brague, Rémi, [1992] 2002, *Eccentric Culture. A Theory of Western Civilisation*. South Bend, IN: St Augustine's Press.

Cacciari, Massimo, 2002, 'Digressioni su Impero e tre Rome', in Heidrun Friese, Antonio Negri and Peter Wagner (eds.), *Europa politica. Ragioni di una necessità*. Rome: Manifestolibri, pp. 21–42.

Castoriadis, Cornelius, 1990, 'Pouvoir, politique, autonomie', in *Le monde morcelé. Les carrefours du labyrinthe III*. Paris: Seuil, pp. 113–39.

Chakrabarty, Dipesh, 2000, *Provincialising Europe. Postcolonial Thought and Historical Difference*. Princeton, NJ: Princeton University Press.

Derrida, Jacques, 1994, *Specters of Marx*. New York: Routledge.

1997, *Politics of Friendship*. London: Verso.

Donzelot, Jacques, 1984, *L'invention du social. Essai sur le déclin des passions politiques*. Paris: Fayard.

Dumont, Louis, 1983, 'Une variante nationale: le peuple et la nation chez Herder et Fichte', in *Essais sur l'individualisme. Une perspective anthropologique sur l'idéologie moderne*. Paris: Seuil.

Ferry, Jean-Marc, 2000, *La question de l'État européen*. Paris: Gallimard.

Fiegle, Thomas, 2003, *Von der Solidarité zur Solidarität. Ein französisch-deutscher Begriffstransfer*. Münster: Lit Verlag.

Jean Fourastie, 1979, *Les trente Glorieuses*, Paris: Fayard.

François, Etienne and Hagen Schulze (eds.), 2001, *Deutsche Erinnerungsorte*. Vols. I–III. Munich: Beck.

Friese, Heidrun, 2000, 'Silence – Voice – Representation', in Robert Fine and Charles Turner (eds.), *Social Theory after the Holocaust*. Liverpool: Liverpool University Press, pp. 159–78.

2002, 'L'Europa a venire', in Heidrun Friese, Antonio Negri and Peter Wagner (eds.), *Europa politica. Ragioni di una necessità*. Rome: Manifestolibri, pp. 59–75.

2003, 'L'Impero e l'Europa a venire', in Giuseppe Bronzini, Heidrun Friese, Toni Negri and Peter Wagner (eds.), *Europa, costituzione e movimenti sociali*. Rome: Manifestolibri, pp. 25–45.

2004, ' "The word passed away, as that world awakened". On the (Im)possibility of Representation', in Ronit Lentin (ed.), *Re-presenting the Shoah for the Twenty-first Century*. New York: Berghahn.

Friese, Heidrum and Peter Wagner, 2002, 'The Nascent Political Philosophy of the European Polity', *The Journal of Political Philosophy*, Vol. 10(3), 342–64.

Galli, Carlo, 2002, 'L'Europa come spazio politico', in Heidrun Friese, Antonio Negri and Peter Wagner (eds.), *Europa politica. Ragioni di una necessità*. Rome: Manifestolibri, pp. 43–58.

Habermas, Jürgen, 2001, 'The Postnational Constellation and the Future of Democracy', in *The Postnational Constellation*. Cambridge: Polity, pp. 58–112.

Hardt, Michael and Antonio Negri (eds.), 2000, *Empire*. Cambridge, MA: Harvard University Press.

Henningsen, Manfred, 1974, *Der Fall Amerika. Zur Sozial- und Bewußtseinsgeschichte einer Verdrängung*. Munich: List.

Jászi, Oscar, [1929] 1971, *The Dissolution of the Habsburg Monarchy*. Chicago, IL: University of Chicago Press.

Kristeva, Julia, 2000, *Crisis of the European Subject*. New York: Other Press.

Lamont, Michèle and Laurent Thévenot (eds.), 2000, *Rethinking Comparative Cultural Sociology. Polities and Repertoires of Evaluation in France and the United States*. New York: Cambridge University Press.

Lefort, Claude, 1999, *La Complication. Retour sur le Communisme*. Paris: Fayard.

Majone, Giandomenico, 1996, *Regulating Europe*. London: Routledge.

Manent, Pierre, [1987] 1995, *An Intellectual History of Liberalism*. Princeton, NJ: Princeton University Press.

Marramao, Giacomo, 2003, *Passaggio ad Occidente. Filosofia e Globalizzazione*. Turin: Bollati Boringhieri.

Meier, Christian, 1990, *The Greek Discovery of Politics*. Cambridge, MA: Harvard University Press.

2002, *Von Athen bis Auschwitz*. Munich: Beck.

Nancy, Jean-Luc, 1991, *The Inoperative Community*. Minneapolis, MN: University of Minnesota Press.

Narr, Wolf-Dieter and Claus Offe (eds.), 1975, *Wohlfahrtsstaat und Massenloyalität*. Cologne: Kiepenheuer und Witsch.

Oestreich, Gerhard, 1982, 'The Structure of the Absolute State', in Gerhard Oestreich (ed.), *Neostoicism and the Early Modern State*. Cambridge: Cambridge University Press, pp. 258–73.

Offe, Claus, 1998, 'Demokratie und Wohlfahrtsstaat: Eine europäische Regimeform unter dem Streß der europäischen Integration', in Wolfgang Streeck (ed.), *Internationale Wirtschaft, nationale Demokratie*. Frankfurt/M: Campus, pp. 99–136.

Palmer, Robert Rosell, 1959, *The Age of the Democratic Revolution*. Princeton, NJ: Princeton University Press.

Patočka, Jan, 1983, *Platon et l'Europe*. Paris: Véridier.

1996, *Heretical Essays in the Philosophy of History*. Chicago and La Salle, IL: Open Court.

Rorty, Richard, 1989, *Contingency, Irony, Solidarity*. Cambridge: Cambridge University Press.

Scharpf, Fritz W., 1999, *Governing in Europe. Effective and Democratic?* Oxford: Oxford University Press.

Schmitt, Carl, [1923] 1985, *The Crisis of Parliamentary Democracy*. London: MIT Press.

Sewell, William, 1980, *Work and Revolution in France. The Language of Labor from the Old Regime to 1848*. Cambridge: Cambridge University Press.

Shin, Jong-Hwa, 2002, 'The Historical Formation of Modernity in Korea. Events, Issues and Actors'. Unpublished PhD thesis, University of Warwick.

Siedentop, Larry, 2001, *Democracy in Europe*. London: Penguin.

Stråth, Bo, 2000, 'Multiple Europes: Integration, Identity and Demarcation to the Other', in Bo Stråth (ed.), *Europe and the Other and Europe as the Other*. Brussels: Peter Lang, pp. 385–420.

Tocqueville, Alexis De, 1994[1835], *Democracy in America*. London: Everyman.

Toulmin, Stephen, 1990, *Cosmopolis. The Hidden Agenda of Modernity*. Chicago, IL: The University of Chicago Press.

Wagner, Peter, 1994, *A Sociology of Modernity. Liberty and Discipline*. London: Routledge.

1999, 'The Resistance that Modernity Constantly Provokes. Europe, America and Social Theory', *Thesis Eleven*, Vol. 58, 39–63.

2001a, *Theorising Modernity*. London: SAGE.

2001b, 'Modernity, Capitalism, and Critique', *Thesis Eleven*, Vol. 66, 1–31.

2002, 'The Project of Emancipation and the Possibility of Politics, or, What's Wrong with Post-1968 Individualism?', *Thesis Eleven*, Vol. 68, February, thematic issue on '1968', 31–45.

5   Is There a European Civil Society?

William Outhwaite

There is a state of uncertainty, not about the desirability of a European civil society (as Gandhi said of Western civilisation, it sounds like a good idea) but about its reality. I have become, if anything, somewhat more tentative about the claims one can make for the existence of anything one might want to call civil society at a European or European Union (EU) level, as distinct from the several and sometimes overlapping civil societies located in the individual member states of the EU. The existence of a section called 'civil society' on an EU website publicising relevant conferences and so forth provides only limited reassurance here.[1] There are of course numerous civil society organisations with a European/EU reference, ranging from the European Trade Union Confederation (ETUC) to more informal social movements and lobbying organisations representing the interests of consumers, cyclists and others. There is also of course the European Social Forum, emerging in 2002 out of the global social movement, the World Social Forum, and playing an equally prominent if occasional role. The question is whether all this amounts to something we might meaningfully call a European or EU civil society.

Two books have had a particular influence on my thinking. One is Michael Billig's *Banal Nationalism*,[2] the other is Larry Siedentop's *Democracy in Europe*.[3] Referring to such everyday examples as national flags outside public buildings, Billig points out the extent to which nation-state categories frame our social experience and our most basic assumptions:

... the term *banal nationalism* is introduced to cover the ideological habits which enable the established nations of the West to be reproduced. Daily, the nation is indicated, or 'flagged', in the lives of its citizenry. Nationalism, far from being an intermittent mood in established nations, is the endemic condition.[4]

This is not nationalism in a strong sense, but rather the unthinking use of national symbols or the adoption (for example in weather forecasts) of a nation-state frame of reference – matched in academic and public social commentary by what Jan-Aart Scholte has called methodological nationalism.[5] Chris Rumford[6] has suggested that this is also true even of many discussions of transnational civil society. And it is clear, as a lot of the literature on globalisation has noted, that international or supranational processes are characteristically experienced at a local (which often means a national) level. In Europe, for example, customs tariffs may be a matter of European-level policy, but they must all be largely imposed by locally employed staff of member states, for reasons of convenience and tradition. So the upshot of Billig's book, I think, for reflection on European integration, is to suggest that the road slopes somewhat more steeply uphill than we may sometimes have thought.

Siedentop's very different book points in political-theoretical terms to the need both for serious constitutional debate and for gradualism in the move towards European integration. As he puts it in his closing sentences:

The danger of premature federalism in Europe – of the rush to political integration which turns federalism into little more than a mask for a unitary superstate – is that it could put at risk the complex textures of European societies. ... The attraction of federalism, properly understood, for Europe is that it should make possible the survival of different national political cultures and forms of civic spirit. But that can be the case only if federalism is approached gradually ... Federalism is the right future for Europe. But Europe is not yet ready for federalism.[7]

European civil society, then, may come to appear not so much as the fertile soil in which more formal European political institutions can be expected to flourish, as a weak soil threatened by aggressive over-exploitation and requiring a good deal of nurturing before it can grow anything but the sickliest of plants.

The concept of civil society has itself come in for a good deal of critical scrutiny in recent years. First, there has been an understandable reaction against an inflationary use of the term in the early 1990s, associated with unrealistic expectations about postcommunist transition. Civil society movements did not live up to the expectation that they would offer a new, higher form of democracy in part at least of the postcommunist world; instead, they were rapidly elbowed out by reconstituted or reinvented political movements and institutions. In Ferenc Miszlivetz's classic formulation: 'We dreamed of civil society and we got NGOs.'[8] Second, these disappointments, together with others about the fate of Western civil society movements, led to a rethinking of some of the implications of civil society thinking, pointing critically to its over-moralisation in 'neat' models which exclude anything distasteful. A useful collection of papers from a conference in 1998, for example, defines civil society in terms of 'self-organisation' presupposing 'corresponding resources such as trust, communication skills and education' and 'the recognition of diversity and the legitimacy of regulated conflict'.[9] But while something like this may be a requirement for a functioning civil society as a whole, it should clearly not be automatically imputed to individual components of civil society. Neo-Nazi groups which are authoritarian and intolerant both in their public activities and in their internal organisation are no less components of civil society, as I understand the term, than the more attractive and friendly movements that students of social movements have tended to concentrate on. Those who object to the normative inflation of the concept of civil society have also often pointed to its possibly illiberal uses in certain contexts. Robert Fine has illustrated some of these, notably in South Africa.[10] More recently, Graham Pollock has argued, like Fine, that civil society theory has been constructed in opposition to a somewhat caricatured negative image of nationalism and national identity and sometimes acted as an ideological support to what he calls 'banal state nationalism' such as that displayed by much of the Spanish political class in its backlash against Catalan and Basque nationalism.[11]

It is easy to retort that partisans of civil society have rather little to offer in the way of political murder, war, deportations and genocide compared to champions of the nation or Volk and the state, but some contemporary uses of civil society theory should give pause for thought. Despite all this, however, I continue to think both that we require some concept of civil society for Tocquevillian reasons and that civil society politics in both its Western and Eastern European forms from the 1970s onwards remains one of our most fruitful political experiences and resources. What we need, I think, is a model of civil society which is critical but not moralistic, avoiding setting the entry costs too high while being more than the mere descriptive category of public administrative discourse as illustrated by the Europa website or invoked by Hartmut Kaelble in his brief outline of the development of European civil society in the 1980s and 1990s.[12]

Conceptions of civil society can be roughly divided into broader and narrower understandings of the term; Pérez-Díaz distinguishes between 'generalists' and 'minimalists'.[13] In the former conception, as for example in Larry Siedentop's book, it is principally conceived as a form of society, characterised by, *inter alia*, individualism, the rule of law, some sort of public sphere and so forth.

> For what is fundamental to the idea of a civil society? It is that the equality of status attributed by states to their subjects creates, at least potentially, a sphere of individual liberty or choice, a private sphere of action.[14]

In the latter, narrower understanding of the term it is presented as a form of associational life independent of the state and economy, the base of a pyramid, as it were, whose apex is formed by public intellectuals and commentators and social movement activists. Whereas Pérez-Díaz favours a broader understanding of the term, Jeff Alexander has argued for many years for a more restricted one.[15] My preference is for a weaker version of Alexander's usage, in which civil society is taken to mean associational life at a variety of levels, shading off into conceptions of the public sphere.[16] I would however be less restrictive than Alexander in that I would include low-level economic exchanges such as the reciprocal visits by market traders in the framework of the INTERREG programme, despite the fact that it involves economic activity and is sponsored by a state-like body, the EU.[17]

However one specifies these concepts, however, the important point, I think, is that a discussion of European civil society necessarily hangs between the two poles of questions about broadly conceived European cultural identities on the one hand, and European-level economic and political institutions and practices on the other. My approach is therefore something like that advanced by Habermas in 1974 in an early reflection on the possibilities of social identities not tied to territorial states and their membership. A collective identity, Habermas argues, can only be conceived in a reflexive form, in awareness that one has opportunities to participate in:

> processes of communication in which identity formation occurs as a continuous learning process. Such value and norm creating communications ... flow out of the 'base' into the pores of organisationally structured areas of life. They have a subpolitical character, i.e. they operate below the level of political decision processes, but they indirectly influence the political system because they change the normative framework of political decisions.[18]

I am assuming that, despite all the vicissitudes of the concept of civil society and of the reality of civil society politics,[19] one can meaningfully talk about the existence of civil socie*ties*, however embattled, in most if not all of Europe. Whether there is also an emergent *European* civil society is a further question. Without overplaying conceptions of identity and pursuing the chimera of a European *Staatsvolk*, I think that to talk of a European civil society does presuppose some minimal version of a European identity, perhaps a weak or 'thin' cultural identity based on a particular modulation of modernity. As Reinhold Viehoff and Rien Segers put it in the introduction to their edited collection on this theme, many of the conflicts accompanying the European integration process have a cultural content, wherever they may formally be located in institutional structures.[20] At the same time, however, to frame the question of civil society in this way raises the stakes since, as Klaus Eder points out in the same collection, to start from the premise that there should be some sort of European identity and to look for ways of adequately representing it is 'to turn the logic of collective identity formation on its head'.[21] Nevertheless, Eder insists, if it is to be more than an instrumental association of nation-states dressed up as a 'community', 'Europe needs culture in order to found a transnational order on a consensus'[22] – even if, as he goes on to stress, this may be as much as anything a consensus on how to handle conflicts. The British historian Keith Middlemas offers a similar analysis of informal cooperation within the European Community (EC)/EU:

The game also induces a process of socialisation, habituating players to each other, forcing them to think through other points of view and subsequently live with them. Indeed, this Euro-civilising aspect may come to be seen ... as informal politics' largest contribution to the European Union.[23]

It is of course conflicts as much as anything else that have shaped the vague sense of Europeanness, which can be seen as operating like a musical ground-bass in relation to the shrill rise and perhaps incipient fall of national identities in the nineteenth and twentieth centuries. In reflecting on the defining events of European history, perhaps the most difficult issue is to decide at what point they are appropriately called European. Ancient Greek polyarchy as a form of intra- and interstate organisation clearly deserves a mention, as do the Macedonian and, much more importantly, Roman empires. The latter of course intersects with a third crucial element, the somewhat unexpected rise of Christianity in the Empire and subsequently as a defining element of Europe as a whole, just as Islam became a defining element of the 'Middle East'.

Yet just as it is artificial to separate out English history from the rest of European history before the fifteenth century, it is similarly anachronistic to think of Europe as a distinct entity before that time.

Charlemagne's empire of the early ninth century may have covered the territory of the original EC and lent his name to a building and a prize, but it had nothing to do with Europe as such. The Crusades of the thirteenth century are resented, with some justification, as inaugurating Europe's continuing domination of the Middle East, but they are more appropriately seen, like the rest of the history of that half-millennium (and arguably the following one too), in a broader Eurasian context. A recent popular book[24] features a map of the Hanseatic League labelled 'The EU of the middle ages', but the irony is of course intentional.

In what Europeans call the fifteenth and sixteenth centuries, however, something distinctively European begins to emerge, marked by the conjuncture, roughly speaking, of the Renaissance, the Reformation and the beginnings of the voyages (anticipated of course by the Vikings) of discovery and conquest. These were not, to say the least, unique or endogenous 'European' developments, but they do initiate a distinctive path: a line of development from the Renaissance to the scientific revolution and the Enlightenment, from the Reformation to the religious wars and the 'European' state model consecrated in 1648 after perhaps the first genuinely European war, and from Columbian adventures to the European colonial and semi-colonial empires of the eighteenth, nineteenth and twentieth centuries. The 'discoveries' were reflected in the culture shock experienced by Europeans confronted by alterity and perceiving themselves in its mirror.[25] A different form of alterity closer to home was provided by the confrontation with the Turks at Mohács in 1526.

Whatever one might say about the more diffuse development of European conceptions of human and political rights and freedoms, the French Revolution clearly deserves a central place as the defining feature of the European political imaginary. This is no less true of the conservatives who rejected it or of the socialists and communists for whom it was just a prelude to a full social democratic and anti-capitalist revolution. Concurrently, the American Revolution inaugurated another form of republican constitutional government and, perhaps more importantly, the first major postcolonial state. For progressive Europeans, it was one more victory over the old aristocratic order, while geopolitically it marked the beginning of the provincialisation of Europe, the relativisation of its power in between the USA and Russia, which Tocqueville foresaw less than forty years afterwards (and an even shorter time since Napoleon's short-lived European empire)[26] and when Europe's imperial power was still on the rise. Imperialism was of course a European transformation both of Europe itself and of much of the rest of the world, running alongside the generalisation of capitalist production and industrialisation. From now on, though no-one was yet thinking in these terms (except perhaps in relation to the contrast between the old and the new worlds), there were multiple modernities and a post-European future.

Back at home, Europe experienced three further transformations, all in one or another way associated with notions of citizenship. First, the slow extension of political democracy, finally reaching adult women in most parts of Europe in the early twentieth century. Second, the nationalism that arose in part as a reaction to Napoleon and consolidated the (Western) European nation-state model. This, with its prioritisation of nation-state citizenship as a defining identity, swept the world wherever the European states had not established colonies or, as in South America, were expelled from them. Third, the dual response to the 'social question' in the form of welfare states and social democracy. The former is the beginning of the 'European social model' and social conceptions of citizenship, the latter of what can be called the European political model, the left–right division between ostensible opponents and defenders of capitalism, which structured European politics and tendentially the politics of much of the rest of the world at least until the end of the twentieth century. In Russia, of course, after the Bolshevik Revolution, there was only the left left. The thoroughly European ideology of Marxism took hold in Russia, China and elsewhere, with the Russian export model reimported into much of Europe in the aftermath of the Second World War.

The world wars of the twentieth century were both quintessential expressions of Europe at its worst, practising techniques of warfare often tried out earlier on colonised populations, and stages of its geopolitical decline. Earlier European wars had of course been fought outside Europe, but now wars could only be fought as world wars. The (nuclear) third world war which we escaped more by luck than anything else would of course have been a further and no doubt final example. Geopolitically, the provincialisation of Europe was marked by the subordination of most of the two halves of the divided continent into the Cold War military alliances firmly controlled from Washington and Moscow and by the withdrawal from almost all the colonised territories. Domestically, the three processes identified above modulated into the configuration in which we now live. Democracy was briskly extinguished in the communist bloc, only to bounce back forty years later. In the West, there was a more diffuse democratisation of social relations, particularly in the wake of the 1968 movements. Welfare states were further developed in both parts of Europe, though more slowly after the capitalist economic crisis of the mid-1970s. In the richer parts of the West rights of abode and citizenship were more or less grudgingly accorded to the short- or long-term immigrants recruited to help out with the postwar boom of the thirty glorious years. In another major social change, with the transformation of agriculture after the Second World War, the peasants who had been 'nationalised' in Eugen Weber's sense in the late nineteenth century[27] or collectivised in most of the Soviet bloc in the 1950s were increasingly displaced into manufacturing or service occupations, leaving agricultural policy looking more like a disguised social policy to support the vestiges of rural life.

Finally, and perhaps most dramatically, what began as a reaction to the consequences of nationalism in the two world wars developed gradually and haltingly into a new political model in Europe, an 'ever closer union' of more and more European states whose ultimate destination or *finalité* remains more or less as unclear as when Andrew Shonfield examined it in 1965. Briefly, however, and to anticipate what I shall say later, the EU is incipiently postnational, despite or because of its continuing symbiotic relationship with its member states. It is post-imperial, in that however much it might superficially come to resemble the Austro-Hungarian Empire it will surely retain principles of democracy more characteristic of the national state. And it is perhaps (and this is part at least of its appeal), the beginning of a form of post-European cosmopolitan democracy attractive not just to Europe but to many other parts of the world.

It is not enough to point to distinctiveness or commonality in cultural or social forms within Europe, nor even to the frequency and intensity of inter- or transnational interaction. What matters is a more reflexive shaping and incorporation of these common patterns into some sense of identity. A European identity might be seen as taking shape in opposition to, on the one hand, national or subnational identities of a traditional kind and, on the other, alternative supranational identities such as an Anglo-American atlanticist identity, a Francophone (or Hispanophone or Lusitanophone) or a Mediterranean one. A former supranational candidate, based on the Soviet bloc or 'socialist community of nations' and backed up by the knout of the Brezhnev doctrine, is clearly eliminated. But none of the others seems particularly salient either; the structural relations emerging from the European integration process have probably dealt the *coup de grace* to these anyway somewhat factitious identities. For the core states of the EU, the euro will probably be a more powerful integrative force than any of these, though even a currency union is not necessarily much more of a *Heimat* than was the German customs union, the Zollverein.[28]

Despite 'banal nationalistic' residues of the kind noted by Billig, low levels of migration and intermarriage between the European countries and the massive presence of national infrastructures of all kinds, one should not overlook the growing affinities between inhabitants of the main metropolitan centres in Europe or within some of the Euroregions. Border regions such as Mosel-Rhine, for example, seem to have a real identity, marked in a slightly macabre fashion some years ago when after a bad motorway pile-up casualties were divided between the nearest hospitals, which happened to be in three different countries. But local regional groupings such as the one in which I live, East Sussex/Seine-Maritime, have more obstacles to overcome – the direct ferry service was only restored with the sale of Newhaven port to Seine-Maritime.

Despite the rise of the transnational manager, the political classes of Europe remain strikingly national in their composition. The bi-national Daniel Cohn-Bendit, who has pursued a political career in both France and Germany, the Czech MEP for Italy the late Jiri Pelikan, or the German-born MP for Birmingham Gisela Stuart remain fairly isolated exceptions. Even in the supranational EU institutions, national quotas exist for appointments, including senior positions such as European commissioner or judge in the European Court. Siedentop's reflections about the need for a European political class are highly pertinent here;[29] as well as more Madisons, we need more Dahrendorfs – people pursuing multinational political as well as academic careers. Social movements are somewhat less bound by nation-state boundaries, though for many of course the local nature of their concerns militates against their Europeanisation, and environmental or human rights movements may often, for good reasons, adopt a global rather than European frame of reference. There is also no genuinely European newspaper, published in the major languages, and the *European* (1990–8), published in English and owned for most of its brief life by the notorious Robert Maxwell, made a poor showing compared to the *Herald Tribune*, *Financial Times* or *The Economist*. Schlesinger and Kevin give a somewhat more positive analysis of the European presence of these three.[30] They point also to *Euronews*, launched in 1993 on a transnational public service broadcasting base and transmitting in the major West European languages; this however is very uneven in its European reach.

To repeat the point with which I began, I take one of the most important elements in recent theorising about and for civil society to have been the realisation that it must be conceived not so much in opposition to as in conjunction with state and other systemic structures, whether or not the term is extended to include them, and it is to these that I now turn rather more explicitly. I am offering therefore one element of a reply to Charles Turner's critique of Gellner and Habermas for what he sees as their undue economism and constitutionalism respectively.[31] There may be good reasons, *pace* Turner, for focusing not just on the associational dimension of civil society but on its interaction with other political and economic (and even military) structures in relation to the integration process. This is not to justify the dangerous elitism of much European integration politics, with its shameless technocratism, its somewhat sinister reference to the *acquis communautaire* and its neglect or patronising of the benighted natives, but it does suggest an open-minded and broad-spectrum approach to Europe-level activities. A European identity may emerge from conflicts in agricultural negotiations and public health concerns as well as from more lofty exercises in pursuit of common values; as Bernhard Giesen has suggested, we should be thinking perhaps in terms of Simmel's model of the integrating effects of conflict rather than a more ambitious conception such as one derived from Durkheimian sociology of religion.[32] Eder, too, as noted earlier, has stressed the importance of (the management of) dissensus, as much as consensus.[33]

A European identity will also be something highly mediated in the sense of virtual, where the real agents are likely to remain predominantly drawn from a limited number of social circles; as Münch puts it, somewhat brutally, 'the elites of top managers, experts, political leaders and intellectuals ...'.[34] This applies *par excellence*, of course, to the EU's own elites: As Ulrich Beck and Edgar Grande note in *Das kosmopolitische Europa*, the EU embodies the paradox of a civil society from above aiming to establish one from below. More optimistically, they suggest, the concept of European civil society offers the EU the opportunity of opening up a transnational space in such a way that it organises itself.[35]

There is of course a further issue here: that of the division between a broadly geographical and cultural *Grosseuropa*, stretching from the Atlantic to at least the Urals and arguably the Russian Pacific, and the *Kleineuropa* made up of the member states of the EU at any given point in time. I have always been irritated by the sloppy equation of 'Europe' with the EC/EU, and the concomitant neglect, until the 1990s, of the 'other Europe'. Conversely, it is clear that this distinction is on the way out and that the integration process within the EU is the leading edge of European integration as such, leaving the remaining non-members (and for that matter members who have not yet adopted the euro or signed up to Schengen) as inevitably an outer circle or set of circles. More broadly, the EU has become, as Rainer Lepsius puts it:

> ... an object which possesses a normative content and immediately structures behaviour in the member states. If the extension of a European identity presupposes a specific object relation, this has come into existence with the development of the European Union.[36]

We may wish, then, for a 'people's Europe' beyond the glass and print temples of the EU institutions, but this will have to develop in some sort of relation with them, rather as communists used to have to define themselves, whether positively or negatively, in relation to the Soviet Union. For most Europeans inside the EU, and to some extent outside it as well, it is now the dominant European political form, even if they rightly feel that there is more to Europe than the EU.[37] The old slogan 'Yes to Europe, no to Maastricht' was still of course a contribution to the Maastricht debate. This puts the emphasis back again on the EU and its democratic deficit, and here I can simply associate myself with the position advanced in different ways by Habermas and Siedentop – the former advocating a *Flucht nach vorn* towards constitution-building, the latter advocating extreme gradualism.[38]

With the collapse of the 'people's democracies', and the eclipse of revolutionary socialism, the liberal democratic state, like capitalism, has no obvious practical alternative. If anything, and despite very important elements of disillusionment or political alienation,[39] it has acquired stronger roots with the democratisation of everyday life: the growing acceptance, exemplified in spheres as diverse as media interviews with politicians and child-rearing practices, that all our decisions and ways of life are in principle open to question. They become in Habermas's sense 'post-conventional'. Individualism of this kind may also, as Münch has suggested,[40] favour the development of a European identity. The more sovereign and reflexive we are in the construction of our individual identities, the easier it may be for us to incorporate, or even to foreground, a European one.

Reflexive identities need not of course be cosmopolitan. In conditions of advanced modernity, misunderstanding and prejudice have become reflexive, in the sense that an awareness of the possibility that they may occur, and of ways in which they might be understood, conditions their occurrence. Even the internationalist, cosmopolitan or European identity can perhaps only be defined by way of opposition. *They* are localists, parochial, blinkered or xenophobic, *borné* or *borniert: we* are cosmopolitan, etc., at the cutting edge of the internationalisation or Europeanisation of our disciplines and of their institutional embodiment in our universities. But this universality can produce an intolerance of those who have not universalised themselves sufficiently, and this is an important root of one form at least of reflexive stereotyping. We irritatedly complain that the British or the Germans have dragged their feet or dug their heels in on some issue or other; they have been – well, German, or British or French. In such contexts, the blame is of course placed on the others. *We* would never have thought of using such reductionist categories, even half-seriously; if *they* had not previously othered themselves, in such an inappropriate and irritating manner.[41] This reflexive reconstruction of exclusivist identities is one danger, much played on by Eurosceptics of all kinds. Another is that postconventional individualism may weaken people's willingness to do anything more than 'bowl alone'.[42] In this context, it is unrealistic to expect a 'banal supranationalism' to supplant the much more entrenched banal nationalism.

Banal supranationalism, transnationalism or postnationalism is however arguably what we need: the increasing adoption, though not necessarily unreflectively, of a Europe-wide frame of reference for the discussion of political and other social issues. Like Tocqueville, we can go to the USA to see what this would look like in a European context. Or we can look at countries such as Italy where, for historical and ongoing reasons to do with the nature of the Italian state, regional and European identities and reference-points are stronger than in many other member states of the EU. Hilary Wainwright has argued for the importance of knowledge in the (inherently cosmopolitan) activity of new social movements.[43] Building on her analysis, it is possible to construct a model of cosmopolitan knowledge which has certain similarities with interdisciplinary knowledge – a kind of *savoir sans frontières* that social movements and political activists may find it easier to develop than state-bound or discipline-bound party politicians or over-professionalised academics.

Once again, Europe is pioneering a mode of governance, this time transnational rather than national, which gives some practical embodiment to the current extension of democratic thinking into conceptions of cosmopolitan democracy. This development is as important, I believe, as the earlier extension of liberal democracy into social democracy;

it coexists uneasily, however, with communitarian thinking both in social and political philosophy and in current political practice. As a solution to this dilemma, Habermas has reinvigorated Dolf Sternberger's conception of 'constitutional patriotism' (*Verfassungspatriotismus*) based not on membership of a particular ethnic or national community or Volk but on a rational and defensible identification with a decent constitutional state. But as Habermas has also come to stress, if the liberal democratic nation-state has few internal enemies, it is increasingly seen as inappropriate to the contemporary reality of global processes and challenges as well as to the desire of many citizens for more local autonomy.

In this postnational constellation, as Habermas has called it, the progress of European union, combined as it is with attempts to strengthen regional autonomy under the slogan of 'subsidiarity', becomes a crucial external determinant of the internal reconfiguration of many European states. Larry Siedentop's warning about the possible threat to civil society posed by the European integration process is clearly to be taken seriously, though I incline to a slightly more relaxed vision of these dangers. His critique of over-centralisation is well taken, but centralisation is by definition a part of the integration process, and not without benefits – especially to inhabitants of a member state such as the UK which is relatively backward in its constitutional development no less than in its creaking infrastructure. And while it may be perverse to prefer to be governed by strangers,[44] it is equally odd in the modern world to be afraid of it. The threat to European civil society comes not so much, I suggest, from explicit political initiatives, as from the often more surreptitious efforts of the national governments of member states to circumvent and undermine the emergent institutions of Europe.

Why do we need European unity? In part, as I see it, for the reason Willy Brandt gave for Germany in an explicit value-choice, that what belongs together should grow together. And finally, if there is a drift to something like a global state,[45] it is surely at the European level that we in Europe have the best chance of getting some measure of democratic control over it.

Notes

1 See http://www.europa.eu.int/futurum/evpub-en.htm
2 Billig 1995.
3 Siedentop 2000.
4 Billig 1995, p. 6, original emphasis.

5 See Scholte 2000.
6 Rumford 2002.
7 Siedentop 2000, pp. 230–1.
8 Miszlivetz and Ertsey 1998.
9 Hildermeier 2000, p. 8
10 Fine and Rai 1997.
11 Pollock 2001.
12 Kaelble, incidentally, takes a similarly brisk approach to the fraught
    question, discussed below, of European identity: 'Jedenfalls war in den
    1990er Jahre auch eine europäische Identität entstanden' (Kaelble 2000,
    p. 265). Gerard Delanty (2003, p. 472) takes a more cautious view of the
    1990s: 'Whether in the vision of a 'Europe of regions', a 'postnational
    European civil society', a 'European federation', it began to look
    like a European identity was consolidating and in a largely political form'.
    In a similarly cautious vein, Schlesinger and Kevin ask: 'How does the
    suggestion that we all belong to a global village sit alongside the postulate of
    a European identity? We are compelled to ask *which* communicative
    boundaries are significant for the development of a distinctive political
    identity and political culture in the EU' (Schlesinger and Kevin 2000,
    p. 211).
13 Pérez-Díaz 1998.
14 Siedentop 2000, p. 88.
15 Alexander 1998.
16 Eder 2000.
17 See   INTERREG   website   at: http://www.interreg3c.net/sixcms/
    list.php?page=home_en
18 Habermas 1976, p. 116.
19 Fine and Rai 1997; Alexander 1998.
20 Viehoff and Segers 1999, p. 28.
21 Eder 1999, p. 149.
22 Eder 1999, pp. 152–3.
23 Middlemas 1995, p. 685.
24 Aust and Schmidt-Klingenberg 2003, p. 89.
25 As Beck (2004, p. 432) has noted, the contrast between Fukuyama and
    Huntington in many ways replays the Valladolid conference of 1550,
    between universalistic inclusionism (they too can become Christians) and
    particularistic rejection of the 'savages'.
26 De Tocqueville 1994, p. 434.
27 Weber 1977.
28 The Deutscher Zollverein was a customs union between the German states
    established in 1834. German nationalists aiming at unification (achieved in
    1871) complained that it did not go far enough: 'a customs union is not
    a homeland'.
29 Siedentop 2000, ch. 7.
30 Schlesinger and Kevin 2000, pp. 222–9.
31 Turner 1997.
32 Giesen 1999, p. 145.
33 Eder 1999.

34 Münch 1999, p. 249.
35 Beck and Grande 2004, ch. 4.
36 Lepsius 2001, p. 206.
37 These issues were sharply raised in the debates and non-debates around Eastern enlargement.
38 Philippe C. Schmitter's proposal, in this volume, for a more concrete and participatory route towards a European constitution is a third possibility, rendered more attractive by the 'no' votes in the referenda of 2005.
39 Budge and Newton 1997, ch. 5.
40 Münch 1999, pp. 230–1.
41 Outhwaite 1995.
42 Putnam 2001.
43 Wainwright 1994.
44 Siedentop 2000, p. 22.
45 Shaw 2001.

References

Alexander, J. (ed.), 1998, *Real Civil Societies. Dilemmas of Institutionalisation.* London: SAGE.

Aust, S. and M. Schmidt-Klingenberg (eds.), 2003, *Experiment Europa. Ein Kontinent macht Geschichte. Ein Spiegel-Buch.* Munich: DVA.

Beck, U., 2004, 'The Truth of Others. A Cosmopolitan Approach', *Common Knowledge*, Vol. **10**(3), 430–49.

Beck, U., and E. Grande, 2004, *Das kosmopolitische Europa. Gesellschaft und Politik in der zweiten Moderne.* Frankfurt/M: Suhrkamp.

Billig, M., 1995, *Banal Nationalism.* London: SAGE.

Budge, I. and K. Newton, 1997, *The Politics of the New Europe.* London: Longman.

Crouch, C., 1999, *Social Change in Europe.* Oxford: Oxford University Press.

Delanty, G., 1995, *Inventing Europe. Idea, Identity, Reality.* Basingstoke: Macmillan.

1999, 'Die Transformation nationaler Identität und die kulturelle Ambivalenz europäischer Identität', in R. Viehoff and R. T. Segers (eds.), *Kultur, Identität, Europa.* Frankfurt/M: Suhrkamp.

2003, 'Conceptions of Europe: A Review of Recent Trends' *European Journal of Social Theory*, Vol. **6**(4), 471–88.

Eder, K., 1999, 'Integration durch Kultur? Das Paradox der Suche nach einer europäischen Identität', in R. Viehoff and R. T. Segers (eds.), *Kultur-Identität Europa.* Frankfurt/M: Suhrkamp, pp. 147–79.

2000, 'Zur Transformation Nationalstaatlicher Öffentlichkeit in Europa', *Berliner Journal für Soziologie*, Vol. **10**(2), 167–84.

Eder, K. and B. Giesen, 2001, *European Citizenship between National Legacies and Postnational Projects.* Oxford: Oxford University Press.

Eley, G. and R. G. Suny, 1996, *Becoming National.* New York: Oxford University Press.

Fine, R. and S. Rai (eds.), 1997, *Civil Society. Democratic Perspectives*. London: Cass.

Fischer, M. E., 1996, *Establishing Democracies*. Boulder, CO: Westview Press.

Giesen, B., 1999, 'Europa als Konstruktion der Intellektuellen', in R. Viehoff and R. T. Segers (eds.), *Kultur, Identität, Europa*. Frankfurt/M: Suhrkamp, pp. 130–47.

Habermas, J., 1976, 'Können komplexe Gesellschaften eine vernünftige Identität ausbilden?', in *Zur Rekonstruktion des Historischen Materialismus*. Frankfurt/M: Suhrkamp.

1994, 'Europe's Second Chance', in J. Habermas, *The Past as Future*. Cambridge: Polity, pp. 73–98.

1998, *The Inclusion of the Other*. Cambridge: Polity.

1999, 'The European Nation-State and the Pressures of Globalisation', *New Left Review*, Vol. **235**, 46–59.

2001, *The Postnational Constellation*. Cambridge: Polity.

Hildermeier, M., 2000, *Europäische Zivilgesellschaft in Ost und West. Begriff, Geschichte, Chancen*. Frankfurt/M: Campus.

Hudson, R. and A. M. Williams (eds.), 1999, *Divided Europe. Society and Territory*. London: SAGE.

Kaelble, H., 2000, 'Demokratie und europäische Integration seit 1950', in M. Hildermeier, J. Kocka and C. Conrad (eds.), *Europäische Zivilgesellschaft in Ost und West. Begriff, Geschichte, Chancen*. Frankfurt/M: Campus, pp. 245–71.

Lepsius, M. R., 2001, 'The European Union. Economic and Political Integration and Cultural Plurality', in K. Eder and B. Giesen (eds.), *European Citizenship. Between National Legacies and Postnational Projects*. Oxford: Oxford University Press, pp. 205–21.

Middlemas, K., 1995, *Orchestrating Europe. The Informal Politics of European Union 1973–1995*. London: Fontana.

Miszlivetz, F. and K. Ertsey, 1998, 'Hungary: Civil Society in the Post-Socialist World', in A. van Rooy (ed.), *Civil Society and the Aid Industry*. London: Earthscan.

Münch, R., 1993, *Das Projekt Europa. Zwischen Nationalstaat, Regionaler Autonomie und Weltgesellschaft*. Frankfurt/M: Suhrkamp.

1999, 'Europäische Identitätsbildung', in R. Viehoff and R. T. Segers (eds.), *Kultur, Identität, Europa*. Frankfurt/M: Suhrkamp, pp. 223–52.

Nagle, J. D. and A. Mahr (eds.), 1999, *Democracy and Democratisation. Post-communist Europe in Comparative Perspective*. London: SAGE.

Outhwaite, W., 1995, 'Reflexive Xenophobia', ESSE (European Society for the Study of English) Conference, University of Cologne, March.

Outhwaite, W., 2000, 'Towards a European Civil Society?', *Soundings*, Vol. **16**, 131–43.

Pérez-Díaz, V., 1993, *The Return of Civil Society*. Cambridge, MA: Harvard University Press.

1998, 'The Public Sphere and a European Civil Society', in J. Alexander (ed.), *Real Civil Societies. Dilemmas of Institutionalisation*. London: SAGE, pp. 211–38.

Pohoryles, R., *et al.* (eds.), 1994, *European Transformation. Five Decisive Years at the Turn of the Century.* Aldershot: Avebury.

Pollock, G., 2001, 'Civil Society and Euro-nationalism', *Studies in Social and Political Thought*, Vol. 4, 31–56.

Putnam, R., 2001, *Bowling Alone: The Collapse and Revival of American Community.* New York: Simon & Schuster.

Schlesinger, P. and D. Kevin, 2000, 'Can the European Union Become a Sphere of Publics?', in E. Eriksen and J. Fossum (eds.), *Democracy in the European Union.* London: Routledge, pp. 206–29.

Scholte, J.-A., 2000, *Globalisation: A Critical Introduction.* London: Palgrave.

Shaw, M., 2000, *Theory of the Global State.* Cambridge: Cambridge University Press.

Shonfield, A., 1965, *Modern Capitalism. The Changing Balance of Public and Private Power.* London: Oxford University Press.

Siedentop, L., 2000, *Democracy in Europe.* Harmondsworth: Penguin.

Tocqueville, A. de [1835] 1994, *Democracy in America.* London: Everyman's Library.

Turner, C., 1997, 'Civil Society or Constitutional Patriotism?', in R. Fine and S. Rai (eds.), *Civil Society. Democratic Perspectives.* London: Cass, pp. 115–31.

Viehoff, R. and R.T. Segers, 1999, 'Einleitung', in R. Viehoff and R.T. Segers (eds.), 1999, *Kultur, Identität, Europa.* Frankfurt/M: Suhrkamp.

Wainwright, H., 1994, *Arguments for a New Left. Answering the Free-Market Right.* Oxford: Blackwell.

Weber, E., 1977, *Peasants into Frenchmen. The Modernisation of Rural France, 1870–1914.* London: Chatto and Windus.

Part III

European History and European Culture

6   Plaidoyer pour l'Europe des Patries

John A. Hall

The shape of the new Europe is best appreciated through a particular understanding of the old Europe. My use of these terms does not coincide with Donald Rumsfeld's contrast – designed to divide so as to better control Europe – between the key pioneers of European integration and newer members from Central Europe. Attention focuses instead on the historical sociology of European territory and institutions over the last century. What matters most of all is the national question, for reasons so obvious that they can be stated immediately with both bluntness and force.

The central feature that differentiated the old Europe of a century ago from its contemporary variant was the presence of multinational empires, most notably those of the Habsburgs, Romanovs and Ottomans.[1] These authoritarian regimes were faced with the challenge of modernity, that is, with the complex intertwining of nationalism, democratisation and industrialisation, the precise contours of which we still do not fully understand. None was able to meet this challenge intact; all fragmented into a series of separate nation-states, albeit dissolution in the Russian case was much delayed by the empire being placed under new management at the end of the First World War. The tectonic shift caused by the ending of imperial rule in the European heartland resulted in vicious practices of ethnic cleansing, population transfer and genocide, all carried out in the midst of the fog of world wars. Accordingly, it is entirely appropriate to call twentieth century Europe 'the dark continent'.[2] This hideous and shameful background lay behind and did much to initiate the varied initiatives of European integration. The analytic question that lies behind this chapter follows from this. Is it possible for a Europe made new by the acceptance of democracy to achieve what was beyond the reach of the dynastic empires of a century ago, that is, to create a single political roof within which different nations will be happy to live, function and prosper? It is as well to say immediately that this question is not really that at the heart of Jürgen Habermas's contribution to this volume. He is representative of a school of opinion so convinced of the horrors of nationalism that he hopes to move Europe completely – for he suggests that some movement has *already* taken place – beyond the era of nation-states towards a postnational future. The nature of the disagreement between these positions is for the most part descriptive, albeit with prescriptive overtones.

The character of the argument, of the particular understanding of old Europe already noted, can usefully be highlighted immediately by a comment on Ernest Gellner's celebrated theory of nationalism. Gellner claimed that the break up of empires was made inevitable by the combination of social inequality and ethnic marker. His marvellous parable about Megalomania and Ruritania is accordingly one in which socio-economic factors are privileged as the causal factors at work.[3] While such factors should not be ignored, two reasons suggest the need to develop a rather different position. First, Gellner's attempt to produce a general theory of nationalism must fail, in my view, because nationalism has existences rather than any single essence. It is best understood by analogy to Freud's view of the libido – as something elemental and sticky, whose character depends upon the particular object to which it attaches itself. In this context, it is worth noting that nationalism should not be defined simply as secession. The moments when established states have been captured by the fever of nationalism has marked the historical record to a far greater extent. This first point lies at the back of my disagreement with Habermas. To a very great extent nationalism *was* as repulsive as he imagines between roughly 1870 and 1945. But the mood of nationalism has changed for the better. This beneficent development is much to be welcomed. It makes it less necessary to aim for some sort of post-national constellation; this is something of a relief because that aim is not likely to be realised given that national feelings retain more power than Habermas allows. A second disagreement with Gellner can be pinpointed by subtly changing his parable so as to suggest that Megalomania *breeds* Ruritania. Nationalism results very often from the way that empires treat their nations. Differently put, I prefer a more political – and indeed geopolitical – theory of nationalism that has at its centre the importance of repression and exclusion.[4]

This chapter opens by offering an account of the period in which nationalist excesses were so very apparent. This account serves as background to the three elements of my 'plaidoyer'. The first is entirely descriptive. The process of European integration after 1945 has been driven by intergovernmental agreements; differently put, the European Union (EU) depends upon nation-states rather than replacing them with genuine transnational arrangements. The second element, equally descriptive in essence, concerns a different sense of 'the new Europe'. What matters here are less the achievements of the EU to date but rather the view that Europe will soon *become* transnational, not least because the entry of ten new members in 2004 'must' entail radical restructuring so as to avoid stalemate. I will present banal reasons suggesting that such a move is in fact very unlikely. Continuity is likely to be more important than change. Finally, the third element turns, with some hesitations, from description to prescription.

Heroism and Horror

The best-known challenge that modernity posed to old regimes derived from the impact of industrialisation. The emergence of organised working classes threatened the position of the privileged, especially of course when socialist ideologies were adopted. Further, the fact that the socialist movement boasted of its transnational character and vision made ruling elites feel still more insecure. The very basis of political loyalty – namely acceptance of the legitimate authority of national states – seemed to be placed in question. In fact these were largely matters of perception rather than of reality. For contemporary sociological investigation has made it quite clear that the emergence of working classes did not in itself pose much threat to capitalist industrialism.[5] When left alone, workers certainly fought for higher wages – but that was essentially economistic, mere trade union consciousness as Lenin had it.[6] Roughly speaking, this was the dominant situation in the liberal regimes of the UK and the USA: workers organised for industrial action, but had little political consciousness. But of course workers were often not left alone in this way. Perceptions matter, and the fears of the ruling elites of the authoritarian imperial regimes led to policies which then affected the character of social movements. When such old regimes passed anti-socialist legislation they radicalised workers, giving them political consciousness. In Wilhelmine Germany the working class accordingly became organised both in industrial and political terms, with great loyalty being shown by unions to their Social Democratic Party. In Tsarist Russia matters went even further. The working class became genuinely revolutionary, at least at those moments when the autocracy went beyond anti-socialist legislation to outright repression.[7] One contemporary who appreciated the sociological mechanism at work was Max Weber. In practical politics, he stressed what can be termed a liberal Machiavellian line: incorporation would bring national loyalty, with socialist consciousness being seen merely as the result of regime error.[8]

Weber is of great interest here in a rather different capacity, that is, as exemplar rather than analyst. He was not nearly as acute a sociological analyst about two further factors, deeply entwined both with each other and with industrialisation. In contrast, Weber was a 'Fleet Professor', a member of the Navy League convinced that Germany needed 'a place in the sun'. He was himself a nationalist, albeit one marked by liberalism, and he took for granted the view that it was necessary for his society to have its own sources of supply and its own secure markets.[9] Werner Sombart's treatise of the time suggested that Germany had a choice between 'heroism' and 'trading'.[10] Weber had no doubt that heroism was necessary. In one sense he was wrong: the German economy of the time was prospering without imperial possessions. But rationality is lent to his view when one considers the longer term: the possession of empire was an insurance policy should interdependence fail. Further, it was certainly appropriate to see a measure of hypocrisy in the British advocacy of free trade. The Royal Navy protected British food supplies from abroad; it further had the capacity to starve Germany into submission should it seek to become genuinely interdependent. All this can be highlighted by means of a particular formulation, namely that in these years nationalism was intimately linked to imperialism.

But this is not the only thing to be said about nationalism. For, on the other hand, the young Weber was apparently known to his friends as 'Polish Max', on account of sociological studies of Polish farm workers on the east-Elbian estates – and more particularly because he insisted that the presence of such a minority weakened the German nation-state. In this he was wholly representative of his time: most elites believed that catching up with the leading edge of power required, for reasons of military and industrial efficiency, the creation of national homogeneity. The late Tsarist empire had a majority of Russian ethnics as long as it could ensure that the 'little Russians' became integrated into a Russian nation-state rather than gaining national self-consciousness as Ukrainians. The trouble of course was that attempts at forcible assimilation encouraged secession, in the Ukraine and still more so in the socially more advantaged Polish and Finnish territories. In contrast, the Germans at the core of the Habsburg Empire had no choice, given their demographic weakness, but to tolerate other nationalities. Still, the fact that this empire did not turn itself into a constitutional monarchy meant that the nationalities question was far from being solved before the First World War.

The absence of voice encouraged demands for exit, albeit these might never have succeeded but for defeat in war.[11] These are the examples that justify the theoretical claim made above, namely that the actions of megalomanias bred national consciousness amongst the various Ruritanias. The history of Gellner's own homeland in Bohemia makes the point with especial clarity. Masaryk would have been perfectly satisfied to stay within a more liberal Austro-Hungary; some argue that his conversion to a fully separatist stance came as late as 1916, that is, only in the face of complete intransigence on the part of the Habsburgs.

The link between nationalism and imperialism, together with attempts to homogenise territories and counter-attempts at secession, meant that any war that took place would have enormous scope — as most certainly proved to be the case.[12] But war itself was occasioned by the nature of foreign policy-making inside imperial courts, to which attention must be given for an explanation for the breakdown of order that then allowed nationalism and imperialism to cause disaster. A preliminary, scene-setting point is simply that the late nineteenth-century European great powers were engines of grandeur, whose leaders habitually wore military uniform. The problem that such rulers faced, however, was that making foreign policy was becoming ever more difficult. Jack Snyder has usefully suggested that foreign policy making tends to be rational when states have 'centres' with the capacity to prioritise policy.[13] Examples of such rational states include the rule of traditional monarchs, the collective domination of a revolutionary party so much in control of a late developing society as to have no fear of popular pressure, and the checks and balances on foreign adventures provided by liberal systems. In contrast, late developing societies — which combine authoritarianism with genuine pressures from a newly mobilised population — tend to lack the state capacity necessary to calculate by means of realist principles. What mattered most in the years before 1914 was the inability of the German state to calculate clearly. One symbol of this was the fact that Chancellor Bethmann-Hollweg did not know the extent to which war plans involved invading Belgium — something which he knew would lead to British entry into the war before mobilisation had actually taken place. Crucially, the Kaiser's personal rule allowed for both a *Weltpolitik* aimed at Britain and empire, and a more traditional Eastern policy aimed at Russia to be supported at the same time absolutely contrary to the simple dictum that war on two fronts tends to be disastrous. Germany began a war that it was bound to lose, to escape an encirclement that it had itself created.

The fact that this was an industrial war based on mass conscription led to the toppling of old regimes, to massive boundary changes and to the breakdown of much established social structure. This caused instability such that it is entirely proper to stress the continuity between the First and Second World Wars – best seen, in other words, as Europe's Peloponnesian War of modernity. One element at work was the way in which the legacy of the war created resentful paramilitaries, the human material of fascism.[14] An equally important element was the fact that the link between nationalism and imperialism remained absolutely in place, as can clearly be seen in the mentality of Hitler. The German dictator of course helped create a situation in which national security seemed to require imperial possessions; but his rise to power can in part be seen as a response to the fact that the Treaty of Versailles had not established a legitimate international order. The absence of security undermined economic interdependence, further linked imperialism with nationalism, and encouraged pressure for national homogenisation. When war came, it again tended to the absolute. One consequence of this was a great deal more 'sorting out' of peoples, a process which included both the extermination of the Jews and the expulsion of Germans from Eastern Europe in the immediate aftermath of defeat in war. Gellner's insistence on industrialisation as the prime mover of national homogenisation fails to recognise that the great human agents of the process were Hitler and Stalin.

Explaining a Becoming Modesty

The First World War ended badly despite the making of formal treaties. In contrast, the Second World War ended well without formal agreements. What mattered most of all was consideration given to power politics. Spheres of influence were established between superpowers allowing for ever-increasing levels of mutual understanding. A bipolar system is probably more stable at all times than its multipolar alternative; the creation and refinement of nuclear weapons massively reinforced this logic because their destructive potential was so great that rationality was, so to speak, imposed upon statist calculations. Within this basic structure Europe developed an idiosyncratic but altogether more successful form of life. Attention must be given to two crucial elements in the reconstitution of Europe.

First, Europe's security dilemma at last found a solution. If one element of this was that of the relationship between the two superpowers, another was that of the presence of American forces within Europe. In one sense this was an 'empire by invitation'.[15]

The formulation of Lord Ismay – that the purpose of NATO was to keep the Russians out, the Americans in and the Germans divided – bears repetition and highlighting. The Russian threat was real, and it was felt as acutely by those on the front line as it was in Washington. One could add to this that the Americans took active steps to remove the extreme left of European politics in the years immediately after 1945 – taking particular care, for instance, to support Christian Democracy in Italy against its communist rivals.[16] Less obvious but quite as important was the fact that the Europeans appreciated the American presence for an entirely different reason. European states had fought endlessly, and to the point of absolute exhaustion in the twentieth century. The USA in effect acted as an umpire, or court of last appeal. When distrust is very high there is a great deal to be said for a mediator – and one in this case possessed of powerful means of coercion and persuasion. Finally, the decision to keep Germany divided exemplifies the difference between the way the First and Second World Wars ended: power mattered in 1945, not least since obeisance before the principle of national self-determination in 1919 was considered to have contributed to geopolitical disaster. It is important to stress once again that geopolitical stability is a precondition for investment and economic growth. Just as interdependence was undermined by geopolitical competition in the interwar period, so too was it made possible within Europe after 1945 because a stable international order had been put in place. The ability to become traders rather than heroes rested on secure geopolitical foundations.

Second, Europeans themselves made a major contribution to a newly liberal world. Fascism was thoroughly discredited; beaten in its own chosen arena of military valour. More particularly, French bureaucrats, aware of the devastation caused by three wars with Germany within a single lifetime, effectively changed their country's geopolitical calculation. If Germany could not be beaten militarily, an alternative strategy might be possible: a permanent embrace of mutual co-operation could neutralise aggression. The origin of what is now the EU came from a decision by the two leading powers to give up their geopolitical autonomy, by establishing genuine inter-dependence in coal and steel – that is, in giving up the capacity to make their own weapons. The condominium between these two powers has structured the EU throughout its history: when agreement has been present, movement forward has been possible, with the absence of agreement leading to temporary stalemates.

The most high-powered history of the EU, and of its precursors, is that of Alan Milward. His first general treatment showed how important participation in advanced markets was for European economies, noting that Britain's continued membership in imperial markets did a great deal to damage its chances for economic growth.[17] Much was made in that book of the historical class compromise, of the impact of social democracy and Christian democracy, in creating the social cement that allowed for greater utilisation of the market principle. But Milward's second intervention has still greater importance. He recognises that European states had sought, between 1870 and 1945, to be complete power containers, nationally homogeneous and in possession of markets and secure sources of supply.[18] The fact that this led to complete disaster produced humility, a becoming sense of modesty. But this is not to say for a moment that state power somehow lost its salience. Rather states discovered that doing less proved to give them more, that interdependence within a larger security frame allowed for prosperity and the spread of citizenship rights. Differently put, breaking the link between nationalism and imperialism enhanced rather than undermined state capacity.

At this point; a measure of scepticism as to the depth of European liberalism is in order. For one thing, it may be the case that class peace has been achieved more as the result of regimes learning to leave working classes alone than from incorporation by social democratic means.[19] Many academics and commentators had expected that Thatcherite neo-liberal policies designed to create flexible labour markets and to curtail corporatist arrangements would lead to powerful political reactions from below. In fact, there was very little response. It may be that corporatist arrangements breed more intense political reactions precisely because they involve working classes with the state. Liberalism without much social democratic gloss seems to be more stable than had been thought, which is not to say that neo-liberalism has equivalent appeal in every European country.[20]

Something even more troubling can be said about the other form by means of which the people entered the political stage – that is, as nations rather than just as classes. Geopolitical peace makes possible liberal consociational arrangements of all sorts largely because the 'unitariness' of the state is less important when there is no immediate prospect of war. To that extent liberalism has contributed, for example, to the consolidation of multinational Spain. But the brute fact about nationalism remains that ethnic cleansing has taken place within Europe in the last century, most recently of course during the last Balkan wars. Nearly every member of the EU – Spain and the UK are obvious exceptions – now has a dominant ethnic majority. This generalisation most definitely applies to the new members

who gained entrance in 2004. Let us take as an example Prague, the city
of Gellner's childhood. The Jews and Germans were killed during or
expelled after the war, while the end of communism saw the secession of
the rich Czechs from the Slovaks and systematic discrimination against
Gypsies. The Czech Republic is now utterly homogeneous — and, in
comparison to its past, somewhat boring. This reference to Gellner is
not accidental. His theory of nationalism privileges a functionalist style
of explanation: a society works best on the basis of a single culture.
Gellner made the most of this in economic terms, but the same point
was made about liberty by no less a figure than John Stuart Mill.[21]
While there may be ways in which liberal democracy can be combined
with the presence of many nations within a single state, this does
not detract from the force of the Gellner–Mill position. Liberal
democracy is more secure within European nation-states because
of increased homogeneity. One can only feel morally uneasy about
this, as Gellner himself certainly did on his return to the homogenised
Czech Republic in the last years of his life. Nevertheless, it is as well
to admit that there are very often structural limits to liberalism.
In Europe liberalism was made secure only after the politics of mass
viciousness; its capacity to mollify and compromise came into full force
only when there were no great problems left to handle.

Limits to Transnational Development

European integration has had a long and complex history, which
deserves a level of attention and a command of evidence that is sadly
beyond my powers. A particularly notable character of that history has,
however, been its curiously stop–go character: just when stalemate
seemed in place, a sudden lurch forward took place. This unpredictability deserves emphasis as it makes one realise that the future of
Europe is by no means closed. Arguments over the level of integration within Europe often boil down to interpretations as to whether
the glass is half full or half empty. There is no intention here to deny
that some integrative developments have taken place, certainly in the
economic realm and to a lesser extent in the legal sphere. Nonetheless,
the argument here is of the half empty variety. The justification for this
is simple: there are clear constraints on further integration. The purpose
of this section is to specify five home truths that should be borne
in mind by those imagining that transnationalism is likely to increase
within the EU.

The first point is implicit in the account give of the origins of
the European project. The calculation of states created the EU and

its precursors, and those calculations remain in force today. Consider some powerful but banal examples. First, the collapse of communism famously led Mrs Thatcher to get in touch with Mitterand so as to ask 'what should be done with the Germans'. Mrs Thatcher's views about Germany reflected prejudice rather than reality, but the analytic point about state calculation should be retained. For geopolitical calculation was quite as much at work in France's response to this huge change. If one element was the insistence that Germany be tied to Europe by means of the euro, still more striking was France's return to the NATO command structure – a decision that had at its heart the desire to keep Americans in Europe so as to balance a greater Germany. A second example is the bargaining at the December 2002 Nice summit on enlargement, some details of which were provided thanks to leaks published in *The Economist*. This was a forum at which Bismarck would have felt at home: 'if you give me this, then I'll give in on that issue' was the characteristic tone of the meeting, especially as far as voting rights for new states were concerned. Three, scepticism needs to be shown to the claim, frequently made, that the Franco-German condominium is losing its salience within Europe. When crucial issues to do with enlargement had to be faced at the end of 2002, it was only agreement between France and Germany that broke through what had seemed an insurmountable set of obstacles. Further, in early 2003 a plan for the future of Europe was announced by these two powers alone. The plan itself was ill thought-out, but the power of the relationship was made evident by the fact that the members of the Bundestag travelled to the Hall of Mirrors at Versailles to endorse it. The entry of ten new members in 2004 does present a challenge for the Franco-German condominium, but it may yet be met by encouraging Britain to enter into closer relations with the leading pair, so as to set an informal agenda for the EU as a whole. Finally, attention should be given to empirical work probing behind the ideology of harmonisation so as to examine its realities. Francesco Duina's work is exemplary in this regard. His first book took two directives, those on equal pay and on air pollution, and then examined the extent to which different countries actually implemented rules suggested to them. Analysis of three countries per directive produced a picture of very considerable variety. Implementation was likely to succeed when it fitted with previous policy choices and had the support of national pressure groups; when the history and group organisation of a nation-state pointed in a direction opposed to the directive, implementation was likely be fudged, delayed or ignored.[22] A similar story is told in a more recent study over tobacco control: both the initial blocking and eventual acceptance of the directive on advertising for tobacco depended upon the particular constellation of national interests in place at the time.[23]

Second, it is crucial to remember that the EU is in a fundamental sense weak, not the Leviathan made much of by most Eurosceptics. Fiscally the EU extracts well below 2 per cent of the national product of the member states, that is, far less than the proportion − characteristically 30−45 per cent − that the various nation-states take from their societies. In 2003 the Commission requested that its share rise to 1.25 per cent, but the request was resisted by several states that wish to limit that share to a ceiling of just 1 per cent.[24] It is worth noting in this context that plans to allow for direct taxation were dropped from the final version of the constitution promulgated in 2004. Further, it remains the case that the EU by and large has only one policy on which it spends large amounts of money, indeed most of its own budget, namely the Common Agricultural Policy (CAP). Remembering this basic fact gives a sense of perspective about the key question of identity. These fiscal considerations suggest that it is very unlikely there will be very many significant European political movements in the near future. For one of the most firmly established generalisations of comparative historical sociology − already noted and made use of in this chapter − is that social movements arise and gain force when state demands are placed upon civil society. Perhaps the key social process creating identity has traditionally been that of citizenship struggles over taxation. As the EU makes few fiscal demands, a sense of European identity is unlikely to be created through popular struggles.

Very much the same point derives from a consideration of a third basic fact about the EU. The EU may be economically powerful, but it remains insignificant in geopolitical and military terms. The inability to reach a common policy when Yugoslavia broke up, in the face of Balkan ethnic cleansing and over the invasion of Iraq makes the first point clear. So too does the 2004 constitution. The proposal in the draft constitution was for a foreign minister to devise a policy and then to seek its ratification; the final version requires unanimity before a policy can see the light of day. Attempts are now being made to create a European defence force, but it is very unlikely that this will amount to a great deal − certainly nothing like a force capable of giving the EU genuine autonomy so as to change the unipolar ordering of the contemporary international order. There is no sign that Europeans are prepared to pay the very high price that would be required to gain geopolitical autonomy. If citizenship struggles over taxation gave shared identity, so too did military involvement in a common project. It seems unlikely that war will forge a European identity.

Fourth, a sense of European identity is, as already explained, limited. All opinion polls show that national identities trump those of Europe in every single country of the EU. Of course, there are great differences between countries, with loyalty to the European project characteristically being higher in countries that suffered badly in the war compared to those that did not. Further, identities are not simple, with many having multiple, overlapping and changing identities. In general what is noticeable is that attitudes to Europe are path dependent: they follow the characteristic histories of the nation-states involved.[25]

Finally, opinion polls also make it quite clear that the EU is essentially an elite affair, with strong support throughout Europe habitually being related to high socio-economic status. In this connection, it is worth considering language. David Laitin has suggested that the linguistic repertoire that Europeans would need in the future would be a 'two plus or minus one' language regime.[26] One necessary language would be English, the world language used most often in EU affairs, with the second being that of one's nation-state. The minus in his formula refers to the UK and Ireland, where English is the national language, with the plus being the need to speak a minority language when one's nation-state has a different tongue. Laitin's claim is that such a repertoire will help solve European problems. I am not so sure. Europeans are indeed very good at learning languages. But to be really sophisticated, to be able to perform at a high level in other languages is difficult. It depends upon education, and perhaps requires sending your children off to other countries. This is likely to be something that elites can manage better than can their peoples. At a minimum, this suggests that there will be a limit to popular enthusiasm for the EU – as seems apparent from the decline in numbers of those voting at European elections. At a maximum, one might expect something worse. The mood of nationalism may be about to change once again. Nineteenth- and early twentieth-century nationalism was in large part a strategy of late development and as such it had very great appeal to elites.[27] In Europe it now seems that elites wish to be part of the action with a territorial frame larger than that of a single nation-state, albeit they doubtless feel that this is the best strategy for their countries. The rise of varied social movements opposed to further integration suggests that those who are left behind, caged within national borders, resent the creation of a world that disadvantages them. Nationalism may yet gain new force as a reactionary project.

It is worth concluding this section by repeating what was said at its start. The fact that the limits to integration have been stressed here should not be taken as a claim that integration has no significance. In this matter, the work of Duina is exemplary. For all his stress on the varied ways in which different nation-states react to directives of the Commission, he nonetheless recognises the novelty of a situation in which a single agenda is placed before so many states at the same time. He certainly does not rule out the possibility that this may in the longer run diminish the range of variation between nation-states within the EU. Still, it is worth looking carefully at the constitution promulgated in 2004. The very first article makes it clear that powers derive from nation-states, while further clauses allow for withdrawal and for the transfer of certain competences back to the member states. Adding to this some of the other points made in this chapter – the limit to foreign policy making and the absence of direct taxation, and the continuing presence of veto rights – suggests that one is a long way from any sort of creeping transnational arrangement. And, of course, this was most pertinently exemplified by the 'no' votes in the referenda in France and the Netherlands in 2005.

From Description to Prescription

The central argument that I have made is that Europe is not a fully developed transnational entity.[28] Rather, it is a place where heads of government meet, with its key institution remaining the Council of Ministers. In substantive terms, the EU provides regulations for capitalism: states have agreed to let the market rule, so as to increase prosperity. Beyond that economic basis stands splendour and shame. Splendour resides in the protection for minorities that any new member must accept, a vital piece of legislation, sure to limit ethnic conflict throughout the European zone, and the inclusion of Central European countries – saved at last from the vicious practices of their recent histories. Shame refers to the CAP, able to protect rich farmers at the expense of the developing world, and to the determination to exclude peoples from the South and East.

Let me conclude first by issuing two warnings and then by offering an overall assessment as to where the EU stands.

An initial warning is simple: if Europe starts to feel in any way like an empire, like Megalomania, then there will be Ruritanian reactions in consequence. I do not have in mind here the extraordinary Euroscepticism of the British Conservative Party – for that reflects the situation of a formerly great state having trouble adjusting to a more limited role. Rather, what may well matter is the feelings of small nations and nation-states. The Scots and the Catalans have already noticed that Estonia, with a population of about a quarter of their own, looks set to have three votes in EU affairs while they will have none. Then there is the reaction of the Danes, most notably their vote against joining the euro. There is a certain sort of irrationality here. The Danish Krone was tied to the Deutsche Mark for many years, and it has always been pegged to the euro, so there has not been any monetary autonomy for some considerable time. Belonging to the euro would in fact increase autonomy because it would allow Danes to influence the European Central Bank. In a sense this very irrationality proves the point, that suspicions that greater union will diminish the power of a small state are very great indeed. They are likely to be shared by most of the new members from Eastern and Central Europe. Experience of life in imperial systems — Tsarist, Habsburg and Soviet — has made these states deeply sensitive to any limits to their autonomy. In this context attention can usefully be drawn to Brendan O'Leary's powerful demonstration that successful federalism has always depended upon the presence of a *Staatsvolk*.[29] In the absence of a dominant people, federalism can only work when it is combined with consociational arrangements designed to reassure minorities — as was historically the case in Canada, where care was taken to alternate between anglophone and francophone Prime Ministers. Given that there are not enough Germans to form a *Staatsvolk* in Europe, stability may well depend upon allowing the blocking powers of small states to remain in place.

Second, Jürgen Habermas is correct when he notes that the USA does not provide a proper model for the future of Europe. For one thing, it behoves us to remember American unity was established through a civil war. For another, the USA is still — as is often the case with 'civic' nations — a powerfully homogenising society.[30] Most obviously, there is a great deal of evidence to suggest that the USA will remain monolingual. 'If English was good enough for Jesus Christ', a recent Texas election stump orator declared, 'it's good enough for Texas'. All the evidence suggests that Spanish is being lost as a language quite as fast as was Italian a century ago. To make this point, it should be stressed, is not to engage in facile anti-Americanism. For one thing, the American capacity to integrate is remarkable. For another, there is a completely admirable facet to life in the USA. Rates of inter-marriage are incredibly high, for every group except African Americans. These considerations make it clear that arrangements for Europe must differ from those of the USA.

These two warnings can be highlighted with reference to the title of this chapter. The EU is made up of co-operating nation-states. Little should be done to change something that is working. This is especially so given that against potential dangers can be set forces making for stability, to which we can now turn.

A first point concerns differences in economic levels within the EU. Roughly one-third of the budget of the EU is spent on Structural Funds and Cohesion Funds, both designed to level the economic playing field within Europe. Such funds have worked rather effectively, thereby undercutting the possibility that backward areas will play the nationalist card. It is only fair to admit that this source of stability may yet be threatened, should such funds be significantly cut for the ten new members who joined in 2004. Second, the change in the history of nationalism, the sundering of the link between nationalism and imperialism, is fundamental. How many people believe that Russian economic success is going to be assured by maintaining control of Chechnya?[31] Europeans, at the end of the Second World War, gave up their empires and, against all expectations, entered into the most fabulous period of economic growth in their history. The nationalism of Scots and Catalans is 'free trade nationalism' in the sense that remaining part of the EU is an absolute priority. Third, the American presence is likely to remain, thereby providing considerable stability. There is an opportunity and a cost here: Europe will be stable without high levels of identification but, equally, high levels of identification will be curtailed by the absence of any real need for self-defence. Fourth, there is every sign that elites wish to be part of the large European world, rather than being prisoners inside their own nation-states. The desire to be 'part of the action' is, of course, overwhelmingly present in Central Europe: this world has produced no ideas since 1989, merely a visceral desire to 'return to civilisation'. Finally, the tension created by smaller nations, with or without their states, should not be exaggerated. Central Europeans accepted the harsh terms imposed on them with enthusiasm so that they could gain entry, not surprisingly given that their memories are of truly vicious imperial rule. The Danes voted no once before, and then reversed themselves. They inhabit a small nation-state, bereft in the end of many options, and it is likely that they will soon reverse themselves on the euro. Finally, the fact that taxation demands from the EU are very limited is likely to limit the force of Europe-wide social movements: this may put a cap on the creation of a shared identity, but it will equally contribute to social stability.

Let me conclude with two maxims. Despite being a very enthusiastic European, I find it hard to propose any rousing call to action. A first maxim must be 'Consumers of the world, unite': this does not warm the blood like wine, but perhaps there is something to be said for placing reason above passion. My second maxim must be 'Down with Descartes'. There is a good deal to be said for messiness, mild confusion, differing levels of integration, a certain lack of clarity. Austro-Hungary thrived in this way, and only fell because of defeat in war. The EU thrives too, and is not in imminent danger of disabling defeat. A constitution may be needed, given new and future entrants to the EU. But let it not be too clear: for clarity from anything like Megalomania might yet produce Ruritanians.

Notes

1 For a brilliant recent account, see Lieven (2000). Lieven's analysis includes Wilhelmine Germany and Great Britain – the latter in part because of its treatment of Ireland.
2 Mazower 1998.
3 Gellner 1983.
4 For a good deal more along these lines, see the papers in Hall (1998).
5 Mann 1993.
6 Lenin 1961.
7 McDaniel 1987.
8 Weber 1968.
9 The desire for geopolitical autonomy is well illustrated in Sen (1984). Sen demonstrates that each European country sought to have the same set of basic industries, namely those needed for military purposes. From this came oversupply, dumping practices and international trade rivalry.
10 Sombart 1915.
11 These terms are of course drawn from Hirschman 1978.
12 Kaiser 1990.
13 Snyder 1991. Cf. Mann 1993, ch. 21.
14 Mann 2004.
15 Lundestad 1986.
16 Maier 1981.
17 Milward 1984. There is a touch of unjustified anti-Americanism in this book. It may well be that capital formation was more European than American, but it remains the case that the establishment of security was a precondition for investment.
18 Milward 1992.
19 Hall 1994, ch. 1.
20 Smith 1992.
21 Mill 1875.
22 Duina 1999.

23 Duina and Kurzer 2004.
24 'The existing budget ceiling', the European enthusiast Loukas Tsoukalis (2003, p. 136) notes, 'is simply unrealistic and inconsistent with officially stated objectives'.
25 On this matter, see the brilliant empirical investigation by Medrano (2003).
26 Laitin 1997.
27 Szporluk 1991.
28 Moravscik 1998.
29 O'Leary 2001.
30 Hall and Lindholm 1999.
31 Brooks 1999.

References

Brooks, S., 1999, 'The Globalisation of Production and the Changing Benefits of Conquest', *Journal of Conflict Resolution*, Vol. **43**, 646–70.
Duina, F., 1999, *Harmonising Europe: Nation-States within the Common Market*. Albany, NY: SUNY.
Duina, F. and P. Kurzer, 2004, 'Smoke in Your Eyes: The Struggle over Tobacco Control in the European Union', *Journal of European Policy*, Vol. **11**, 57–77.
Gellner, E., 1983, *Nations and Nationalism*. Oxford: Blackwell.
Hall, J. A., 1994, *Coercion and Consent*. Oxford: Polity Press.
 (ed.), 1998, *The State of the Nation. Ernest Gellner and the Theory of Nationalism*. Cambridge: Cambridge University Press.
Hall, J. A. and C. Lindholm, 1999, *Is America Breaking Apart?* Princeton, NJ: Princeton University Press.
Hirschman, A. O., 1978, *Exit, Voice and Loyalty*. Cambridge, MA: Harvard University Press.
Kaiser, D., 1990, *Politics and War*. Cambridge, MA: Harvard University Press.
Laitin, D. D., 1997, The Cultural Identities of a European State, *Politics and Society*, Vol. **25**, 277–302.
Lenin, V. I., [1902] 1961, *What is to be Done? Burning Questions of Our Movement*, in *Collected Works*, Vol. V. London: Lawrence and Wishart.
Lieven, D., 2000, *Empire. The Russian Empire and Its Rivals*. London: John Murray.
Lundestad, G., 1986, 'Empire by Invitation?', *Journal of Peace Research*, Vol. **23**, 263–77.
McDaniel, T., 1987, *Autocracy, Capitalism, and Revolution in Russia*. Berkeley, CA: University of California Press.
Maier, C., 1981, 'The Two Postwar Eras and the Conditions for Stability in Twentieth-Century Western Europe', *American Historical Review*, Vol. **86**, 327–52.
Mann, M., 1993, *The Sources of Social Power. Vol. II: The Rise of Classes and Nation-States, 1760–1914*. Cambridge: Cambridge University Press.
 2004, *Fascists*. Cambridge: Cambridge University Press.

Mazower, M., 1998, *Dark Continent*. London: Allen Lane.

Medrano, J. D., 2003, *Framing Europe. Attitudes to European Integration in Germany, Spain and the United Kingdom*. Princeton, NJ: Princeton University Press.

Mill, J. S., 1875, *Considerations on Representative Government*. London: Longmans Green.

Milward, A., 1984, *The Reconstruction of Western Europe, 1945–51*. Berkeley, CA: University of California Press.

   1992, *The European Rescue of the Nation-State*. Berkeley, CA: University of California Press.

Moravscik, A., 1998, *The Choice for Europe: Social Purpose and State Power from Messina to Maastricht*. Ithaca, NY: Cornell University Press.

O'Leary, B., 2001, 'An Iron Law of Nationalism and Federation? A (Neo-Diceyan) Theory of the Necessity of a Federal Staatsvolk, and of Consociational Rescue', *Nations and Nationalism*, Vol. 7, 273–96.

Sen, G., 1984, *The Military Origins of Industrialisation and International Trade Rivalry*. London: Frances Pinter.

Smith, M., 1992, *Power, Norms and Inflation*. New York: Aldine de Gruyter.

Snyder, J., 1991, *Myths of Empire*. Ithaca, NY: Cornell University Press.

Sombart, W., 1915, *Händler und Helden*. Leipzig: Duncker & Humblot.

Szporluk, R., 1991, *Communism and Nationalism. Karl Marx versus Friedrich List*. Oxford: Oxford University Press.

Tsoukalis, L., 2003, *What Kind of Europe?* Oxford: Oxford University Press.

Weber, M., 1968, 'Parliament and Government in a Reconstructed Germany', in *Economy and Society*, Vol. II. Berkeley, CA: University of California Press, pp. 1381–469.

7 Europe Becoming: The Civilisational Consequences of Enlargement

Gerard Delanty

The Eastern enlargement of the European Union (EU) has important implications for our understanding of the meaning of Europe. Although the precise nature of this process is uncertain, the very fact that it is underway is in itself of major significance. Indeed the very term integration may be inadequate when it comes to the current scale of Europeanisation, which consists not of one but several logics and not all of which can be understood in terms of integration. Europeanisation is not leading to a society, a state or a clearly definable geopolitical entity that rests on a cultural foundation, as is often assumed. Moreover, there is not one 'Europe', but several. In this respect, what is central is the question of modernity, or modernities and their civilisational forms.

The categories that are used to make sense of Europeanisation tend on the whole to be either descriptive or normative – 'widening', 'deepening', 'integration', 'convergence' – and thus fail to appreciate the dynamics of a multi-directional process. There is relatively little theoretical literature exploring the wider significance of the Eastern enlargement, which is generally seen only in terms of intergovernmentalism and of institutional design.[1] The constitutional debate instigated by the Convention on the Future of Europe in February 2002 has, to a degree, opened a wider perspective on the emerging face of a bigger Europe, but the issues at stake go beyond what can be addressed by a constitution. In order to advance theorising on Europe, this chapter borrows concepts from social theory as a basis for a civilisational approach to European modernity.

First, following Habermas[2] and several other authors, such as Jacques Derrida,[3] Hans-Georg Gadamer[4] and Alain Touraine,[5] Europeanisation entails postnational developments of a cosmopolitan nature. This is relevant to an understanding of the emergence of distinctly European as opposed to national forms of consciousness and identification, and might be related to critical and reflexive forms of communication that do not presuppose an underlying consensus but the discursive thematisation of differences. This approach to cosmopolitanism emphasises its cultural and communicative dimension and does not reduce cosmopolitanism to straightforward globalisation or transnational politics.[6]

Second, in Habermas's particular approach such forms of communication are embedded in forms of social integration as opposed to system integration.[7] In the most general sense, the idea of social integration refers to integration through normative and symbolic processes, such as cultural values, beliefs systems, media of communication, as well as deeper processes of socialisation. System integration refers to integration achieved through the institutional imperatives of money and power operating in markets and states. Until now, Europeanisation has been largely achieved through system integration, but increasingly questions of social integration have come to the fore. The precise relationship between these forms of integration is far from clear but tensions between them are likely to be important in the future.

Third, to take up an idea of Niklas Luhmann's, Europeanisation can be seen as an autopoietic process in a system that reproduces itself by internal and highly differentiated logics of development. His approach puts the emphasis less on integration than on differentiation, for it is through differentiation that integration is achieved.[8] Differences – distinctions, exclusions – do not precede integration but are produced by the very logic of differentiation. But integration and all orders of interpretation and communication have to be seen as specific to the subsystems from which they emanate. What emerges from Luhmann's social theory is precisely a sense of several and largely incommensurable orders of interpretations emerging and producing different logics of exclusion. In this view 'society' does not exist as such, for it is merely the flow of different systems of communication. If society exists, it is only at the level of the global society.[9] This is an approach that is very applicable to an understanding of certain aspects of Europeanisation as a process of becoming in which the entire process produces its own terms of reference.

Fourth, globalisation theory argues that Europeanisation cannot be attributed exclusively to European developments.[10] According to Castells,[11] Europeanisation is now being shaped by wider global processes and takes the form of a network society; the state is being transformed along the lines of a transnational framework of governance and the emergence of new state–society relations. The basic idea is also found in Bauman's notion of a modernity, which is becoming more 'fluid'.[12] Avoiding the dualism of systemic versus social integration, it locates cosmopolitan possibilities in new forms of communication, which are as integral to the economy and the state as they are to the life-world. In this view, Europeanisation can be reproductive and it can be transformative, working through social and systemic forms of integration and creating new logics of differentiation.

Fifth, following Bourdieu we can see Europeanisation as a field of symbolic conflicts in which culture becomes a major site of contestation. This is particularly pertinent to conflicts over belonging and identity, but also to struggles over material capital. For Bourdieu, culture is not just reproductive but generative of social realities. This suggests a view of Europeanisation as generating symbolic discourses in which new realities are cognitively defined in cultural conflicts.[13] In these discourses about Europe, it is not just a matter of an identity being found for a project that is already in existence, but is a matter of the shaping of the project through and by discourses in which competing claims are worked out.[14]

In the context of the enlargement of the EU, these different perspectives all point to a way of thinking about Europe as an indeterminate process of becoming and one in which its latest expressions reflect a deeper transformation of modernity. In my view the modernist project of European integration is reaching its historical limits, and other projects are beginning. Some of these are older and have their origins in earlier modernities, but the societal outcome is highly indeterminate. In short, the EU does not exhaust the field of Europe, which has become open to many new interpretations and projects. This is paradoxical, for the enlargement project, on the one hand, is spear-headed by Brussels and various bilateral arrangements, but on the other hand, has opened up a whole range of discourses that cannot be contained by a state-dominated project. The more the EU advances eastwards and southwards the more difficult will it become to sustain the existing modernist project of Westernisation. The result is that Europeanisation enters into a decisive phase in which more diverse expressions of Europe will become the norm.

The enlargement of the EU to include central and Eastern European and Baltic states and indeed eventually Turkey – along with the continued engagement with Russia – is a major challenge for our understanding of the meaning of Europe as a geopolitical, social and cultural space based on a common or shared identity. Enlargement is not just about getting bigger but is crucially a matter of cultural transformation and in this respect it differs from all previous dynamics of Europeanisation. The *acquis communautaire* cannot define Europe any more than any state can define a society. Europeanisation is a process of differentiation as much as it is of integration, but it is also more than this. The central thrust of my argument is that Europe is best conceived of as a civilisational constellation, or more precisely, as a constellation of at least three civilisations.

Theorising Europeanisation

Europeanisation is a process driven both by political-administrative and economic dictates and by democratic and cultural currents. Until recently the first — systemic forms of integration — was the primary logic of Europeanisation, determined by the twin needs for political coordination and economic integration. The cultural and democratic dimensions were largely secondary. Today such forms of social integration have become powerful counter-logics to the point that Europeanisation can no longer be conceived in terms of a model of straightforward system integration in the sense of administrative steering or the imposition of a model of statehood. Questions of the democratic deficit, citizenship and identity loom large in discussions about European integration. This is not just a backlash against excessive bureaucratic regulation because the enlargement into Central, Eastern and Southern Europe has forced this reappraisal.

There are four major logics of Europeanisation currently unfolding. The first logic is one of postnational developments entailing a transformation of societies in a cosmopolitan direction. National societies are no longer entirely separate from each other but interconnected for reasons that can be explained by processes of globalisation (migration, information and communication technology, Americanisation), European integration and in many cases de-colonisation. In addition to political, economic and legal interpenetration, there is a growing cultural interpenetration of national societies, especially in the countries of the EU. Tourism, educational exchange programmes, European transport systems, changing forms of consumption, sport, even crime, as well as the euro, contribute to this interpenetration.[15]

However, this is not to suggest that there is a European society emerging. Indeed, with John Urry it can be argued that the very category society — suggesting something culturally cohesive and bounded — is inadequate for a description of the interconnections between societal processes.[16] Furthermore it makes little sense to assume that societies — the UK, Belgium, Canada, Ireland — are culturally cohesive in a way that 'Europe' is not. This is why Luhmann has argued that society exists ultimately only as the global society and takes the form of communication rather than an underlying reality.[17] Indeed one interesting application of this idea applied to Europe is that Europe exists only in the modes of communication about it. However, for present purposes, it will suffice to state that a European society is emerging not as an alternative to national societies, as in some kind of transnational suprasociety, but as an expression of interconnections between postnational societies.

The second logic is one of a transnationalisation of the state. This is separate from the question of the meaning of the term society. The EU is a historically unique transnational polity.[18] As has been pointed out in numerous studies, it transcends the nation-state without becoming a federation or confederation. According to Majone, its system of governance resembles that of a regulatory state.[19] The EU has brought about a form of transnational governance in which powers are shared between national and transnational regimes. To a degree, too, a transnational civil society is emerging based on the interaction of many social actors, ranging from national governments, the EU, regulatory agencies, non-state actors such as NGOs, social movements and activists of different kinds. In addition, a new kind of citizenship is emerging, called 'European citizenship'.[20] But this civil society is not necessarily located in a specific transnational space; it is a multilevelled civil society, part transnational, part national and part regional; and it is also linked into global civil society.

The third logic is a cultural process of construction entailing the articulation of new discourses, expressions of collective identity and social imaginaries. The nation no longer exclusively defines the imaginaries of peoplehood and the state lacks the capacity to create new collective identity. This is also true of the EU. We are witnessing new discourses in which competing claims are being worked out. Examples are the various right and left discourses of Euroscepticism, anti-Americanism, fortress Europe, social exclusion and the democratic deficit.

The fourth logic is that of a geopolitical reconfiguration of the EU as an ever-larger entity. This spatial transformation of the EU will have major implications for the other two logics in that their 'deepening' tendencies will not merely be diluted by 'widening' processes but will take more indeterminate forms. In this way several 'Europes' will emerge.

The first two logics are related in that the transnational governance of the EU has enhanced the interpenetration of European societies, which have in turn brought onto the political agenda demands that exceed the original rationale of the EU. For Castells this means that the EU has become more like a network than a traditional state.[21] Furthermore, for Habermas and Derrida this has strengthened cosmopolitan tendencies and may allow Europe to escape its Eurocentrism. Such postnational developments do not mean that nations and nation-states are disappearing. Millward's argument that the original European Economic Community (EEC) enhanced the capacity of the state to sustain itself still applies.[22] What has happened, however, is that the state has lost its capacity to define the nation with the result that societies are becoming more 'postnational'. The equation of nation – state – society has broken down.[23] It is in this context that we can consider the question of the enlargement process.

In addition to state-directed processes, other forces can be identified which are shaping the emerging geopolitical field of Europeanisation. In this field capitalism and state-driven interests meet the resistance of popular currents in which issues of democracy and identity are central. Much of this is an expression of postmaterial values, such as fears about the loss of democratic and cultural autonomy. But it is also fuelled by fears of material losses, and the loosening of social securities and stability that the nation-state has been able to offer.

Where some theorists, such as Castells and Habermas, see cosmopolitan possibilities indicative of a new European 'Enlightenment' based on a democratic civil society and citizenship, others see instead the signs of a different version of Europe emerging around xenophobia, anti-democratic currents and fast capitalism.[24] In contrast to the well-known views of 'Eurosceptics',[25] the sociological approach of Bourdieu offers a more interesting appraisal of the current enlargement process. Bourdieu's sociological theory points to an approach that sees Europeanisation as a site of multiple symbolic conflicts over power and inequality.[26] Europe would be a discourse that has the capacity to construct reality. With the enlargement process, a number of symbolic discourses emerges, none of which can become dominant.[27]

Luhmann's social theory reinforces this view of Europeanisation as an indeterminate process. He shares with Bourdieu a conception of culture in which distinctions are made and legitimated. However, in contrast to Bourdieu, Luhmann's social theory stresses functional differentiation in which the political moment is diluted and does not have the capacity to impose a logic of integration based on normative principles or cultural values. Europeanisation is confronted with competing interpretative frameworks that presuppose one another.

The dominant *acquis communautaire* is a system of interpretation that will have to contend with others.

The Reshaping of Europe

Until now Europeanisation has been shaped by internal factors. Following Eastern enlargement in 2004, external factors will be more decisive in shaping it. Europe will increasingly compete with the USA as a player in the global society. Under Putin there is already a growing interest in Europe rather than the USA as a reference point to define Russian foreign policy. The EU's diplomatic and military role is likely to increase in the coming years.

The main facts of the enlargement process can be stated simply. Enlargement entered the agenda of the EU in 1993 with the Copenhagen European Council, which made the historic promise that 'the countries in Central and Eastern Europe that so desire shall become members of the Union. Accession will take place as soon as a country is able to assume the obligations of membership by satisfying the economic and political conditions.'[28] This was also stated in the Maastricht Treaty but it was not until the Nice Treaty in December 2000 that steps were put in place to prepare the EU for a twenty-five member union by 2004.[29] In addition to the existing fifteen members, the Czech Republic, Cyprus, Estonian, Hungary, Latvia, Lithuania, Malta, Poland, Slovakia, and Slovenia joined the EU in 2004. The decision on membership of Bulgaria and Romania has been delayed. Although Turkey, which has been on the candidacy list since 1999, has not yet been given a date for consideration, it is widely believed this is only a matter of time. At its meeting in Santa Maria da Feira in June 2000 the European Council agreed that all of the countries in the Western Balkans are 'potential candidates' for membership of the EU. The Stabilisation and Association process, which is the EU's policy in this region, allows these countries to move towards integration and to do so with financial support from the EU. Russia has expressed an interest in opening discussion with the EU on the consequences of enlargement, but membership is unlikely ever to happen, despite Gorbachev's promulgation of the idea of a 'common European home'. Currently the Commission intends to use the institutions of the Partnership and Co-operation Agreement to explore the implications of enlargement for Russia and to strengthen the integration of Russia into a common European economic and social space. Since the accession of Finland and the more recent accession of the Baltic States and Poland, Russia has been a direct neighbour of the EU, which consequently will be drawn increasingly into cross-regional controversies.

The recent territorial increase of the EU has seen a population increase of 75 million, bringing the total EU population to 450 million and the addition of some twelve languages and political and legal systems. The implications for political representation remain unclear. On the surface it would appear that small countries will benefit, but the Nice Treaty suggests that this is not the case. This is hardly surprising as many of the new members – with the exception of Poland with a population of almost 39 million – are small countries. This institutional reshaping may have adverse effects for existing smaller member states, such as Ireland, Greece and Portugal. There can be little doubt that the major Western countries will continue to dominate an enlarged EU and will economically benefit from it. However, what is likely to change in a significant way is the cultural composition of the EU. What is going on in Central and Eastern Europe cannot be so-easily called 'Westernisation' in the sense of the imposition of a coherent structure and culture. Although many people in Central and Eastern Europe, as well as people further into Eurasia, see themselves as Western and want to have more not less of the 'West', they all mean different things by this. The debate about joining the EU in the ten new member states was in almost all cases a deeply divided one, with different collective identities coming to the fore. Europeanisation entails resistances, reconstructions, negotiations; it is not a unilateral and unidirectional process.

Geographically the centre is more likely to be Budapest than anywhere in Western Europe. Central Europe is coming more and more into prominence in the reshaping of Europe that enlargement entails. Where the earlier enlargement of the EU has been largely shaped by the incorporation of the European Mediterranean countries of Portugal, Spain and Greece, it is arguably the case that the political traditions of central Europe – especially as represented by Hungary, Poland and the Czech Republic – are closer to the core values of the European political tradition. Christianity has figured centrally in their historical memories and throughout the communist era a political culture of civil society preserved a strong link with European modernity. Nevertheless, there are differences between Western and Central Europe and also between Central Europe and Eastern Europe, to follow a distinction made by Jeno Scüzs in a classic essay on the three historical regions of Europe.[30] Eastern Europe, a less specific term and one which does not have a clear geographical foundation, now no longer refers to *Mitteleuropa*, but – and depending on who uses the designation – it clearly includes Bulgaria and Romania and arguably the Baltic countries.[31] Despite the great differences between these parts of Europe, to varying degrees they all represent regions that are products of European modernity and of Latin Christianity, with the exception of Bulgaria and Romania. However, once we look at Europe in this broad view what is striking is not just a mosaic of regions and nations, but a civilisational constellation. In this constellation Russia and Turkey are key reference points, having partly defined the patterns of modernity in Eastern and Central Europe. Obviously, this is to look beyond the current enlargement. But while it is unlikely that Russia will join the EU, it is playing an increasingly important role in the wider European area.

As the borders of the EU now partly impinge on Russia and, with the eventual entry of Turkey, will extend to Asia, the identity of Europe will become increasingly post-Western, a condition defined by the legacy of an earlier modernity which will have to be negotiated with other modernities. Turkey's close relationships with the countries of central Asia will also have implications for the present countries of the EU, which will have borders with Iran, Syria and Iraq. In short, the borders of the EU will no longer be within Europe, but will be with Asia. In this respect it could be suggested that the Eastern enlargement is different from all earlier enlargement processes since it will raise new questions concerning the very identity of Europe. Enlargement in this case is not only about getting bigger, but also about cultural transformation in terms of both the identity of Europe and in terms of the rise of new kinds of symbolic conflicts over identity, belonging and the meaning of national autonomy.

Enlargement means in effect that the EU embraces societies which have experienced quite different routes to modernity; for instance the new member states – with the exception of Malta and Cyprus – have been former communist countries. Most of the new states have been engaged in the treble transition to capitalism, democracy and national autonomy. Many of these countries have disputed territories and major ethnic divisions. The incorporation of the Central and Eastern European countries will be quite different from the earlier assimilation of the British Isles, the Scandinavian countries and the Iberian Peninsula and Greece because of the scale of the operation and the fact that the enlarged EU will be more politically and culturally diverse than was previously the case. Enlargement means too that the European North–South axis will be overshadowed by the expanding West–East axis, where closure will be more difficult to achieve, for there are no natural Eastern frontiers.[32] Moreover, the earlier enlargement processes were largely responses to economic and political aspiration, a fact which to a degree made possible the deepening and ever closer union of the EU. This will not necessarily be the case with further expansion. Previously the incorporation of new members did not greatly challenge the fundamental assumptions of the EU. The goals of balancing efficiency with social justice and democratic legitimacy may now be overshadowed by issues of security, immigration and crime.

Religion is also likely to become a site of cultural contestation. Despite its apparent secular and republican nature, the EU in fact rests on very Christian cultural assumptions. Most countries have Christian political parties and several (Denmark, the UK, Greece) have state churches and quite a few are monarchies (Spain, the UK, Belgium, the Netherlands, Denmark, Sweden) based on Christian culture. Catholic social teachings have been influential in shaping some of the ideas of the EU. They have played a major role in the vision of the EU as based on solidarity, integration and subsidiarity. With the entry of Poland and Hungary the Catholic underpinning of the EU is likely to be strengthened.

In addition, the EU will have to accommodate Islamic and Orthodox populations. To be sure there has already been within the fifteen-member EU a major Orthodox tradition as represented by Greece. However, with the inclusion of other Orthodox populations, such as Bulgaria and Romania, religion is likely to become more visible in the public sphere, especially where it is more closely tied to national identity. Even though the Turkish state is highly secular, the inclusion of a large Islamic population will certainly have implications for the definition of European identity as one framed in the Christian tradition. Within Turkey main support for Turkish membership has come from the Islamic-based Justice and Development Party, a moderate Islamist Party, which in the historic election of 2002 won two-thirds of parliamentary seats and forms the present government.[33] While the rise of a modern Islamic movement within Turkey demonstrates that Islam and European democratic traditions are compatible, the view persists that Europe is Christian and that Turkey, despite its official secularism, cannot therefore be European.[34]

The Eastern frontier is being pushed in different directions, opening up new borders as well as liminal zones, as the example of Kaliningrad illustrates, and unsettled border disputes. With the entry of Poland, the Polish–Ukrainian border may become significant, as will the border with Russia. However, separate agreements between Russia, Belarus and Ukraine confirm the existence of more than one Europe.

Hungary's membership of the EU may make it less able to look after the interests of Hungarian minorities in non-EU countries, such as Romania, Serbia and Ukraine. In this case, it is a matter of borders becoming on the one hand more porous, but on the other hand more closed.[35] Already the question of Cyprus joining is inseparable from the question of border with the Turkish occupied territory. It is indeed paradoxical that as borders have been diminishing within the existing EU, they are becoming more visible in Central and Eastern Europe. Major symbolic conflicts are being fought around these borders by societies in which national autonomy has been relatively recent and in which it is often associated with the need to deny large minorities of rights.

Within the older member states, the question of borders has taken on a new symbolic significance. Polls indicate that support for enlargement is mixed. Not all opposition is xenophobic. For example, the initial Irish rejection of the Nice Treaty in June 2001 may have been a result of the growing importance of postmaterial values, such as concerns about the erosion of democratic liberties that the Nice Treaty apparently implies. Similarly the 'no votes' in the French and Dutch constitutional referenda in May 2005 resulted from a variety of motives. As the primary justification for the EU is no longer prosperity, other values are entering the political agenda. The extreme right have placed security on the agenda, and have attached it to fears about the erosion of the welfare state. However, not all of the opposition is about security. Democracy for many people is under threat by the enlargement process which has put in place measures that will transfer more power away from elected representatives and civil society into unelected forms of power.[36] The EU is faced with the dilemma that, although its crisis must be measured by the equally pervasive crisis in the legitimacy of national governments, it cannot appeal to democracy as such. It can claim only legitimacy in terms of legality and efficiency.

It thus appears that the enlargement process has opened up a variety of logics of differentiation, especially in terms of culture and democracy. Symbolic conflicts over identity and belonging, new borders within and beyond the EU, cultural differences between East and West, different legitimating principles are coming to the fore. The EU will undoubtedly sustain its integrative drive, but this will not halt the internal differentiation of Europe.[37] The differences between the new Eastern member states and the existing fifteen member states fall within the extremes that already exist within the latter group. The civilisational perspective invoked here sees Europe in fact consisting of a civilisational constellation that is a juxtaposed rather than a fixed or integrated cluster of changing elements, which do not have a common foundation or underlying meaning.

Europe and Its Modernities: a Civilisational Approach

The enlargement process is not based on a model of integration that presupposes either an underlying reality called 'Europe' or the possibility of attaining an overarching regulative ideal. There are several cultural models of Europe, which can be related to the different trajectories of modernity in European history, but these go beyond national and regional traditions and take the form of civilisational traditions. Of particular importance are three, which constitute what might be called the European civilisational constellation: Western European, Russian-Slavic and Islamic-Turkish civilisations. European modernity has been shaped by not one, but by all three civilisations, which open up different geopolitical routes to modernity.[38]

The dominant civilisation that has shaped European and indeed Western world history is the Occidental Christian civilisation. The secularisation of this tradition led to the emergence of modernity based on the ideas of the Enlightenment, the rise of the nation-state and the social movements of the nineteenth century. This is the civilisational model of modernity to which the EU has owed its identity. However, in the context of the enlargement of the EU, the assumptions upon which identity are based may need to be reconsidered. It is worth recalling that the civilisational roots of this Western civilisation – Athens, Rome and Jerusalem – were not particularly European in the Western sense of the term 'European'. Classical antiquity and origins of Christianity were Mediterranean in the sense in which Fernand Braudel used the term.[39] It was only from the sixteenth century that Europe became gradually associated with the West.

With its roots in the Byzantine tradition, the Russian model of modernity represents another major part of the European civilisational constellation. One of the most important aspects of the emergence of modernity in Russia was its peculiar mixture of European and Asian perspectives. In Russia modernity unfolded through an active and close engagement with the West and earlier with the Byzantine tradition. As a Eurasian civilisation deeply rooted in the Orthodox tradition, Russia warrants being called a civilisation distinct from Western civilisation.[40] The creative combination and translation of traditions – Western (the national state tradition), Eurasian (Slavic) and classical (Byzantine) – provided a framework for the emergence of modernity in Russia in the twentieth century. It may be asked whether this civilisation is re-emerging from the ruins of communism. In Russia today for example we can identify three collective actors: Western liberals; secular nationalists; and those fundamentalist nationalists who look to the Slavic tradition and orthodoxy are reconstructing Russian civilisational identity. The negotiation of these differences within Russia will be critical in the shaping of a European identity in the twenty-first century. Current indications – the apparent rise of the Eurasian idea – suggest that Russia is not seeking to assert its Europeanism.[41]

Since the fall of Constantinople in 1453 and the expansion westwards of the Ottoman empire, it is possible to venture the claim that a third major component of the European civilisational constellation is constituted by the Islamic Mediterranean, and principally represented by modern Turkey as the inheritor of the Ottoman legacy. The Ottoman Empire brought Islamic civilisation to Europe and while a later arrival it is an important – but an all too neglected – part of the European civilisational constellation. According to Jardine and Brotton, the Renaissance was formed out of encounters between the Orient and the Occident and in the fifteenth and sixteenth centuries East and West met on more equal terms than was later the case.[42] These authors have shown how some of the most potent symbols in European culture derived from the East and how the borders between East and West were more permeable than was later thought. The conventional approach is to see Russian civilisation as the inheritor of the Byzantine tradition in the aftermath of the fall of Constantinople, which ceases to be European, except in the narrow geographical sense. The civilisational approach adopted here on the contrary would suggest that the Ottoman tradition represents a third European civilisation and one based on Islam.[43] Today this is represented principally by Turkey, which is a reminder of a third route to modernity.[44]

The civilisational perspective in this analysis[45] suggests a transformation in the modernity of Europe. If the foundation of the EU reflected a particular and singular model of modernity – based on the nation-state, capitalism and democracy – the current situation challenges us to rethink modernity, since what is coming into focus is a constellation of multiple modernities. The civilisational context reveals something more far-reaching than different political traditions, such as different state traditions, and also extends beyond a focus on cultural differences, such as religion.[46] To reiterate a point made earlier, this is not a matter of a clash of civilisations, since the civilisations in question are interlinked and have been throughout history as a result of borrowings, translations, negotiations and migrations. Moreover, the movement towards modernity has given rise to tensions of different kinds and the conflicts produced by modernity cut across all civilisations. Europe is best viewed as a constellation of civilisations rather than just one.

A broader view of the present enlargement project suggests, then, that what we are currently witnessing is the coming into being of what might be cautiously called a post-Western Europe, that is, a Europe that is no longer based on a singular, Western modernity, but multiple modernities. In the broader perspective of history we can see a European civilisational constellation emerging and the confluence of different modernities, which will be critical in shaping the identity of Europe for some time. We are witnessing something more than simply institutional enlargement. Rather, what is significant about the current juncture is a redefinition of the very meaning of Europe. It is unlikely that the EU and its enlargement project will entirely dominate all the discourses that are currently emerging. The Europe of the EU will have to contend not with just different national and regional cultures, but also with diverse understandings of the European heritage. Those countries shaped by the Eastern and Mediterranean civilisation will have different historical memories and definitions of the European. Central to these will be different relations to Asia. As the EU extends more and more into Eurasia, the very terms of a European identity will have to be rethought. It is unlikely to be a 'Scandinavian' Europe, as Therborn argued a few years ago.[47]

Since 1989 with the collapse of the second project of modernity – communism – and as a result of wider processes of globalisation, modernity in Europe enters a new phase. In the former communist countries the consequences of an abortive second route to modernity remain.[48] One of the enduring alternative paths to modernity in Europe, the Turkish route, despite the advanced movement towards Westernisation in the twentieth century in that country, represents one of the most important challenges to the dominant Western model. In it at least three kinds of nationalism collide: republican, Kurdish and Islamist nationalism.[49] These represent different versions of the conflict of modernity in Turkey, ranging from Western to anti-Western and Asian values. Straddled across Europe and Asia, Turkey – which cannot be viewed as a periphery – challenges the dominance of the Western-centric view of Europe. The assimilation of Turkey into the EU will require a rethinking of a European identity based on a common European culture that is Christian. Turkey evolved a modernity based on being part of the West, but not self-consciously of Europe, but that is now changing. Turkish modernity is reflected in the paradox of political modernity developing alongside a bifurcated cultural modernity in which Islam is playing a growing role in politics and in business. Recent work on Turkey suggests that in addition to political Islam, there is an emerging and important model of economic Islam which is putting its stamp on a new Turkish modernity.[50]

In this respect a new European dilemma is emerging: Europe is increasingly occupying a middle ground between the American-led West and the East. Perhaps in this ground, a new European identity will emerge. It is no longer a question of overcoming internal borders but rather one of renegotiating external frontiers. The outside is becoming less easy to separate from the inside. Within the EU and its member states, there is a growing presence of the non-European, a presence that creates a new reality, namely a postnational Europe. As the community of reference is widened, it is also diluted, as witnessed by the decision not to include a reference to Christianity in the Preamble to the European constitution. This inevitably creates crises of identity and belonging but it also suggests more cosmopolitan societies can be created. Europe is becoming polycentric with multiple historical origins. Europeanisation is multidirectional, takes place at different speeds and is highly indeterminate.

To use a term borrowed from Luhmann, we can speak of this process as one of self-creation. Europeanisation defines and redefines itself in a constant process of construction in which different models of interpretation emerge defining and being defined by the process of construction itself. But we can go beyond Luhmann's radical constructivist approach in one respect. While it is true that the construction of Europe as a self-creative process cannot be seen as the narrative of a subject or the expression of a historical logic, it can be interpreted in Habermasian terms as opening up postnational possibilities in which communicative forms of social integration may be possible. In a large and multifaceted entity such as the EU, or indeed any modern polity, social integration cannot rest on tightly defined cultural values. More important are communicative links between different parts of the polity, beginning with individual citizens. From the point of view of Habermas's social theory, this indicates the centrality of the public sphere as a means of social integration.

However, Castells's notion of a network society suggests that a European public sphere is more likely to resemble a mosaic of communicative links. Indeed what is emerging is a diffuse 'society' based on mobilities and discourses rather than a clearly defined territory. In Bourdieu's terms this also entails new fields of symbolic struggles as competing and emergent cultural models clash. The EU will not be able to reproduce the nation-state's ability to achieve closure and identity.

Globalisation, of which Europeanisation is an expression, is a quite different scenario from that of modernisation and nation-state formation. Where modernisation was spear-headed by the nation-state and reflected universalistic values and a linear conception of history, globalisation is expressed through an intensification of links in which local and global levels interact according to many different logics and velocities.

Conclusion

The argument of this chapter is that the contemporary project of Europeanisation must be situated in the broader perspective of modernity and the encounter of its different civilisations. The kinds of modernities to which these gave rise are coming closer together today. The enlargement of the EU is one very significant factor in this, but the EU should not be taken to be the primary actor or force shaping the current situation.[51] Viewed in the longer perspective of history we get a more differentiated picture of civilisational transformation in modernity. Central Europe, for instance, while constituting a separate historical region of Europe to the Western one, from a civilisational perspective is closer to the Western tradition and part of this Occidental civilisation. In civilisational terms, Europe extends well into Eurasia and the wider Mediterranean cannot be excluded from it. The interaction with Russia and Turkey and those countries shaped by them is critical in this respect.

A conclusion might be the following: 'Europe' is becoming a free-floating signifier. It no longer reflects a stable body of ideas, institutions or territory. It is being redefined in the actual process of Europeanisation. In this it is possible to see a certain de-Westernisation of Europe. The future may see Europe becoming more 'European' and less American. As the logic of Europeanisation extends eastwards and southwards, driven by the enlargement process and by various partnerships, Europe will become more and more post-Western.

Notes

1 Cederman 2001.
2 Habermas 1998, 2001.
3 Derrida 1992.
4 Gadamer 1992.
5 Touraine 2000.
6 Delanty 2000.

7 See Habermas 1987 and 1996. This is a distinction several theorists have made, see Lockwood (1964).
8 Luhmann 1998; Rasch 2000.
9 Luhmann 1990.
10 Rumford 2002.
11 Castells 1996.
12 Bauman 2001.
13 Holmes 2000; Shore 2000.
14 Delanty 1995; Malmborg and Stråth 2002.
15 Roche 2001; Rumford 2002.
16 Urry 2000.
17 Luhmann 1990.
18 Chrysochoou 2001.
19 Majone 1996.
20 Eder and Giesen 2001; Soysal 1994.
21 Castells 1998.
22 Milward 1992.
23 Delanty and O'Mahony 2002.
24 Holmes 2000.
25 See for example Tierney 2001 and Smith 1995.
26 See, for example, Bourdieu 1991.
27 An example is the new symbolic construction of borders in Central and Eastern Europe. See Meinhof 2002.
28 Cited in the Regular Reports from the Commission on Progress towards Accession, 8 November 2000. Available at: http://www.europa.eu.int/enlargement/report_report_11_00/index.htm
29 This broad vision of Europe is also reflected in the quite separate intergovernmental organisation, the Council of Europe, which consists of forty-three member states, including Russia, which joined in 1996.
30 See Scűzs 1988; Scűzs argued that Europe consists of three geopolitical units, which were formed out of a deeper East–West divide: a western Carolingian Europe, *Mitteleuropa* and Eastern Europe (including the western parts of Eurasia).
31 The Baltic countries do not fit into any clear category; while being closest to Central Europe, they are not generally regarded as part of Central Europe and yet cannot be easily defined as Eastern European in the sense in which this term is being used today.
32 This is not to suggest that the Mediterranean is a natural frontier. In the 1980s the Moroccan government raised the question of possible membership of the EU. It is interesting to observe that the existing EU already contains two enclaves in North Africa in the form of the Spanish territorial regions of Ceuta and Melilla. The original EEC contained Algeria, which prior to its independence was a region of the French republic. See Hansen 2002.
33 Keyman and Önis 2003.
34 Robbins 1996.
35 Dingsdale 2002.
36 Siedentop 2000.

142   *Gerard Delanty* / European History and European Culture

37 Zielonka 2002 and Laitin 2002.
38 The civilisational approach used here follows the suggestions of S. N. Eisenstadt (2003).
39 Braudel 1972–3.
40 Buss 2003.
41 Neumann 1996.
42 Jardine and Brotton 2000.
43 This is not to neglect the importance of the earlier history of Islam in Spain. However, whether this constitutes a separate civilisation is questionable, since after the defeat of the Moors there was little historical continuity.
44 Bozdogan and Kasaba 1997; Göle 1996; Kaya 2003. Furthermore, the Mediterranean geopolitical face of Europe is becoming more important. Malta is an example of this, albeit of a Christian country that has played a role in mediating the civilisations and cultures of the Mediterranean.
45 A definition of the term civilisation might be appropriate. Western Christendom, the Eastern Byzantine, Russia and the Ottoman Empire in their historical and in the contemporary forms exhibit the key features of civilisation in that they are characterised by distinctive geopolitical or spatial configurations, which are generally related to major empires, distinctive cultural models, which in turn are linked to a universalistic religion, and a dominant social imaginary, such as a historical narrative. The Russian and Ottoman Empires were major imperial powers in which distinctive civilisations emerged. Other important empires, such as the central European Habsburg Empire or earlier the Polish Lithuanian state, did not have the same civilisational significance and were mostly regional variants of one of the main civilisations.
46 Sčűzs's (1988) model is an important one, but is limited in that it failed to see a wider civilisational order in which *Mitteleuropa* can be viewed as part of the Western European civilisation and the Russian and Ottoman Islamic civilisations constituting other expressions of the European civilisational constellation. Moreover, Scüzs did not link these conceptions of Europe to modernity and to global processes. The civilisational approach, in contrast, stresses the wider civilisational context of the major regions of Europe and to relate these to different models of modernity.
47 Therborn 1997.
48 Arnason 1993.
49 Houston 1999.
50 Özbundun and Keyman 2002, p. 303.
51 To the extent to which the EU is important, more attention needs to be given to EU relations with North Africa and Asia. See Featherstone and Kazamias 2001; Hall and Danta 2000; Rumford 2002.

References

Arnason, J., 1993, *The Future that Failed. Origins and Destinies of the Soviet Model.* London: Routledge.
Bauman, Z., 2001, *Liquid Modernity.* Cambridge: Polity Press.

Bourdieu, P., 1991, *Language and Symbolic Power*. Cambridge: Polity.

Bozdogan S. and R. Kasaba (eds.), 1997, *Rethinking Modernity and National Identity in Turkey*. Seattle, WA: University of Washington Press.

Braudel, F., 1972−3, *The Mediterranean and the Mediterranean World in the Age of Philip II*, Vols. I (1972) and II (1973). London: Collins.

Buss, A. E., 2003, *The Russian Orthodox Tradition and Modernity*. Leiden: Brill.

Castells, M., 1996, *The Information Age. Vol. I: The Rise of the Network Society*. Oxford: Blackwell.

1998, 'The Unification of Europe', in *The Information Age. Vol. III: End of Millenium*. Oxford: Blackwell, pp. 310−34.

Cederman, L.-E. (ed.), 2001, *Constructing Europe's Identity. The External Dimension*. London: Lynne Rienner.

Chrysochoou, D., 2001, *Theorising European Integration*. London: SAGE.

Delanty, G., 1995, *Inventing Europe. Idea, Identity, Reality*. London: Macmillan.

2000, *Citizenship in a Global Age. Culture, Society and Politics*. Buckingham: Open University Press.

Delanty, G. and P. O'Mahony, 2002, *Nationalism and Social Theory*. London: SAGE.

Dingsdale, A., 2002, *Mapping Modernities. Geographies of Central and Eastern Europe, 1920−2000*. London: Routledge.

Derrida, J., 1992, *The Other Heading. Reflections of Today's Europe*. Bloomington, IN: Indiana University Press.

Eder, K. and B. Giesen (eds.), 2001, *European Citizenship. National Legacies and Transnational Projects*. Oxford: Oxford University Press.

Eisenstadt, S. N., 2003, *Comparative Civilisations and Multiple Modernities*. Vols. I and II. Leiden: Brill.

Featherstone, K. and G. Kazamias (eds.), 2001, *Europeanisation and the Southern Periphery*. London: Frank Cass.

Gadamer, H.-G., 1992, 'The Diversity of Europe. Inheritance and Future', in D. Misgeld and G. Nicholson (eds.), *Hans-Georg Gadamer on Education, Poetry, and History. Applied Hermeneutics*. Albany, NY: SUNY, pp. 221−36.

Göle, N., 1996, *The Forbidden Modern. Civilisation and Veiling*. Ann Arbor, MI: University of Michigan Press.

Habermas, J., 1987, *The Theory of Communicative Action*, Vol. II. Cambridge: Polity Press.

1996, *Between Facts and Norms. Contributions to a Discourse Theory of Law and Democracy*. Cambridge: Polity Press.

1998, *The Inclusion of the Other. Studies in Political Theory*. Cambridge, MA: MIT Press.

2001, *The Postnational Constellation*. Cambridge: Polity Press.

Hall, D. and D. Danta (eds.), 2000, *Europe Goes West. EU Enlargement, Diversity and Uncertainty*. London: The Stationery Office.

Hansen, P., 2002, 'European Integration, European Identity and the Colonial Connection', *European Journal of Social Theory*, Vol. 5(4), 483−98.

Holmes, D., 2000, *Integral Europe. Fast-Capitalism, Multiculturalism, Neofascism*. Princeton, NJ: Princeton University Press.

Houston, C., 1999, 'Civilising Islam, Islamist Civilising? Turkey's Islamist Movement and the Problem of Ethnic Difference', *Thesis Eleven*, Vol. **58**(1), 83–98.

Jardine, L. and J. Brotton (eds.), 2000, *Global Interests. Renaissance Art between East and West*. London: Reaktion Books.

Kaya, I., 2003, *Social Theory and Later Modernities. The Turkish Experience*. Liverpool: Liverpool University Press.

Laitin, D., 2002, 'Culture and National Identity: "The East" and European Integration', *West European Politics*, Vol. **25**(2), 55–80.

Lockwood, D., 1964, 'Social Integration and System Integration', in G.K. Zollschan and W. Hirsch (eds.), *Explorations in Social Change*. Boston, MA: Houghton Mifflin, pp. 244–57.

Luhmann, N., 1990, 'The World Society as a Social System', in *Essays in Self-Reference*. New York: Columbia University Press, pp. 175–90.

1996, *Observations on Modernity*. Stanford, CA: Stanford University Press.

Majone, G., 1996, *Regulating Europe*. London: Routledge.

Malmborg, M. and B. Stråth (eds.), 2002, *The Meaning of Europe*. Oxford: Berg.

Meinhof, U. H. (eds.), 2002, *Living (with) Borders. Identity Discourses on East–West Borders in Europe*. Aldershop: Ashgate.

Milward, A., 1992, *The European Rescue of the Nation-State*. London: Routledge.

Neumann, I., 1996, *Russia and the Idea of Europe*. London: Routledge.

Önis, Z. and F. Keyman, 2003, 'Turkey at the Polls: A New Path Emerges', *Journal of Democracy*, Vol. **14**(2), 95–107.

Özbundun, E. and F. Keyman, 2002, 'Cultural Globalisation in Turkey: Actors, Discourses, Strategies', in P. Berger and S. Huntington (eds.), *Many Globalisations*. Oxford: Oxford University Press, pp. 296–321.

Rasch, W., 2000, *Niklas Luhmann's Modernity. The Paradoxes of Differentiation*. Stanford, CA: Stanford University Press.

Robins, K., 1996, 'Interrupting Identities: Turkey/Europe', in S. Hall and P. du Gay (eds.), *Questions of Cultural Identity*. London: SAGE, pp. 61–86.

Roche, M., 2001, 'Citizenship, Popular Culture and Europe', in N. Stevenson (ed.), *Culture and Citizenship*. London: SAGE, pp. 74–98.

Rumford, C., 2002, *The European Union: A Political Sociology*. Cambridge: Polity Press.

Szücs, J., 1988, 'Three Historical Regions of Europe', in J. Keane (ed.), *Civil Society and the State. New European Perspectives*. London: Verso, pp. 291–332.

Shore, C., 2000, Building Europe. *The Cultural Politics of European Integration*. London: Routledge.

Siedentop, L., 2000, *Democracy in Europe*. London: Penguin.

Smith, A., 1995, *Nations and Nationalism in the Global Era*. Cambridge: Polity Press.

Soysal, Y., 1994, *The Limits of Citizenship*. Chicago, IL: Chicago University Press.

Therborn, G., 1997, 'Europe in the Twenty-first Century', in P. Gowan and P. Anderson (eds.), *The Question of Europe*. London: Verso, pp. 357–84.

Tierney, R. (ed.), 2001, *Euro-Skepticism*. New York: Rowan and Littlefield.

Touraine, A., 2000, *Can We Live Together? Equal and Different*. Cambridge: Polity Press.

Urry, J., 2000, *Sociology Beyond Societies. Mobilities for the Twenty-First Century*. London: Routledge.

Zielonka, J. (ed.), 2002, *Europe Unbound. Enlarging and Reshaping the Boundaries of the EU*. London: Routledge.

8   Gaia and Europa: Religion and Legitimation Crisis in the 'New Europe'

Richard H. Roberts

> Convinced that, while remaining proud of their own national identities and history, the peoples of Europe are determined to transcend their former divisions and, united ever more closely, to forge a common destiny.... Convinced that, thus 'United in its diversity', Europe offers them the best chance of pursuing, with due regard for the rights of each individual and in awareness of their responsibilities towards future generations and the Earth, the great venture which makes of it a special area of human hope....[1]

The Preamble to the Treaty Establishing a Constitution for Europe contains the expressions 'transcend', 'common destiny', 'rights of each individual' and 'responsibilities towards future generations and the Earth', and these words are framed by a conception of Europe as a 'great venture which makes of it a special area of human hope'. While this does not quite attain the exalted level of an American belief in a 'manifest destiny', the intentions of the *Président de la Convention*, Valéry Giscard d'Estaing and his colleagues are nonetheless apparent. The 'new Europe' is not to be understood merely as bureaucracy or as an expanded market, but as a vital entity, the bearer of intellectual, cultural and spiritual continuities. In this chapter, I explore some of the dimensions that such aspirations touch upon, once they are emancipated from high-flown intention and anchored in the matrix of tensions and contradictions that afflict all efforts to define and defend identity in an era of globalisation and religiously inspired terror. In broad terms this representation of the 'venture' of Europe confronts the reader with the question of legitimation. Here I outline a strategy of response inspired by anthropological insights that seeks to supplement and in certain respects outflank the efforts of sociology, both in terms of grand theory and as applied to the study of religion as such.

Jürgen Habermas has dedicated a lifetime to the general legitimation crisis (or crises) of Western modernity, the resolution of which has taken on a specific form as regards the 'future of Europe' as this is currently represented in debates pertaining to the adoption of a Constitution for Europe.[2] Indeed, the wider legitimation crisis is subject to differentiation within the European Union (EU) between an 'old' and a 'new Europe', and this split has hardened into clearer contours as a result of the Second Iraq War. From the specific standpoint of the UK the fraught history of the British relationship with the EU has also been characterised by contrasting images of 'Europe'. On the one hand, there has been a broad and growing 'Europe' of multilingual consensus comprising most nations other than the UK that has recognised to a greater or lesser degree the need, albeit problematic, for a cultural and symbolic, non-material dimension in the European Constitution. On the other, there is the essentially monolingual British (i.e. Westminster Conservative and Anglo-Scottish New Labour) 'Europe' that has, historically speaking, resisted the cultural and political integration of Europe. This British mono-lingual strategy is dedicated to the extension of the European open market and opposes any notion of federalism. This is a tendency reinforced by government policies that have embedded Britain as subaltern in an Anglo-American axis committed to a global war against terrorism.[3]

However, the Madrid and London bombings of March 2004 and July 2005 and the popular responses to them seemingly provided an opportunity for the symbolic integration of European solidarity and the Anglo-American war against terrorism. Both Europe and Anglo-America are thus now seen and felt to be confronting a common 'other'. The 'old European' concerns with cultural consensus in the face of historic enmities (above all that between France and Germany) as opposed to British pragmatism, has now, perhaps, found an enemy capable of uniting these divergent tendencies. An uncritical integration of purpose in the face of terror would have implications for the possibility of a common legitimating identity, but the tacit and uncri-tical assumption of a generic 'new European' self-image could amount to the re-assimilation of what Al-Qaeda sources refer to as a Christian 'Crusader' *mentalité*. Such a response based upon polarisation provoked by terror would not, in reality, do more than satisfy North American Neo-Conservative and European political ideologues, and those Abrahamic religionists on all sides with strong confrontational agendas who seek to co-opt elements drawn from tradition in the service of threatened male power.[4]

The consolidation of identity through reification of the other implies a dangerous repetition of past patterns. Yet as the distinguished German jurist Kurt Biedenkopf has argued, if the new European Constitution is to 'guide Europeans through periods of change and yet unknown threats, its roots must reach the foundations of European history and identity as they are embodied in the shared culture that Europe's citizens freely acknowledge as their own'.[5] As I shall argue, the 'foundations' are to be found in the zone beyond traditions, in the consciousness-, identity- and norm-forming processes that attend the 'making of humanity'.

Habermas on Europe and religion

One of the most distinguished social and political philosophers of post-Second World War Europe, the German thinker Jürgen Habermas has recently pushed questions as to the cultural dimension of the European project a stage further, arguing that if the further political integration of Europe is to succeed then it would require legitimation. The necessary 'symbolic crystallisation' could, he maintains, be brought about through the promulgation and collective acceptance of a European constitution.[6] Habermas has made this proposal on the assumption that the religious inheritance of the West to which the original founders of the EU held an allegiance is, for the most part, no longer plausible. But present circumstances would surely indicate that the question of the religious inheritance of the West is now, however, no longer merely to be regarded as a premodern embarrassment to sociologists, but as a pressing issue. In effect, both global and locally manifest militant Islam is requiring Europe to own, decline, or modify its received identities. This process of reappraisal has, I believe, to be both fundamental and total.[7]

The crisis of legitimation is not, however, a straightforward matter of the juxtaposition of premodern modes of identity with a rational, benign modernity, because modernity has in certain crucially important ways failed. For example, in *Modernity and the Holocaust*, Zygmunt Bauman attributed the extermination of the Jewish population of Europe to the moral vacuity that surrounds the unrestrained power of *Technik*, and in the *Dialectic of Enlightenment*, Adorno and Horkheimer traced the catastrophic history of Enlightenment in its instrumentalist version. The Second Iraq War has compounded this sense of moral bankruptcy in an exceptionally public way through (for example) the global circulation of images of the sexual humiliation of Iraqi prisoners. In contrasting and positive terms, Habermas has dedicated himself to the propagation and elaboration of modes of communicative action designed to counter the totalitarian outcomes of 'enlightened' modernity as first exemplified in the mutual threats of National Socialism and Marxist Communism. The extension of the principle of meeting the crisis of legitimation through effective democratic communication from postwar Germany to the EU is a consistent step. The EU possesses one of the most complex bureaucracies in human history. To a sociological thinker of the stature of Jürgen Habermas, educated in the interpretative traditions of Max Weber and Emile Durkheim, the discernment and countering of the ineluctable tendency of bureaucracy to stifle human spontaneity through routinisation represents a unique challenge.

As Eduardo Mendieta has convincingly demonstrated, Habermas's attitudes to religion are complex.[8] While it is important to recognise this complexity, in the following argument we are concerned to discover and outline the existence of a mechanism of repression and thus to subvert the superficiality of the representation of the contemporary religio-spiritual field as it pertains to the legitimation of 'Europe'.

Running through late twentieth-century sociological thought there are two conflicting societal tendencies. On the one hand, there is the pervasive routinisation associated with bureaucratic rule, and, above all, the diminution of humanity into the banal vacuity of the inhabitant of the iron cage. On the other hand, within the overall framework of globalisation, conflictual identity politics on (for example) the levels of ethnicity, nation, race, gender, sexual orientation and place threaten to fragment any meaningful social solidarity. When what Theodor Hanf has called the 'sacred marker' is superadded as an intensification of either alternative, that is either to bureaucracy (or, as I would prefer to characterise it, 'managerial modernity')[9] or to identity politics in the context of societal change, then a radicalisation may take place which rightly alarms the informed observer.[10] Yet, without a measure of 'hot' legitimation capable of articulating what the architects of the Constitutional Treaty for Europe regard as a 'special area of human hope', how will it be possible to achieve the required 'crystallisation'?[11] Indeed, deep socialisation is likely to fail if societal stresses exceed the capacity of 'cold' legitimation – the common bonds of legality, welfare and personal security – to sustain solidarity. In a scenario of stress, in this instance the expansion of the EU eastwards (to which has now to be added an awareness of the possible consequences of the so-called 'war on terror'), will the summation of 'cold' legitimation in the form of a European Constitution meet present and likely future needs? In reality, this is not merely a passing crisis of legitimation as a consequence of expansion; it is a matter of the re-definition of the 'soul of Europe' itself.

More directly, will the dissemination of communicative reason in a supranational form as theorised and advocated by Jürgen Habermas be an adequate and feasible means of achieving legitimation in the context of an agreement between nations theoretically on a convergent path towards an ever greater union? Now these questions give rise to many others, but in the interests of manageability I confine myself to a critical consideration of the religious dimensions of legitimation. This I undertake on the assumption that Habermas and others now have to take this factor into consideration in terms which modify the commonly held sociological view that 'tradition' is an inherently unreflexive residuum possessing no utility in advanced modernity. Similarly, the reduction of the field of contemporary spiritualities to 'new spiritual outlets' in a marketplace fails to take account of the importance of developing a full cultural explanation. Clifford Geertz's much discussed definition still has relevance to this argument, albeit as a starting point:

A *religion* is: (1) a system of symbols which acts to establish (2) powerful, pervasive, and long-lasting moods and motivations in men by (3) formulating conceptions of a general order of existence and (4) clothing these conceptions with such an aura of factuality that (5) the moods and motivations seem uniquely realistic.[12]

Europe and the dialectic of aggrandisement

As I have argued elsewhere,[13] religiously or anti-religiously grounded 'ideas of Europe' are longstanding, contradictory and much contested. These 'ideas' include, for example, the modernising accommodatory Europe of Ernst Troeltsch's *Protestantism and Progress*,[14] the nihilistic 'morphology' of national quasi-Darwinian struggle propounded by Oswald Spengler, the traditional Catholic apologetic for a greater Christian Europe controversially revivified by Pope Jean Paul II, and the essentially secular, Enlightenment Europe extending from the Atlantic to the Urals advocated by Mikhail Gorbachev.[15] My earlier work, based upon history, sociology and theology, led to negative conclusions as regards the possibility of a workable *episteme* for theology which could be understood in parallel with the multiple and no less problematic 'souls of Europe'.

The standard modern (i.e. from around 1780 onwards) religious and philosophical renditions of the 'idea of Europe' and the cultural identities of 'Europe', associated with, for example, Goethe, Hegel, Nietzsche, Christopher Dawson, Karl Löwith, Max Horkheimer and Theodor Adorno, Pope John Paul II, and so on, expose what George Steiner some thirty years ago depicted as the evolution of a 'dialectic of aggrandisement' underlying both the internal operations and the external relations of a primarily Christian and post-Christian 'Europe'.[16] Centralised and hierarchical epistemic power is set over against the 'others' of the once peripheral Muslim and internally subordinate Jew. The consuming power of the Lord (*Herr*) is set over against the weakness of the slave (*Knecht*) as represented in social and mythic terms in the existence *an sich* of the proletariat in the *Communist Manifesto*, as confrontation between Prometheus and Christ by Karl Löwith in *Meaning in History*,[17] and in the parallel between the *Phänomenologie des Geistes* and *Faust I* developed by Ernst Bloch.[18]

In the final, mythopoetic analysis, this is a tension between the Promethean *huplo logo tous pantas exthairo theous* (Aeschylus as cited by Marx in his doctoral dissertation), that is to say a principled hatred of all those gods who might demean the expression of the will-to-power that informs the self-identity of man, and *agape*, the self-giving love (contrasted in turn with *eros* by the Swedish theologian Anders Nygren)[19] that Nietzsche identifies with slave-morality. The uneasy dialectic of mutual negation, the construction and probing of identity created through the encounter of self and negated 'otherness' poses many challenges to a perpetually creative, yet perpetually, even pathologically unstable condition of culture. This oppositional dialectic has been received in various ways through figures as diverse as Ernst Jünger (*Der Arbeiter*), Sartre (*Being and Nothingness*), and from the latter through Simone de Beauvoir (*The Second Sex*) to second- and then third-wave feminism (Judith Butler), in psychoanalysis (Jacques Lacan), and not least to the late Edward Said (*Orientalism*) and Francis Fukayama (in *The End of History*).[20]

With the dissolution of much mainline institutional religion in Western Europe, both Protestant and now Catholic (as evident in the extraordinarily rapid evolution of 'post-Christian Ireland'), the fragmentation of value-systems, and the relentless driving force of commodification, consumerism and managerialism, religious minorities, both old and new, form redoubts, however societally problematic, of internalised psychic order and identity sustenance (as seen notably in some Muslim and other ethnic communities). These stand out in stark contrast as inner-directed communities that contrast with the *anomie* of post-Christian cultures. These latter increasingly rely, above all in Anglo-America, upon the external imposition of order through the psycho-social oversight of the 'modernised' managerial order and the technological Panopticon of 'surveillance society'[21] and the 'Homeland security' state.[22]

In the Christian East, Orthodoxy maintains a non-reflexive patriarchal premodernity and rejoices in its apparent freedom from the Western corruptions of Renaissance, Reformation and Enlightenment. Orthodoxy is often enough prepared to endorse the recovery of regressive nationalistic ethnicities and a Pan-Slavism that might restore its pre-communist monopolistic spiritual hegemony in the face of the marketisation of the religio-spiritual field. Yet both Latin West and Orthodox (especially the Russian) East are seemingly disengaged from some of the fundamental issues that cut right across an expanded Europe, at the core of which is the question, highlighted in a life's work by Jürgen Habermas, of adequate, apposite legitimation. The latter is not merely the formal legitimation that consolidates the acceptance of a common ideological basis of consent, but also implies a deeper socialisation.

'Cold' and 'Hot' Legitimation

We may concede with Jürgen Habermas that religiously configured ideological legitimations grounded in 'ideas of Europe' are deeply conflictual,[23] and that, given the secularisation of mainline religion they also lack wide plausibility.[24] Conversely, there are grounds for doubting whether the constitutional legitimation he envisages, even that leading, perhaps, to a European surrogate for 'civil religion' enacted in the conviviality of European summit meetings,[25] would either have the required societal efficacy or be capable of avoiding the difficulties of discord and credibility analogous to those of the traditional Abrahamic faiths.

In addition to the resurgence of regional identities on the part of minority 'nations' within larger unitary national entities that characterised the last decade of the twentieth century, there is now growing public and political hostility towards the encroachment upon the national specificities of European host populations when they are confronted with the full implications of multiculturalism. Now 'indigenous' peoples can no longer simply be represented as small minorities within host populations (for example the Basques, Bretons or Scots in their respective contexts), but as local majorities with low birth-rates who perceive themselves as being 'swamped' by asylum-seekers and economic migrants, above all those of Muslim origin (as controversially in France, the Netherlands and northern English towns).[26] The present political enthusiasm for mass migration of skilled but low-wage workers across Europe and from further afield to serve the needs of ageing populations may well exacerbate these tensions.[27]

This new indigenous resistance has found a measure of political expression through the progress across Europe of the extreme right. The general political situation is now increasingly unstable as Third Way politics has relied upon the communication and marketing of policies based upon responses to interest group pressure driven by party-political funding requirements and (notably in the UK) by the extensive use of focus groups as means of ascertaining likely grassroots responses. This further problematises legitimation in the 'hot', socialisation sense in which the term is used in this chapter. In response to Habermas, we shall suggest possibilities for the renewal of a symbolic legitimation, which might well be *a priori* inadmissible from the standpoint of a German thinker all too aware of the mythopoeic aberrations of National Socialism.

In his advocacy of a constitution for Europe, Habermas has maintained that the contemporary socio-political and cultural challenge is not to '*invent* anything but to *conserve* the great democratic achievements of the European nation-state, beyond its own limits'.[28] The conservation and enhancement of civic rights, besides levels of social welfare, education and leisure is the preserve of the relevant specialists and the correlative expert systems. Even the inclusion of lawyers and political scientists in an ongoing and important constitutional debate does not, in my view, really address what Habermas calls the 'power of symbolic crystallisation' which 'only a political act of foundation can give'.[29] Yet we need to ask if a 'political act of foundation' is really adequate to the likely task, not least given the increased salience and now the critical importance of religion. Furthermore, could European legitimation take place successfully at a supranational level without a symbolic crystallisation which goes beyond that of a rational-ethical Constitutional Treaty?

The Ritual Function and Socialisation

In his advocacy of legitimation, Habermas appears to relaunch an aspect of the classical sociological task in rational modernity, namely the quest for legitimation as the adjunct of social science. This complements the scientific task of providing government and the public with informed social knowledge. However, in suggesting the means of gaining legitimation Habermas is touching upon the 'priestly' role of the sociologist in a way which invites responses from those traditionally charged with this task of mediation. The reaction of former Cardinal Joseph Ratzinger is instructive: 'religion needs new translators'.[30] Habermas concedes that while the 'Judeo-Christian understanding of history in terms of salvation' is fundamental to the European 'concepts of morality and ethical life, persons and individuality, or freedom and emancipation', without 'transmission through socialisation and the transformation through philosophy' this 'semantic potential could one day become inaccessible'.[31] In my judgement this anomic state of affairs has already come about in areas of Europe where, as a result of rapid and unmediated post-Communist marketisation or as a matter of deliberate social policy as in Britain, the cultural base has been fundamentally eroded. In the light of this might Habermas be tempted to reconsider the creative implications of his own depiction of the ritual act? In *The Theory of Communicative Action* he argued that:

> [T]he core of collective consciousness is a normative consensus established and regenerated in the ritual practices of a community of believers. Members thereby orient themselves to religious symbols; the intersubjective unity of the collective presents itself to them in concepts of the holy. This collective identity defines the circle of those who understand themselves as members of the same social group and can speak of themselves in the first person plural. The symbolic actions of the rites can be comprehended as residues of a stage of communication that has already been gone beyond in domains of profane social cooperation.[32]

It is just such a teasing possibility that informs this chapter, given that there are now areas of Europe in which the 'semantic potential' is either dangerously vibrant or in reality exhausted. Most critical, however, is the contemporary failure of the benign elective affinities that need to exist between extant forms of tradition and the wider socio-cultural *Sitz-im-Leben*. It is these affinities and their discovery that permit religious or spiritual intensification to energise deep socialisation and the achievement of both individual and collective human maturity. Their absence informs the sense of deeper crisis that pervades my observations here.

The original main aims of European integration, deliverance from internecine warfare, the containment of a potentially dangerous Germany and economic growth cannot drive further forward the European project; nor, indeed, can any explicitly ideological integration rely upon a shared past. In this regard, Habermas dismisses the religious dimension of this inheritance: 'The "Carolingian" background of the founding fathers — Schuman, De Gasperi, Adenauer — with its explicit appeal to the Christian West, has vanished'.[33] The crowning achievement on the level of economic integration, the introduction and acceptance of the euro (a process from which the UK has pointedly excluded itself), has become a unifying symbol in everyday life and may contribute to stability, but 'economic expectations alone can hardly mobilise political support for the much riskier and more far-reaching project of a political union – one that deserved the name. The Europe of the "mere market" cannot sustain the goal of ultimate political union: this will require the legitimation of shared values'.[34]

A complex dilemma arises here. The desired political goal of further integration requires an intensity of symbolic legitimation that economic and social welfare (however desirable) and the 'national diversity of a multi-secular culture' based upon a 'glistening material infrastructure' cannot provide.[35] Such legitimation normally emerged in national settings from historic religious, quasi-religious or mythopoetic factors; yet, these latter means are no longer plausible, or indeed desirable given their negative and conflictual elective affinities. In the words of the former French Prime Minister Lionel Jospin, the defence of the 'European way of life' against the threats of globalisation (and, we might add, since the events of the 11 September 2001 in New York, Madrid in 2004 and London in 2005) and global terrorism ideologically inspired by fundamentalist Islam requires a dimension beyond that of the 'mere market'.[36] What can, indeed what should, this dimension be?

We have already noted Habermas's recognition of the significance of the ritual function, but the anthropologist Roy Rappaport goes further and construes ritual in terms that have even more direct implications for the legitimatory deficit that we are seeking to address. In his posthumously published book, *Ritual and Religion in the Making of Humanity*, Rappaport argued that:

in attending to ritual's form we must not lose sight of the fundamental nature of what it is that ritual does as a logically necessary outcome of its form. In enunciating, accepting and making conventions moral, ritual contains within itself not simply a symbolic representation of social contract, but the tacit social contract itself. As such, ritual, which also establishes, guards, and bridges boundaries between public systems and private processes, is *the* basic social act.[37]

The stakes could scarcely be higher. Having largely lost touch with traditions which, even where they survive, possess resonances and capacities that are all too close to the dynamics of the patriarchal fundamentalism that now underlies much religious terrorism, the inherent nihilism of Euro-American modernity is intoxicating itself with absolute military power. Moreover, 'post-emotional society' proffers the narcotics of ever-expanding virtuality, all-embracing consumerism and the compulsory commodification of the production of identity.[38] As regards the necessary societal space, time and competence, what opportunity now remains for what Rappaport described as *'the* basic social act'?[39]

Legitimation and the Recomposition of the Religio-spiritual Field: Regression and Bricolage

In relation to this crisis of religious legitimation the contemporary recomposition of the religious field exhibits a range of phenomena and attendant styles of reflexivity. Once the interpretation of this field as a whole is prised out of the grasp of the sub-discipline of the sociology of religion and brought into closer contact with mainline social and cultural theory, it becomes more salient than it might first appear. For example, at one extreme, within elite Christian theology in the Latin West a highly marketable, regressive Christian theology self-identified as 'radical orthodoxy' has emerged, associated with such names as the French Roman Catholic theologian Jean-Luc Marion and the English Anglican John Milbank. 'Radical orthodoxy' tends to reiterate and reinforce psycho-spiritual patriarchy, and asserts a postmodern 'order' grounded proleptically in the eschatological overcoming of the so-called 'violence of difference'. This strategy lays emphasis upon the rhetorical plausibility of forms of non-negotiable 'cultural-linguistic practice', that is, a zone pointedly divorced from any human 'utility' or truth-in-use that might be represented through the 'heretical' discourses of 'social theory' and their adjuncts.[40] By contrast with this theological intransigence the field of alternative spiritualities has grown and differentiated in a remarkable way. The ever-extending market place of alternative spiritual practices, has now, somewhat paradoxically, become increasingly mainstream. If we assume that these developments can no longer be adequately understood within the 'orthodox' theory of secularisation,[41] then neither can they be fully assumed into the market model.

Recognised authorities on so-called 'New Age', such as the anthropologist Paul Heelas, represent contemporary religiosity as mediated through market-differentiated 'new spiritual outlets' in a generational development (and thus the eventual demographic disappearance) of the alternative, neo-Romantic 'New Age Movement'.[42] A corollary of this approach is to regard this subjective religiosity grounded in the 'sacralisation of the self' as spiritual bricolage, an essentially trivial phenomenon throughout its cycle of emergence, development and decay. Within the ambit of the sociological study of contemporary religion and religiosities, experts more sympathetic to the religious factor such as Grace Davie and Danièle Hervieu-Léger defend a *réligion de l'émotion* and the indispensable, yet critically threatened transmission of societal *memoire*.[43] Neither the more dispassionate observers of religiosities such as Heelas,[44] nor the sociological defenders of the persistence of religion as source of solidarity,[45] nor again the erstwhile proponents of the secularisation paradigm[46] are prepared to place the religious factor in the wider context represented in this chapter. I suggest that the societal 'effervescence' required to remedy the contemporary deficit in legitimation and socialisation goes far beyond what sociologists of religion are prepared to conceive of – or to concede.

The standard sociological approach to contemporary religiosity assumes the centrality of detraditionalised modernity, the correlative decay of mainline religious organisations and the growth of 'alternative' forms as an adjunct to the activity of an exceptional, now ageing generational cohort. One new line of interpretation, offered by Roland Robertson and Peter Beyer, takes globalisation, rather than secularisation, as the basis of a new comprehensive paradigm.[47] Both perspectives assume a causal, rather than a mutual or reciprocal set of connections between dominant societal factors and changing patterns of religiosity. Whilst the globalisation perspective is indispensable,[48] Beyer's causal schematisation of the relationship between globalisation and reactive religious change is weakened by his appeal to the intrinsic character of the religious function as communicative practice.[49]

If we were to look at an entire historical episode in terms of the theory of ritual, then the defeat of Germany in 1945, the extinction of National Socialism and the subsequent self-awareness on the part of an entire nation that it was passing through 'Year Zero' may, I suggest, be regarded as the analogue of a national, albeit catastrophic rite of passage. The imposition by the Allies of the Federal German Constitution can then be understood as the provision by (as it were) *deus ex machina* means of the context for reaggregation after liminal extinction. In this setting of relative consensus, legitimation through communicative practice was both plausible and successful when it took place within well-defined boundaries. Do, however, those conditions pertain that might support a similar process across an expanded Europe as Habermas is proposing? My suggestion would be that they do not, and that the contrasting modernities experienced across an enlarged EU prevent this on the level of informed discourse endorsed by Habermas. Far more probable is a banalisation of difference through the emergence of a 'Euroglot' trans-European *lingua franca* that corrodes cultural distinctiveness through a commodified popular culture. This is homogenisation, not legitimation. While such debasement and cultural de-differentiation may well be inevitable as driven forward by the monolingualism of Anglo-America, expressed through the global media, we may also find the possibility of a more authentic legitimation than the mere routinisation of banality, or regression into conflictual religious identities. It is to this possibility of a different form of 'hot' legitimation to which we now turn.

Post-patriarchal Religious Legitimation and the 'New Europe'

Recent research exposes further differentiations within the recomposing religious field that are not readily made congruent with either the secularisation or market models that dominate sociological explanation. I have characterised one strand within this matrix as the 'chthonic imperative' within a re-emergent 'nature religion' that is simultaneously and ambiguously both archaic and new.[50] It is this resurgent shamanic or neo-shamanic consciousness that may be connected with other aspects of the cultural field, in specific terms with factors such as the renewal of ritual, the 'feminisation' of social theory as a response to 'post-emotional society', an eco-psychological shift from fragmenting *animus* to inclusive *anima*, the promotion of a 'global ethic', and a Gaianic spirituality of embodied *eros*. Taken together, these amount to intimations of a 'human ecological', ethical, somatic, even a potentially tantric 'new Europe', capable of the democratic legitimation sought by Habermas. They even suggest possibilities for the epistemic renewal of Christian theology as genuine embodiment. These are bold claims, the full exposition of which lie outside the remit of this chapter, but they suggest the possibility of a critique of patriarchal thought and practice, practice that comprises both the problematic rationalities of modernity and the negative aspects of warring Abrahamic theologies. The context of these assertions is well expressed by the German sociologist Klaus Eder, whose account of the age of postenvironmentalism reconnects our argument with Habermas's project and its limitations:

... the ideological systems and institutional solutions of the nineteenth century are still functioning, but the public discourses centred around these elements never solved the problem of identity construction. Liberalism and socialism failed in this task. Ecology as a political and social world-view could therefore become a way of carrying out this overdue modernisation of one of the most consequential aspects of social life. This also means that the age of environmentalism, the collective mobilisation for a cause is over. The age of post-environmentalism begins where ecology is established as the master frame thus laying the ground for a further development of the cognitive, moral and aesthetic rationality inherent in the culture of modernity.[51]

An expanded rationality might also comprise the rationality of ritual, charisma and the possibility of an embodied and en-natured sacred, and thus a richer mode of legitimation. This would imply processes of human maturation that challenge the banality of a managerial modernity.[52] Yet, and this is critically important, Eder has assimilated ecology into instrumental rationality as the new 'masterframe' and with this word he has reinscribed patriarchy. This appropriation inhibits the ritual function, the 'basic social act'.[53]

It is my contention that there is a significant convergence between a European anchoring of what the Swiss Roman Catholic theologian Hans Küng calls the 'global ethic',[54] the practical, symbolic and spiritual elective affinities of radical environmental concern in 'deep ecology', and the development of a corresponding feminist critique of the mainline Abrahamic traditions of Christianity, Judaism and Islam. With the growing environmental crisis and the development of the (not undisputed) Gaia hypothesis by the scientist James Lovelock,[55] the only religious option in the Western world which would appear unambiguously to endorse a positive attitude and practice towards Nature as bearer of an immanent sacred would appear to be (neo-) paganism. There is a strong elective affinity between environmental activism, deep ecology and paganism. In particular, a paganism of the shamanic type, serving local religious needs and centring on connections with the specific trees, hills, rivers and animals of any given place, through which life may be understood to flow, could provide a sense of the immanent sacred and inform and energise a critical, holistic human ecology.

The contemporary context of this convergence may be understood as the analogue of the religio-spiritual situation of the late Roman Empire. The equivalent of neo-Hellenistic cultural syncretism is the modern/postmodern matrix now held in the grasp of an imperial ambition that informs the major features of globalisation. This totality is perceived to be under challenge by the equivalent of the barbarian hordes both outside the gates and within. Moreover, what E.R. Dodds said of the ancient Graeco-Roman world is true of ours: this is an age of anxiety and internal emigration, and thus of retreat from political involvement.[56] Contemporary neo-Fordist managerial modernity requires the internalisation of identity-forming protocols and the sacrifice of the relatively autonomous intellect, and these measures of inward conformity go far to eliminate the residual possibility of inner emigration.[57]

Mainline Abrahamic religious traditions have, through their early persecution of nature religion, and then through the evolution of patriarchal theologies of textual and institutional mediation, repeatedly repressed and displaced human awareness and connection with nature and the body, and with the primal ritual function fundamental to the 'making of humanity' out of mere biological existence. Mircea Eliade's contentious, yet still valuable representation of shamanism reinforces our awareness of the closure, repression and dispersal that afflicts modernity:

> In accounting for the formation of the shamanic complex in Central and North Asia, we must keep in mind the two essential elements of the problem: on the one hand the ecstatic experience as such, as a primary phenomenon; on the other, the historico-religious milieu into which this ecstatic experience was destined to be incorporated and the ideology that, in the last analysis, was to validate it. We have termed the ecstatic experience a 'primary phenomenon' because we see no reason whatever for regarding it as the result of a particular historical moment, that is, as produced by a certain form of civilisation. Rather, we would consider it fundamental to the human condition, and hence to the whole of archaic humanity; what changed and was modified with the different forms of culture and religion was the interpretation and evaluation of the ecstatic experience.[58]

As I have argued, it is not only those who would seek the means of legitimation sufficient to consolidate a fragmenting European identity but also the theologians of the Abrahamic God who will have to come to terms with the contemporary analogates and displacements of the shamanic primality of which Mircea Eliade wrote. To fail to undertake this would amount to failure to invoke the 'power of symbolic crystallisation' in its fullest sense. As the anthropologist Charles Lindholm has argued in his notable (and very hostile) study of charismatic action, even the rationalistic Durkheim could believe that:

> . . . all human communities must retain the potential for charismatic experience, since without it they are mere aggregations of highly intelligent but rapacious beasts, plundering and destroying one another. Only the sharing of *communitas* in the ritual can give an inner sense of higher purpose, and this is necessary not only for the foundation of society but for individuals as well, who need a transcendent object to escape from despair and isolation.[59]

Lindholm rules out this possibility as too dangerous to risk enactment, and inevitably prone to evil. All we can do, he suggests, is resign ourselves to the failure of modernity to produce community, and all we can hope for is the solidarity of the romantic dyad. I have sought to challenge these despairing assumptions.

Conclusion: Towards Global and European Indigeneity

Jürgen Habermas has drawn attention to the 'troubled discourse among intellectuals' about the possibility of joining a Europe-wide political sphere with a political culture shared by all.[60] The main religion in Europe, Christianity, obeyed its missionary imperative and expanded all over the world, followed by modern science and technology, Roman law and the Napoleonic Code, human rights, democracy and the nation-state. Within the setting of the quest for further integration, the EU Charter of Fundamental Rights moves well beyond rights to market participation expressed through the free movement of persons, goods, services and capital. My contention is that such a consolidation and strengthening requires what Habermas has called 'symbolic crystallisation'. A fully owned legitimation of further European integration is indeed desirable, but this cannot be derived exclusively from a secularised economic, social, legal or cultural sphere, but from a dual re-engagement with the pre-traditional dimensions of Europe and its contemporary analogues. Moreover, mainline religious traditions will also have to re-engage with this residuum and the contemporary task of the 'making of humanity'.

There are those who, given the opportunity, would rework the process of European convergence in the cultural sphere. Now, however, is the time for a belated recognition and exploitation of the latter in order to reactivate a spiritual and symbolic substratum potentially capable of energising further political integration and legitimising a European constitution. This might also reconnect these traditions with the deep socialisation of societies now exhibiting increased evidence of anomie. Uncritical regression, be it theological in 'radical orthodoxy' or experiential in neo-paganism, would amount to little more than the politics of nostalgia. However, a conscious and deliberate re-engagement with the 'hot' legitimation and deep socialisation necessary for the transition from brute animality and anomie to community of life and benign purpose would, as outlined in this chapter, be something different. It could provide the 'symbolic crystallisation' for which Habermas has asked, and moreover, lead us further on the path towards re-finding the means through which to generate a global indigeneity. The hot legitimation of Europe could be an important 'making' that might do justice to the aspirations of the authors of the Preamble to the Treaty Establishing a Constitution for Europe.

Notes

1 Preamble to the Treaty Establishing a Constitution for Europe.
2 Roberts 2001, ch. 8. I first addressed the question of European religious identities in a paper published in Heelas (1998). This originated in an Inaugural Lecture as Professor of Divinity at the University of St Andrews, entitled 'The Souls of Europe', and was focused in the search for an *episteme* for Scottish 'Divinity' in the setting of the range of resolutions, both religious and consciously anti-religious, of the quest for a European identity.
3 And of course by such banal directives as the abolition of the compulsory teaching of modern languages in secondary schools in England and Wales after the age of fourteen, a measure against which the German ambassador protested in 2003.
4 The line of interpretation underlying these observations owes much to Martin Riesebrodt's (1993) brilliant analysis of fundamentalism as 'patriarchal protest movement'.
5 Biedenkopf 2003, p. 26.
6 Habermas, in this volume.
7 See Samuel 1990 and 1993; Roberts 2001. The standpoint of my research programme has a strong affinity with that of my collaborator, the anthropologist Geoffrey Samuel, who investigates the relationship between pre-traditional experience, traditions and post-traditional or detraditionalised societal conditions through a multi-disciplinary anthropology of mind–body in the context of the emergence and sustenance of community. Samuel has studied Tibetan Buddhism and extended his approach to Indic religions in his recent Wilde Lectures (2003) given at the University of Oxford. I am seeking to develop a parallel and contextually appropriate approach to Western modernities in the setting of the globalisation process.
8 I am much indebted to Eduardo Mendieta's (2002) fine introduction to Habermas.
9 For a recent account of the questionable consequences of 'managerial modernity' for British higher education see Roberts 2004.
10 See Hanf 1994.
11 See Roberts 1990 and also Mendieta 2002, pp. 6, 30 on Habermas. My views on the nature of 'hope' and our responsibility to 'matter' and 'the body' owe much to Ernst Bloch (1986).
12 Geertz 1966, p. 12, original emphasis.
13 Roberts 2001.
14 Troeltsch 1986.
15 Roberts 2001, ch. 8.
16 Steiner 1971; Roberts 2001.
17 Löwith 1949.
18 Roberts 1990.
19 Nygren 1953.
20 I deal with this inheritance in Roberts 2001, ch. 1.
21 Lyon 2001.

22 The fuller implications of this are now becoming apparent with (e.g.) the proposed prior databank 'mining' of personal information and tracking of all visitors to the USA.

23 Roberts 2001, ch. 8.

24 See Mendieta 2002, pp. 6–8, 16, 21.

25 Or for that matter in the celebratory rendition of Beethoven's setting of Schiller's *Ode to Joy* in the Ninth Symphony.

26 The British National Party is gaining ground in northern England precisely because it discerns and capitalises upon the well-grounded fears of local, postindustrial indigenous communities whose socio-economic and cultural plight plays no significant role in mainstream politics. The cultural apartheid between the residual postindustrial white ex-working-class and Muslim communities is virtually complete.

27 The Scottish First Minister's welcome to skilled migrants from mainland Europe to come to Scotland is an example. Whether migration will follow predicted paths and the desired ethnic composition and (e.g.) prevent to the mass inward movement of (say) what the 2001 British Census form used in Scotland refers to as 'other Whites' (i.e. the English) remains to be seen. For an indication of present Scottish attitudes, see McIntosh *et al.* (2004).

28 Habermas, in this volume, original emphasis.

29 Ibid.

30 Cardinal Ratzinger's article, 'Religion braucht neue Übersetzer', was a response to Habermas' assertion that 'Ihr Glauben ist intakt geblieben'. See *Rheinischer Merkur Online* 2003. Available at: http://www.merkur.de (Nr. 04.22.01.3004), accessed in March 2004.

31 Habermas 1992, p. 15.

32 Habermas 1987, p. 60.

33 Habermas, in this volume.

34 Ibid.

35 Ibid.

36 Jospin 2001.

37 Rappaport 1999, p. 138, original emphasis.

38 See Roberts 2001.

39 Again, this is the basis of my objection to the systematic routinisation of worship in mainline Establishment Christianity which holds sacred space in trust for the whole population. See Roberts 2001, ch. 5.

40 Milbank 1989.

41 Bruce 1992.

42 Heelas 1996.

43 Davie and Hervieu-Léger 1996; Davie 2000 and Hervieu-Léger 2000.

44 Heelas 1998.

45 Davie and Hervieu-Léger 1996.

46 Bruce 1992.

47 Robertson 1992; Beyer 1994.

48 Roberts 2001, ch. 9.

49 Taken in large part, as it happens, from Niklas Luhmann and Jürgen Habermas. See Beyer 1994.

50 Roberts 1998a.

51 Eder 1996, p. 191.
52 See Roberts (2001) for an initial account of 'managerial modernity' and its religio-spiritual consequences, and Roberts (2006) for a critical expansion.
53 Rappaport 1999.
54 Küng 1991.
55 Lovelock 1979.
56 Dodds 1965.
57 Vaclav Havel (1987) is one the few writers to have discerned the fuller implications of this process of internal colonisation under what he describes as 'post-totalitarian conditions'. Since 11 September 2001 Anglo-America seems to be entering a 'pre-totalitarian condition'.
58 Eliade 1964, p. 505.
59 Lindholm 1990, p. 33.
60 Habermas, in this volume.

References

Bauman, Zygmunt, 1989, *Modernity and the Holocaust*. Cambridge: Polity.
Beyer, Peter, 1994, *Religion and Globalisation*. London: SAGE.
Biedenkopf, Kurt, 2003, 'Making Culture Count', Commentary, Reflection Group 'The Spiritual and Cultural Dimension of Europe'. Vienna: Institut für die Wissenschaft vom Menschen. Available online at: http://www.iwm. at/index.php?option=com_content&task=view&id=90&Itemid=33
Bloch, Ernst, 1986, *The Principle of Hope*. Oxford: Blackwell.
Bruce, Steven, 1992, *Religion and Modernisation. Sociologists and Historians debate the Secularisation Thesis*. Oxford: Clarendon Press.
Davie, Grace, 2000, *Religion in Modern Europe. A Memory Mutates*. Oxford: Oxford University Press.
Davie, Grace and Danièle Hervieu-Léger (eds.), 1996, *Identités religieuses en Europe*. Paris: La Découverte.
Dodds, E. R., 1965, *Pagan and Christian in an Age of Anxiety*. Cambridge: Cambridge University Press.
Eder, Klaus, 1996, *The Social Construction of Nature*. London: SAGE.
Eliade, Mircea, 1964, *Shamanism: Archaic Techniques of Ecstasy*, Princeton, NJ: Princeton University Press.
Geertz, Clifford, 1966, 'Religion as a Cultural System', in Michael Banton, (ed.), *Anthropological Approaches to the Study of Religion*. London: Tavistock, pp. 1–46.
Habermas, Jürgen, [1973] 1976, *Legitimation Crisis*. London: Heinemann.
    [1982] 1987, *The Theory of Communicative Action*. Vol. II: *Lifeworld and System: a Critique of Functionalist Reason*. Cambridge: Polity.
    [1988] 1992, *Postmetaphysical Thinking: Philosophical Essays*. Cambridge: Polity.
    2001, 'Why Europe Needs a Constitution', *New Left Review*, Vol. **11**, 5–26.
    2002, *Religion and Rationality. Essays on Reason, God, and Modernity*. Cambridge: Polity.

Hanf, Theodor, 1994, 'The Sacred Marker. Religion, Communalism and Nationalism', *Social Compass*, Vol. **41**(1), 9–20.

Harvey, Graham, 1997, *Listening People, Speaking Earth: Contemporary Paganism*. London: Hurst and Company.

Havel, Vaclav, 1987, 'The Power of the Powerless', in Jan Vladislav (ed.), *Living in Truth*. London: Faber, pp. 36–122.

Heelas, Paul, 1996, *The New Age Movement. The Celebration of the Self and the Sacralisation of Modernity*. Oxford: Blackwell.

(ed.), 1998, *Religion, Modernity and Postmodernity*. Oxford: Blackwell.

Hervieu-Léger, Danièle, 2000, *Religion as a Chain of Memory*. Cambridge: Polity.

Horkheimer, Max and Theodor Adorno, 1972, 'The Concept of Enlightenment', in Max Horkheimer and Theodor Adorno (eds.), *Dialectic of Enlightenment*. London: Allen Lane, pp. 3–80.

Hutton, Ronald, 1998, 'The Discovery of the Modern Goddess', in Joanne Pearson, Richard H. Roberts and Geoffrey Samuel (eds.), *Nature Religion Today. Paganism in the Modern World*. Edinburgh: Edinburgh University Press, pp. 89–100.

Jospin, Lionel, 2001, 'On the Future of an Enlarged Europe'. Speech of the French Prime Minister to the Foreign Press Association, 28 May 2001, Paris. Available at: http://europa.eu.int/constitution/futurum/documents/speech/sp280501_en.htm

Küng, Hans, 1991, *Global Responsibility. In Search of a New World Ethic*. London: SCM.

Lewis, James R. (ed.), 1996, *Magical Religion and Modern Witchcraft*. New York: State University of New York Press.

Lindholm, Charles, 1990, *Charisma*. Oxford: Blackwell.

Lovelock, James, 1979, *Gaia. A New Look at Life on Earth*. Oxford: Oxford University Press.

Löwith, Karl, 1949, *Meaning in History. The Theological Implications of the Philosophy of History*. Chicago, IL: University of Chicago Press.

Lyon, David H. S., 2001, *Surveillance Society. Monitoring Everyday Life*. Milton Keynes: Open University Press.

Marion, Jean-Luc, 1991, *God Without Being. Hors-texte*. Chicago, IL: Chicago University Press.

McIntosh, Alastair, 2001, *Soil and Soul*. London: Aurum Press.

McIntosh, Ian, Duncan Sim and Douglas Robertson, 2004, ' "We Hate the English, Except for You, Cos You're Our Pal". Identification of the "English" in Scotland', *Sociology*, Vol. **38**(1), 43–59.

Mendieta, Eduardo (ed.), 2002, 'Introduction', in Jürgen Habermas, *Religion and Rationality. Essays on Reason, God, and Modernity*. Cambridge: Polity, pp. 1–36.

Mestrovic, Stjepan G., 1997a, 'The Disappearance of the Sacred', in Stjepan Mestrovic (ed.), *Postemotional Society*. London: SAGE, pp. 101–22.

1997b, *Durkheim and Postmodern Culture*. New York: Aldine de Gruyter.

Milbank, John, 1989, *Theology and Social Theory Beyond Secular Reason*. Oxford: Blackwell.

Nygren, Anders, 1953, *Agape and Eros*. London: S.P.C.K.

Pearson, Joanne, Richard H. Roberts and Geoffrey Samuel (eds.), 1998, *Nature Religion Today. Paganism in the Modern World*. Edinburgh: Edinburgh University Press.

Primavesi, Anne, 1991, *From Apocalypse to Genesis. Ecology, Feminism and Christianity*. London: Burns and Oates.

Rappaport, Roy, 1999, *Ritual and Religion in the Making of Humanity*. Cambridge: Cambridge University Press.

Riesebrodt, Martin, 1993, *Pious Passion. The Emergence of Modern Fundamentalism in the United States and Iran*. Berkeley, CA: University of California Press.

Roberts, Richard H., 1990, *Hope and Its Hieroglyph. A Critical Decipherment of Ernst Bloch's 'Principle of Hope'*. Atlanta, CA: Scholars Press.

——— 1992, *A Theology on Its Way. Essays on Karl Barth*. Edinburgh: T. T. Clark.

——— 1995, 'Globalized Religion? The Parliament of the World's Religions (Chicago 1993) in Theoretical Perspective', *Journal of Contemporary Religion*, Vol. **10**, 121–37.

——— 1998a, 'The Chthonic Imperative. Gender, Religion and the Battle for the Earth', in Joanne Pearson, Richard H. Roberts and Geoffrey Samuel (eds.), *Nature Religion Today. Paganism in the Modern World*. Edinburgh: Edinburgh University Press, pp. 57–73.

——— 1998b, 'The Construals of "Europe". Religion, Theology and the Problematics of Modernity', in Paul Heelas (ed.), *Religion, Modernity and Postmodernity*. Oxford: Blackwell, pp. 186–217.

——— 1998c, 'Time, Virtuality and the Goddess', *Cultural Values*, Vol. 2(2–3), 270–87.

——— 2001, *Religion, Theology and the Human Sciences*. Cambridge: Cambridge University Press.

——— 2004, 'The Quest for Appropriate Accountability. Stakeholders, Tradition and the Managerial Prerogative in Higher Education', *Studies in Christian Ethics*, Vol. 17(1), 1–21.

——— 2006, *Critique of the Social-Scientific Study of Religion*. Cambridge: Cambridge University Press.

Robertson, Roland, 1992, *Globalisation. Social Theory and Global Culture*. London: SAGE.

Samuel, Geoffrey, 1990, *Mind, Body and Culture. Anthropology and the Biological Interface*. Cambridge: Cambridge University Press.

——— 1993, *Civilized Shamans. Buddhism in Tibetan Societies*. Washington, DC: Smithsonian Institution Press.

Spiro, Melford E., 1966, 'Religion. Problems of Definition and Explanation', in Michael Banton (ed.), *Anthropological Approaches to the Study of Religion*. London: Tavistock, pp. 85–126.

Steiner, George, 1971, *In Bluebeard's Castle. Some Notes Towards a Re-Definition of Culture*. T. S. Eliot Memorial Lectures. London: Faber.

Troeltsch, Ernst [1906], 1986, *Protestantism and Progress. The Significance of Protestantism for the Rise of the Modern World*. Philadelphia, PA: Fortress Press.

9 A Postnational Council of Isles? The British–Irish Conflict Reconsidered

Richard Kearney

In the third millennium, postnationalism looks set to replace nationalism as the dominant political paradigm. The twentieth century witnessed the break-up of the great national empires – British, French, Austro-Hungarian, Ottoman, Russian – as well as a number of devastating world wars resulting from the internecine rivalries between nation-states. The terminal death-rattles of nationalist belligerence (on the European scene at any rate) sounded on the streets of Belfast where republicans and loyalists fought their last battles before finally reaching peace in 1998, and in the villages of Croatia, Bosnia and Kosovo where Balkan ethnicities clashed in genocidal hatred before an international accord was secured. Widening the focus, the events of 11 September 2001 made it dramatically clear that wars of the twenty-first century cannot be confined to specific nation-states, or national empires, but traverse boundaries and borders with disturbing ease. Al-Queda is as postnationalist as the American Way of Life it targets.

In several writings over the last two decades, the German philosopher, Jürgen Habermas, argues for what he calls a 'postnational constellation' as a response to the current political situation in Europe. Noting the erosion of the territorial sovereignty of nation-states, Habermas expresses the hope that this may open up a new space for: (1) cultural hybridisation; (2) transnational mobility and emigration; (3) cosmopolitan solidarity, predicated on a neo-republican balance between private and civic liberties opposed to the neo-liberal disregard for social justice; and (4) constitutional patriotism (on a federal European scale inspired by principles of coordinated redistribution and egalitarian universalism).[1] But Habermas is not naïve. He knows that such a postnational project faces many obstacles. One of the most challenging questions of these is, he notes, 'whether the European Union can even begin to compensate for the lost competences of the nation-state'.[2] And the related question of the European Union's (EU) ability to act effectively, motivating citizens towards social solidarity, will depend in turn, he argues, on 'whether political communities form a collective identity beyond national borders, and thus whether they can meet the legitimate conditions for a postnational democracy'.[3] If these questions cannot be answered in the affirmative then no meaningful 'Federal States of Europe' is possible. Or in Habermas's own words: 'If Europe is to be able to act on the basis of an integrated, multilevel policy, then European citizens, who are initially characterised as such only by their common passports, will have to learn to mutually recognise one another as members of a common political existence beyond national borders'.[4]

This calls for a radical rethinking of both (1) identity politics (the question of recognition and belonging) and (2) constitutional politics (the question of rights and justice). I fully agree with Habermas that the most promising context for such rethinking is that of a new postnational paradigm, though I would insist that in the European context, at least, the idea of a postnational constellation is still very much a task, not a *fait accompli*.

The Belfast Agreement and Subsidiarity

If most of our global conflicts and crises today are largely postnational in character so too, I submit, are the possible solutions. In pursuing my argument, I will concentrate most of my remarks on the historic British–Irish Agreement of 1998, suggesting that it may serve as a litmus test for a new politics of international peace.

What we are witnessing on the Irish-British archipelago today is little short of a revolution in our political understanding of the nation-state, marking the coming-of-age of two historically engaged peoples. With the ratification of the Good Friday Agreement in the spring of 1998, the sovereign governments of the UK and the Irish Republic signed away their exclusivist sovereignty claims over Northern Ireland. This signalled the end of the constitutional territorial battle over the province of Ulster – that contentious piece of land conjoining and separating the islands of Britain and Ireland for centuries. The Siamese twins could now begin to live in real peace, accepting that their adversarial offspring in Northern Ireland might at last be 'British or Irish or both'.[5]

Unitary sovereignty could never be enjoyed by two separate nation-states over the same province at the same time, especially if by sovereignty was meant 'absolutist' sovereignty, where this is understood to mean something like 'one and indivisible' (as defined by Hobbes, Bodin and Rousseau). The Agreement spelt the termination of the age-old conflict between a United Kingdom and a United Ireland, a conflict made inevitable by the fact that two into one won't go.

The British and Irish nation-states are now compelled to redefine themselves. The 'hyphen' has been reinserted into their relations, epitomised in the new British–Irish Council of Isles (BIC) which had its first meeting on 18 December 1999, and whose aim, as the Agreement tells us, is 'to promote the harmonious and mutually beneficial development of the totality of relationships among the peoples of the British and Irish islands'.[6] Membership of the Council is drawn from the British and Irish governments, the devolved assemblies of Scotland, Wales and Northern Ireland, the Isle of Man and the Channel Islands. It acknowledges the fact that the citizens of both islands are inextricably intermingled thanks to centuries of internal migration, cultural borrowing and political exchange (positive and negative). And it purports to deal with a whole range of common interests running from the environment and transport to the knowledge economy. Speaking at the launch of the BIC in Lancaster House in 1999, Prime Minister Tony Blair described its inaugural session as:

an extraordinary and historical event that we have all the people of these islands finally coming together and saying we share certain things in common, that we can resolve our differences. The British and Irish people feel closer together now than at any time in their lifetime.[7]

And the veteran Scottish political theorist, Tom Nairn, hailed it as 'an imagined community disconcertingly different from anything in the political arsenal of the old British State'.[8] The fact that the BIC was able to secure the enthusiastic support of not only both sovereign governments but also of the two leaders of the traditionally opposed republican and unionist communities of Ulster – John Hume and David Trimble – was decisive.

The sea change signalled by the establishment of the BIC was reflected in a radical paradigm shift in the constitutional relations between the two islands. The Irish government endorsed the removal of Articles 2 and 3 from the Constitution of the Republic (a move ratified by the vast majority of the electorate); while the British government redrafted the 1922 Government of Ireland Act and held referenda to establish regional assemblies in Scotland, Wales and Northern Ireland. The zero-sum game of mutually exclusive 'national identities' was over.

The emerging postnationalist scenario permits, for the first time in history, the citizens of Northern Ireland to profess differing degrees of allegiance to an expanding range of identifications: from regional townland, parish or province to national constitution (British or Irish or both) and to the transnational union of Europe. As John Hewitt prophetically wrote to his fellow Ulster poet, John Montague: 'I always maintained that our loyalties had an order: to Ulster, to Ireland, to the British archipelago, to Europe, and that anyone who skipped a step or missed a link falsified the total'.[9]

This scenario of extending circles of identity corresponds felicitously, in my view, with the political paradigm of 'subsidiarity' that has become part of the new European thinking, particularly since the Presidency of Jacques Delors in the 1980s and 1990s. The term refers to the principle and practice of never taking a decision at a higher level that can be taken at a lower level. So the ever ascending and descending levels of political responsibility could be said to chime well with the cultural model of mobile, overlapping identities outlined by poets such as Hewitt and Heaney. Though originally deriving from Catholic social philosophy, the concept of subsidiarity has, of course, assumed its own special significance (beyond all denominational or confessional partisanship) in both the aspirational and actual exercise of power by European institutions and in the increasing provisions for regional, subnational decision-making. There is little doubt that the future success of a postnational European project will depend greatly on the degree to which the model of subsidiarity is positively adopted, both politically and culturally, throughout the expanded EU.

Colonisation and National Identity

But how did the game of exclusive nationalities first originate? Like most stories of national genesis, the Irish and British one began with a mirror-stage. The Irish and British peoples first identified themselves as separate and unique by differentiating themselves from one another. One of the earliest chapters in this process, noted by the Welsh historian, R.R. Davies, was the attempt to forge the notion of a British-English nation (*nacio* or *gens*) over and against that of a colonised Irish nation in the fourteenth century.[10] The British-English settlers of the time felt so fearful of mingling with the natives – thereby becoming 'more Irish than the Irish themselves' – that they invented the infamous Statutes of Kilkenny. These Statutes instigated segregation between coloniser and colonised, fomenting political divisions between two supposedly incompatible 'peoples'. Non-observance of the Statutes was called 'degeneracy' – that is, falling outside the Pale of the *gens*.

To marry outside the *nacio* or *gens* was to cease to be a proper English 'gentleman', and to forfeit the attendant virtues of gentility and gentrification. Commingling with the so-called Gaelic natives was, as the old phrase went, 'going beyond the Pale' (literally, exiting from the frontier-walls of the city of settlers, Dublin). To transgress this limit was to betray the tribe. The colonising *gens* thus came to define itself over and against its *de-gens*, its alter-ego: namely the native Irish. Thus, even though it was the Venerable Bede who initially invoked the idea of an English *gens*, and while it was Alfred's expansion of Wessex (871–99) which opened the way, it was actually in the laboratory of Ireland that the English nation first saw itself in the mirror and believed its image. In Ireland England originally earned its credentials and cried victory. If the Irish did not exist, the English would have had to invent them.

By virtue of this mimetic logic, the Irish in turn began redefining themselves as an equally pure and distinct *nacio*. In response to the colonial campaign of segregation, King Donald O'Neill of Ulster wrote to the Pope in 1317 declaring himself heir of the 'whole of Ireland' and affirming an unbroken historical continuity of the Irish people (*gens*) through their laws, speech and long memory of tribulations suffered at the hands of the colonial invaders.[11] Ever since this act of reciprocal invention and definition in the fourteenth century, the Irish and English-British nations have evolved like twins, inseparable in their loves and hates, joined at the hip of Ulster and forever bound to a dialectic of conflict and reconciliation.[12]

The first successful attempt to identify the Irish and British as two radically separate peoples really only took hold after the fourteenth-century invasionary settlement made it in the interests of the colonisers, and the colonised, to differentiate themselves as two distinct *gens*. The criteria of differentiation were conventional rather than natural. They were, in other words, largely of a cultural and legal character – e.g. apparel, residency, name-forms, language, property rights – than of ethnic foundation.[13] The *gens* actually 'looked' almost identical to the *de-gens*. But this absence of conspicuous racial distinguishing marks, made it all the more necessary to compensate at the level of contrived legislation and statute. Where nature could not segregate, law would.

But law in itself was not enough. The border of the Pale separating *gens* from *de-gens* remained constantly shifting, porous and indeterminable, requiring repeated recourse to propaganda. The stereotyping usually took the form of prejudice and snobbery ('the natives are not *gentlemen*'), drawing great ammunition from Giraldus Cambrensis's twelfth-century *History and Topography of Ireland*. Cambrensis himself was, revealingly, a secretary to Prince John on one of his invasionary expeditions to Ireland and his depiction of the natives as 'a wild and inhospitable people who live like beasts' well served its colonial purposes. As the Irish historian, Art Cosgrove, would later observe:

The picture drawn by Gerald was unflattering; the Irish were economically backward, politically fragmented, wild, untrustworthy and semi-pagan, and guilty of sexual immorality. Doubtless the picture was much influenced by the need to justify conquest and dispossession.[14]

But the prize for colonial stereotypes belongs to the British historian, Charles Kingsley, who many centuries after Gerald could still remark on a visit to Ireland: 'to see white chimpanzees is dreadful; if they were black, one would not feel it so much, but their skins are as white as ours!'[15]

The Irish, of course, responded with their own version of self-conscious national pride, their spalpeen poets and bards spinning tales of the virginal motherland being raped and plundered by the invading *Sasannach*. And this widening gender opposition between Ireland as feminine victim or virgin – Roisin Dubh, Cathleen ni Houlihan, *Speirbhean*, etc. – and England as masculine master – fatherland, King and Country, etc. – served to aggravate the divide between the two peoples.[16]

But while ethnic propaganda worked historically, it was as nothing compared to the divisionary power of religion. Arguably, it was not until the seventeenth-century plantation of Ulster, after the Reformation, that the colonisation of Ireland ultimately succeeded. With the disenfranchising of Irish Catholics *en masse* in favour of Planter Protestants, subsequently backed up with the infamous Penal Laws, religion was deployed as a galvanising force of apartheid. Where neither nature, nor ultimately even law or propaganda, could succeed in separating the peoples of these islands, faith in the one true church would! After Cromwellian zeal and Elisabethan ruthlessness had taken their toll, there were many Protestants and Catholics in the island of Ireland who preferred to die rather than to commingle. Even Wolfe Tone and the United Irishmen, with their valiant appeal to a single nation of 'Catholic, Protestant and Dissenter' in the 1790s, could not put the Hibernian Humpty Dumpty back together again. Sectarianism was here to stay.

It would take another two hundred years after the failed Rebellion of 1798 for Britain and Ireland mutually to renounce their separatist claims to Northern Ireland and thereby to permit Irish Catholics, Protestants and Dissenters peaceably to co-habit for the first time since the Reformation. It was only when the Irish and British communities inhabiting Ulster acknowledged that they could be 'British or Irish or both' that they could be united once again. Not as a unitary national identity, of course, as Tone had hoped, but as a multiple postnational one.

The End of Sovereignty

The story of the genesis and evolution of the Irish and British nations might thus be said to run broadly in parallel. As R.R. Davies again points out in his landmark study *Domination and Conquest*,[17] what the English, and later the 'British', had great difficulty accepting was that after the Viking and Norman invasions, the various parts of these islands were already countries of 'multiple' peoples and identities, which included, in part at least, the culture of the coloniser who was so desperately struggling to retain (even if it meant reinventing) his own sense of pure, uncontaminated identity. The settlers in Ireland were so insecure in their ambiguous status as a 'middle nation' – neither fully English nor fully Irish – that they demonised the native Irish as their 'other' in order to more emphatically insist on their belonging to the former. And as the lady did protest too much she bolstered up her protests with accompanying statutes and racist rhetoric, determined to prove to herself and to others that she was right. This scapegoat campaign led to the exacerbation of existing conflicts. Thus the match between people and polity which was achieved in England (and to a lesser extent Scotland) was not replicated in Ireland. But while the peoples of England (including the Normans) were by the fifteenth century welded into an integrative unit by virtue of such strategies of alien-nation – namely, establishing oneself as a single nation over against an alter-native one – the island of Ireland remained a victim of such divisions. What would continue however, to haunt the contrived national unity of Englishness – and of Britishness after the union with Wales and Scotland – was the ghost of their alien and alienated double, Ireland. The very difference from Irishness became part and parcel of English/British identity. Their Hibernian Other was uncannily mirrored in themselves, the familiar spectre hidden in strangeness, the original double they had forgotten to remember, the threatened *revenant* of their own repressed political unconscious.[18]

The British nation thus emerged, like many other nations, as an 'imagined community' which invented itself in dialectical opposition to its 'others' – and none more fundamentally than Ireland, its first, last and most intimate 'other', combining as it did three of the most significant characteristics of alien-nation: (1) Ireland was majority Catholic (non-Protestant); (2) it was a colony (overseas if only a little over – but sufficiently so to be treated like a subordinate, rather than an equal neighbour like Wales or Scotland); and (3) Ireland was a traditional ally of France, the main military rival to British imperial designs, and inspirational insurrectionary model, as was Ireland itself, for rebellious movements in India, Palestine and elsewhere. Thus Ireland came to serve as the untrustworthy 'poor relation' of the UK:

[Ireland's] population was more Catholic than Protestant. It was the ideal jumping-off point for a French invasion, and both its Protestant and its Catholic dissidents traditionally looked to France for aid. And although Irishmen were always an important component of the British armed forces, and individual Scots-Irishmen like Macartney and Anglo-Irishmen like the Wellesley clan played leading imperial roles as diplomats, generals and pro-consuls, Ireland's relationship with the empire was always a deeply ambiguous one. How could it not be, when London so persistently treated the country in a way that it never treated Scotland and Wales, as a colony rather than as an integral part of a truly united Kingdom? Ireland was in many respects the laboratory of the British Empire. Much of the legal and land reform which the British sought to implement in India, for example was based on experiments first implemented in Ireland.[19]

It is of course the very 'ambiguity' of Ireland's insider–outsider relation with Britain that made it at once so fascinating for the British (witnessed in their passion for Irish literature and drama from Swift and Sheridan to Wilde, Yeats and Shaw) and so repellent (evidenced in the Fleet Street portrayals of the Irish as simian-like brutes).

This paradox of attraction and recoil is typical of what Edward Said calls 'orientalism': Ireland serving as Britain's Orient in its own backyard. It also approximates to what Freud describes as the 'uncanny' (*unheimlich*) – the return of the familiar as unfamiliar, of friend as stranger. Ireland served, one might say, as Britain's unconscious reminding it that it was ultimately and irrevocably a stranger to itself, and that its self-identity was constructed upon the screening of its forgotten other – in both senses of 'screen': to conceal and to project.

The nature of this unsettling rapport was evident not only in the mirror-plays of Irish dramatists like Shaw and Wilde, but also in the works of English dramatists who reflected on the neighbour-ing island. Already in Shakespeare we find an example of this.

In *Henry V,* for example, we find Captain MacMorris, the first true-blue Irishman to appear in English letters, posing the conundrum: 'What is my nation?' – thereby recalling not only that Ireland is a nation still in question (i.e. in quest of itself), but that England is too. And we find an even more explicit example in *Richard II,* when the King visits Ireland only to regain the British mainland disoriented and dismayed. Having set out secure in his sovereignty, he returns wondering what exactly his identity is, and by implication, his legitimacy as monarch: 'I had forgot myself, am I not king?' he puzzles. 'Is not the king's name twenty thousand names?'[20] In short, Ireland takes its revenge on the king by deconstructing and multiplying the one and indivisible character of his sovereignty. The sovereign is shaken from his slumber by his sojourn in the Irish colony, discovering that the very notion of a united national kingdom is nominal rather than real, imaginary rather than actual.

Ireland's advantage over England/Britain, then as now, was that it never achieved indivisible sovereignty as a unitary nation – and so never could mistake the illusion for a reality. For the Irish, from ancient legend to the present day, the idea of sovereignty was linked to the notion of a 'fifth province', a place of mind rather than of territory, a symbol rather than a *fait accompli* (the Irish for province is *coicead,* meaning a fifth, but there are only four provinces in Ireland). Or to put it another way: when it came to sovereignty, Ireland had less to lose than Britain because it never had it to lose in the first place. The Irish knew in their hearts and souls that the nation as such does not exist. This, of course, did not prevent icons and dogmas of exclusivist unitary nationality being elevated to the status of theological mystique by both loyalist and republican extremes.[21]

The crisis of British sovereignty reached its peak in recent times. This was brought on by a variety of factors: (1) the final fracturing of the empire (with the Falklands, Gibraltar and Hong Kong controversies); (2) the end of the Protestant hegemony (with the mass immigration of non-Protestants from the ex-colonies – including Ireland); (3) the entry of the UK, however hesitantly, into the European Community, which ended Britain's isolationist stance *vis-à-vis* its traditional alien-nations, Ireland and France; (4) the ineluctable impact of global technology and communications; (5) the devolution of power from over-centralised government in Westminster to the various regional assemblies of Edinburgh, Cardiff and Belfast; and finally, (6) the ultimate acknowledgment that Britain is now a multiethnic, multicultural, multiconfessional community which can no longer sustain the illusion of an eternally perduring sovereignty.

The old Tory vision of Great Britain as a timeless Anglo-Saxon Empire presided over by indomitable 'little Englanders' is at an end. Influential publications such as the Parekh Report *The Future of Multi-Ethnic Britain*[22] demonstrate that new modes of postnational politics are now a necessity.

The Dawn of Postnationalism

The British–Irish 'Council of Isles' is now a reality. This third spoke of the 1998 Agreement's wheel – alongside the internal Northern Ireland Assembly and the North–South cross-border bodies – harbours enormous promise. What the transnational model effectively recognises is that citizens of Britain and Ireland are inextricably bound up with each other – mongrel islanders from East to West sharing an increasingly common civic and economic space. In addition to the obvious contemporary overlapping of our sports and popular cultures, we are becoming more mindful of how much of our respective histories are shared: from the Celtic, Viking and Norman settlements to our more recent entry to the EU. For millennia the Irish Sea served as a waterway connecting our two islands, only rarely as a *cordon sanitaire* keeping us apart. And this is becoming true again in our own time with almost 30,000 trips being made daily across the Irish Sea, in both directions. It is not entirely surprising then that over eight million citizens of the UK today claim Irish origin, with over four million of these having an Irish parent. Indeed a recent survey shows that only 6 per cent of British people consider Irish people living in Britain to be foreigners. And we do not need reminding that almost one-quarter of the inhabitants of the island of Ireland claim to be at least part British. Finally, at a symbolic level, few can fail to have been moved by the unprecedented image of the President of the Irish Republic, Mary MacAleese, standing beside the Queen of England on the battlefield of Flanders commemorating their respective dead.

In view of this reawakening to our common memories and experiences, it was not surprising to find Tony Blair receiving a standing ovation from both houses of the Parliament of the Irish Republic on 26 November 1998, in the wake of the Good Friday Agreement. Such a visitation had not occurred for over a century, and the ghost of Gladstone was not entirely absent from the proceedings. Blair acknowledged openly on this occasion that Britain was at last leaving its 'post-colonial malaise' behind it and promised that a newly confident Republic and a more decentralised UK would have more common tasks in the scenario of European convergence than any other two member states. East–West reciprocity was on the political agenda for the first time since the divisive Statutes of Kilkenny.

Though rarely acknowledged at the official or constitutional level, a practical form of joint sovereignty has been endorsed by the Irish and British peoples. The pluralisation of national identity, epitomised by the provision of the BIC, entails a radical redefinition of the notion of sovereignty. In essence, it signals the deterritorialisation of national sovereignty – namely, the attribution of sovereignty to peoples rather than land.[23] Contrary to what many continue to believe, 'land' is chronologically and historically a much older criterion for sovereignty than ethnic or civic, that is, national or constitutional identity. The term sovereignty (from the Latin *superanus*) originally referred to the supreme power of a divine ruler, before it was delegated to divinely elected 'representatives' in this world – kings, pontiffs, emperors, monarchs – and, finally, to the 'people' in most modern states. A problem arose, however, in that many modern democracies recognise the existence of several different peoples within a single state. And many peoples mean many centres of sovereignty. Yet the traditional concept of sovereignty, as already noted, was always unitary, that is, 'one and indivisible'. Whence the dilemma: how to divide the indivisible? This is why, today, sovereignty has become one of the most controversial concepts in political theory and international law, intimately related to issues of state government, national independence and minority rights. Inherited notions of absolutist sovereignty are being challenged from both within nation-states and by developments in international legislation. The deterritorialising and pooling of sovereignty in the new European project is an example of this.

There are, however, precedents. With the Hague Conferences of 1899 and 1907, followed by the Covenant of the League of Nations and the Charter of the UN, significant restrictions on the actions of nation-states were laid down. A system of international checks and balances was introduced limiting the right of sovereign states to act as they pleased in all matters. Moreover, the increasing interdependence of states – accompanied by a sharing of sovereignties in the interests of greater peace, social justice, economic exchange and information technology – qualified the very principle of absolute sovereignty:

The people of the world have recognized that there can be no peace without law, and that there can be no law without some limitations on sovereignty.

They have started, therefore, to pool sovereignties to the extent needed to maintain peace; and sovereignty is being increasingly exercised on behalf of the peoples of the world not only by national governments but also by organisations of the world community.[24]

If this pertains to the 'peoples of the world' generally, how much more does it pertain to the peoples of the islands of Britain and Ireland? This is why I argued in *Postnationalist Ireland* (1997) for a surpassing of the existing nation-states in the direction of both an Irish-British Council and a federal Europe of regions. The nation-state has become too large and too small as a model of government, too large for the growing needs of regional participatory democracy; too small for the increasing drift towards transnational exchange and power-sharing. Hence my invocation of the Nordic Council as a model for resolving our sovereignty disputes – in particular the way in which these five nation-states and three autonomous regions succeeded in sorting out territorial conflicts, declaring the Aland and Spitsbergen islands as Europe's two first demilitarised zones. Could we not do likewise under the aegis of a new transnational BIC, declaring Northern Ireland a third demilitarised zone?[25]

The Blair government's readiness to acknowledge the inevitable long-term dissolution of Britain qua absolute centralised state was a singular achievement. But it is not a decision taken in a vacuum. There were precedents for sovereignty-sharing in Britain's recent experience, including the British government's consent to a limitation and dilution of sovereign national power in its subscription to the European Convention on Human Rights, the Single European Act, the European Common Defence Policy and the European Court of Justice. If Britain had been able to pool sovereignty in these ways with the other nation-states of the EU, surely it was only logical to do so with its closest neighbour, the Irish Republic. Moreover, the EU principle of subsidiarity as well as the local democracy principle promoted in the Council of Europe's Charter of Local Self-Government, already signalled an alternative to the clash of British-Irish nationalisms that had paralysed Ulster for decades.

Nor should one forget that the forging of Britain into a multi-national state was predicated, at its best, on a civic rather than ethnic notion of citizenship. We need only recall how dramatically the borders of the British nation had shifted and altered in history (e.g. in 1536, 1707, 1800 and 1921) to envisage how they might shift and alter yet again – perhaps this time so radically as to remove all borders from these islands. The fact that British nationalism was often little more than English nationalism in disguise does not detract from its salutary constitutional principle of civic (rather than ethnic) belonging.

The implications of the Good Friday Agreement are especially relevant here: the conflict of sovereignty claims exercised over the same territory by two independent governments — issuing in decades of violence — is now, as we have been suggesting, superseded by a postnational paradigm of intergovernmental power. The dual identities of British-Irish relations have long belied the feasibility of unitary forms of government and shown the necessity of separating nation (identity) from that of state (sovereignty) and even, to some extent, from that of land (territory). Such a separation is, I submit, a precondition for allowing the co-existence of different communities in the same society; and, by extension, amplifying the models of identity to include more pluralist forms of association — a British—Irish Council, a European network of Regions, and the Irish and British diasporas. In sum, it is becoming abundantly clear that Bossuet's famous seventeenth-century definition of the nation as a perfect match of people and place — where citizens 'lived and died in the land of their birth'[26] — is no longer tenable.

The fact is there are no pristine nations around which definitive state boundaries — demarcating exclusivist sovereignty status — can be fixed. The Belfast Agreement recognised the historic futility of both British and Irish constitutional claims on Northern Ireland as a natural and necessary part of their respective 'national territories'. Instead, the BIC promises a network of interconnecting regional assemblies guaranteeing respect for cultural and political diversity and an effective co-management of such practical common concerns as transport, environment, social equity and e-commerce. We are being challenged to abandon our mutually reinforcing myths of mastery (largely British) and martyrdom (largely Irish) and to face our more mundane post-imperial, postnationalist reality. Might the BIC not, as Simon Partridge suggests, even serve as an inspiration to other parts of Europe and the globe still embroiled in the devastations of ethnic nationalism?[27]

What the Belfast Agreement allows, in short, is that the irrepressible need for identity and allegiance be gradually channelled away from the fetish of the nation-state, where history has shown its tenure to be insecure and belligerent, to more appropriate levels of regional and federal expression. In the Irish-British context, this means that citizens of these islands may come to express their identity less in terms of rival sovereign nation-states and more in terms of both locally empowered provinces and larger international associations.

The new dispensation fosters variable layers of compatible identification – regional, national and transnational – allowing anyone in Northern Ireland who so wishes to declare allegiance to the Ulster region, the Irish and/or British nation, the EU, and the cosmopolitan order of world citizenry.

Citizens of these islands are offered the possibility of thinking of themselves as mongrel islanders rather than as eternal inhabitants of two pure, God-given nation-states. There is no such thing as primordial nationality. If the nation is indeed a hybrid construct, an 'imagined community', then it can be re-imagined in alternative versions. The 'postnational constellation' envisaged by political visionaries as diverse as John Hume and Jürgen Habermas, need no longer be considered a utopian dream.

Notes

1 Habermas 2001.
2 Ibid, p. 90.
3 Ibid.
4 Ibid, p. 99. See also Habermas in this volume; Morin 1984; Morin 1994.
5 See The Belfast Agreement, Part 2, para vi.
6 Ibid, Strand 3, para. 1.
7 Cited in Dworkin 2005.
8 Nairn 2001, p. 60; see also Nairn 1977; Nairn 2000.
9 John Hewitt, Letter to John Montague, 1964, extracts available in University of Ulster Libraries John Hewitt Collection. Available at: http://library.ulster.ac.uk/craine/hewitt/work.htm#letter
10 Davies 1990.
11 This move conveniently masked the fact that the 'natives', no less than the colonial settlers, were a mongrelised ethnic mix of successive invasions by Vikings, Anglo-Normans, Scots, Celts, Milesians, etc.
12 McCana 1978. It is of course true that the Irish nation had some primitive sense of itself before this reaction to the fourteenth-century plantation. It has been argued, by Proinsias McCana for example, that some form of centralised unitary government began to emerge as early as the ninth century in response to the Viking invasions, and again in the twelfth century in response to the Anglo-Norman invasion. But these intermittent efforts at all-island structures of self-rule were largely a matter of self-defence rather than any self-conscious assertion of enduring national identity. After all, the term 'scotus' could as easily refer to an inhabitant of Ireland as of Britain up the eleventh century (e.g. John Scotus Eriugena from the former, Duns Scotus from the latter).
13 Indeed it is well accepted that the inhabitants of our respective islands share a virtually homogenous gene pool due to the commonly shared experience of successive invasions and migrations, pre-Celtic, Celtic, Viking,

Anglo-Norman, etc. One of the earliest known volumes of Irish letters was tellingly named the *Book Of Invasions*.

14 Cosgrove 1993, Introduction.

15 Watson 1994, p. 17.

16 One of the most effective remedies for such a history of opposed national narratives is, I believe, what Paul Ricoeur (1996, pp. 3–14) calls an 'exchange of memories': a critical and creative traversal of one's adversary's stories and histories which might provoke, in turn, a new understanding between two rival nations, at a cultural, psychological and political level. For a more detailed analysis of the conflict between opposed gender stereotypes of national identity, see my 'Myths of Motherland', in Kearney (1997, pp. 108–21).

17 Davies 1990.

18 Colley 1992a. Colley also argues that the peoples that made up the British nation were brought together as a national identity by confrontation with the 'other'. In keeping with the theses of the new British history advocated by Hugh Kearney, Benedict Anderson, J. G. A. Pocock and Tom Nairn, Colley suggests that British national identity is contingent and relational (like most others) and is best understood as an interaction between several different histories and peoples. Without necessarily endorsing the Four Nations model of Britain, Colley contends that most inhabitants of the 'British Isles' laid claim to a double, triple or multiple identity – even after the consolidation of British national identity after 1700. It would not be unusual, for example, to find someone identifying him/herself as a citizen of Edinburgh, a Lowlander, a Scot and a Briton. It was over and against this pluralist practice of identification, on the ground, that the artificial nation of Great Britain managed to forge itself, not only by its Tudor consolidation and successive annexations of Wales in 1536, Scotland in 1707 and Ireland in 1800, but by a series of external wars between 1689 and 1815 and also, of course, by its Industrial Revolution. In this manner, Britain managed to expand its empire overseas and to unify its citizens back home by replicating on a world stage what England had first tried out in Ireland in the fourteenth century. It galvanised itself into national unity by pitting itself against an externalised alien enemy. The strategic benefits of British imperialism were not just commercial and political, therefore, but psychic as well. And the biggest advantage of the 'overseas' African and Asian colonies was that, unlike Britain's traditional enemies closer to home (the Irish and the French), these 'others' actually looked entirely different. But as the empire began to fracture and fragment in the first part of the twentieth century, the British resorted to religion once again to cement the sense of national identity. What united the British above all else in their times of trouble and decline, was their 'common Protestantism'. Hence the emblematic importance of the famous photo of St Paul's during the Blitz – the parish church of the besieged empire *par excellence* – 'emerging defiantly and unscathed from the fire and devastation surrounding it (...) a Protestant citadel, encircled by enemies, but safe under the watchful eye of a strictly English-speaking deity' (Colley 1992b, p. 72).

19 Colley 1992b, p. 76.

20 *Richard II*, Act III, Scene ii.

21 Kearney 1997, pp. 99–108.

22 Parekh *et al.* 2000.

23 A fact which finds symbolic correlation in the Agreement's extension of national 'belonging' to embrace the Irish diaspora now numbering over 70 million worldwide.

24 'Sovereignty' in *Encyclopaedia Britannica*, Vol. XI, p. 57.

25 Prior to the Belfast Agreement of 1998 such sovereignty sharing was mainly opposed by British nationalism which went by the name of Unionism. It was, ironically, the Irish republican tradition (comprising all democratic parties in the Irish Republic as well as the SDLP and Sinn Fein in the North) which was usually labelled 'nationalist', even though the most uncompromising nationalists in the vexed history of Northern Ireland have been the Unionists. It was the latter, after all, who clung to an anachronistic notion of undiluted British sovereignty, refusing any compromise with their Irish neighbours; until the British and Irish governmental initiative made moderate unionism realise the tribal march was over and that the UK was no longer united. By contrast, John Hume's 'new republicanism' – a vision of shared sovereignty between the different peoples of Ireland – had little difficulty with the new 'postnationalist' scenario. Indeed Hume had called himself a 'postnationalist' for many years without many taking heed. And, curiously, one might even argue that Michael Collins was himself something of a postnationalist when he wrote that as a 'free and equal country' Ireland would be willing to 'cooperate in a free association on all matters which would be naturally the common concern of two nations, living so closely together' as part of a 'real league of nations of the World' (*Manchester Guardian*, December 1921).

26 Bossuet 1990, p. 12.

27 Partridge 2000.

References

Bossuet, Jacques-Bénigne, 1990, *Politics Drawn from the Very Words of Holy Scripture*. Cambridge: Cambridge University Press.

Encyclopaedia Britannica, 2005. 32 vols. London: Encyclopædia Britannica.

Colley, Linda, 1992a, 'Britishness and Otherness', *Journal of British Studies*, Vol. **31**, 309–29.

1992b, *Britons: Forging the Nation. 1707–1837*. New Haven, CT: Yale University Press.

1999, 'Britishness in the 21st Century', Downing St Millennium Lectures, 8 December 1999. Available at: http//www.number-10.gov.uk

Cosgrove, Art (ed.), 1993, *A New History of Ireland: Medieval Ireland, 1169–1534. New History of Ireland Vol. II*. Oxford: Clarendon.

Davies, R. R., 1990, *Domination and Conquest. The Experience of Ireland, Scotland and Wales 1100–1300*. Cambridge: Cambridge University Press.

Dworkin, Dennis, 2005, 'Intellectual Adventures in the Isles', in Begoqa Aretxaga, Dennis Dworkin and Joseba Gabilondo (eds.) *Empire and Terror. Nationalism/Postnationalism in the New Millennium.* Reno, NV: University of Nevada Press.

Habermas, Jürgen, [1998] 2001, *The Postnational Constellation.* Cambridge: Polity Press.

Kearney, Richard, 1997, *Postnationalist Ireland.* London: Routledge.

McCana, Proinsias, 1978, 'Notes on the Early Irish Concept of Unity', *The Crane Bag Journal*, Vol. 2(1–2), 57–71.

Morin, Edgar, 1984, *Penser L'Europe.* Paris: Gallimard.

1994, *La Complexité Humaine.* Paris: Flammarion.

Nairn, Tom, 1977, *The Break-up of Britain.* London: NLB.

2000, *After Britain.* London: Granta.

2001, 'Farewell Britannia', *New Left Review* 7, January–February, 55–74.

Parekh, Bhikhu, *et al.*, 2000, *The Future of Multi-Ethnic Britain. Report of the Commission on the Future of Multi-Ethnic Britain.* London: Profile.

Partridge, Simon, 2000, 'The British-Irish Council. The Trans-islands Symbolic and Political Possibilities'. *Looking into England Papers.* London: British Council. Available at: http://www.britishcouncil.org/studies/england/partridge.htm

Ricoeur, Paul, 1996, 'Reflections on a New Ethos for Europe', in Richard Kearney (ed.), *Paul Ricoeur. The Hermeneutics of Action.* London: SAGE, pp. 3–14.

Watson, George J., 1994, *Irish Identity and the Irish Literary Revival.* Second edn. Washington DC: The Catholic University of America Press.

Part IV

Europe and The World

10   Unified or Open? The European Alternative

Ralf Dahrendorf

Peace and prosperity in Europe: anyone who remembers the zero hour of 1945 and all that went before it feels grateful every day for these achievements.[1] We also know who and what can take credit for the flourishing landscapes which have replaced trenches and ruins. Above all, it is the people of Europe who have learnt the lesson of history and worked vigorously to create a better world. But then there was also the USA, safeguarding and promoting the new opportunities of the postwar era. NATO and the Marshall Plan are code words for the commitment for which we Europeans are obliged to be eternally grateful. Both the actions of the people and the USA's assistance have now been strengthened and made lasting by the process of European unification, itself one of the remarkable achievements of recent decades.

And yet precisely this process has made headway only falteringly, subject to detours and prone to occasional accidents. Churchill's splendid vision of 1945 fell on ground on which, to be sure, some flowers bloomed but where no-one had the courage – or found the right conditions – to pave the way to this royal road. There has never been political union in Europe. Should there be? This is my question here. If we do not believe in a world spirit – a spirit which was expressed in Churchill's speeches in Strasbourg and Zurich and which, inevitably if not always recognisably, clears the way for a United States of Europe – then we must ask why we should aspire to the 'ever closer union' of Europe as set out in the Treaty of Rome which established the European Economic Community (EEC). Are there not greater values than the unity of Europe? In other words: is not such unity only worthwhile if it serves these greater values? Do we really want a Europe which is not open to that cosmopolitan order which Timothy Garton Ash calls 'Free World'?

The early stages of European unification after the Second World War were marked by the failure of grand projects. Mainly French-inspired attempts at creating a political union were never agreed, and the alternative plan of a European Defence Community failed to secure a majority in the French parliament. The Organisation for European Economic Cooperation (OEEC) was superseded by a Free World organisation, the Organisation for Economic Cooperation and Development (OECD). The Council of Europe became and remained guardian of the European Convention on Human Rights; notwithstanding its limitations, the Council remains a pillar of a free Europe.

The failure of the direct approach saw the beginning of an indirect attempt to unify Europe. The Schuman Plan had several purposes, but was seen by at least one major European – Jean Monnet, the first president of the High Authority of the European Coal and Steel Community (ECSC) – as the concrete beginning of a process of unification. Walter Hallstein, the first president of the Commission of the European Economic Community at its inception in 1957, gave a name to such hopes. He saw an 'inner logic' at stake, 'an anonymous force, but one which works only through the will of the people', that constitutes the decisive driving force of European unification. Its principle is simple: 'Whoever says A must also say B'. Whoever starts with the single market sets in motion a 'psychological chain reaction of integration which will not stop at the boundaries of economic and social policy'. Moreover, within these bounds, inner logic means that the intention of creating 'conditions within the community similar to an internal market' has consequences for those branches of the economy not determined by the market. There is 'no choice but to include policies (for example, in agriculture and transport) under a community discipline'.[2]

And thus the Common Agricultural Policy (CAP) came into being. Anyone who displays the same scepticism towards an inner logic as towards a world spirit will of course ask questions and indeed express doubts. Even such a weighty political decision as monetary union has not as yet led to the common economic policy which an inner logic would suggest it should. We might even go so far as to say that quite the opposite is true and that national economic policies together with the Growth and Stability Pact actually jeopardise the common currency. One problem in the process of European unification lies in a logic quite unlike that for which Monnet and Hallstein were hoping. Some of the forward-looking intentions of Europe's communities from the ECSC to the European Union (EU) have turned in practice into measures for the maintenance of the status quo. Thus protectionism and closure have taken the place of openness.

In the case of the Montan Union, this was no-one's fault. When, in 1951, the Schuman Plan was discussed in the parliaments of the six founding members, one could still assume that coal and steel were industries of the future. And whoever has the raw materials has everything else. Moreover, one of the motives for the terrible wars had been that Germany wanted French iron and France German coal – and both wanted control of the Saarland. Ten years later the situation began to change fundamentally. New materials made their appearance and the old raw materials were cheaper on the world markets than at home. Coal, iron and steel changed from valuable resources to burdens, their industries requiring subsidies to survive. And the growing number of redundant miners and steelworkers needed help, too. In the end, no-one wanted the Saar, and no-one could pin any hopes for the future on even Lorraine and the Ruhr. And so in the way of things, i.e. as a result of an unexpected inner logic, the ECSC changed from the seedbed of European strength to an instrument of subsidy, protectionism and social security.

In agriculture, an analogous process was perhaps already foreseeable in 1957, when the EEC followed Hallstein's logic and set up a CAP alongside the Common Market. Hallstein dared to hope for an even more far-reaching change: common agricultural policy means common prices; the latter have to be expressed in a unit of currency, i.e. the green mark, or rather the green dollar; which leads eventually and inevitably to a common currency.[3] In fact it led above all to enormous costs, once again in part to subsidise agriculture and agricultural trade and in part as aid to rural communities facing unavoidable structural change. Even in 2005, 40 per cent of the European budget is direct expenditure from the CAP.

And so a regressive, protectionist trait established itself in Brussels even in the early days. It led to such absurdities as subsidies for tobacco cultivation even as Europe embarked upon an anti-smoking campaign. It weakened the European position in trade policy, to say nothing of the repercussions of this position for the Third World. But above all it created a climate in which Brussels is always appealed to when countries or even lobbies seek protection from purported external threats.

Perhaps such developments could not but impact upon 'Brussels' – in the slightly intimidating sense which that word has today when it passes anybody's lips. Brussels itself, i.e. the European institutions, gradually became a closed society. Anyone wishing to be a member has to accept all the basic assumptions; anyone who does not accept them, or even merely questions them, is excluded. Gisela Stuart, the German-British Labour MP, who was a member of the Presidium of the Convention for the Constitutional Treaty, provides us with a vivid account of this when she describes the so-called *acquis commu-nautaire* in her article on Europe's Constitution. No-one is allowed to probe the workings and achievements of the Union. 'Discussion concentrated exclusively on where we could do more at a European level. Any representative who called into question the fundamental objective of closer integration was marginalised.'[4] Many such stories could be told.

The tendency of the EU to turn in upon itself, to protect the status quo, to delimit and exclude, has assumed a wholly new dimension of late. Following the end of the Cold War and the accession of post-Communist countries, many feel that peace and prosperity are not enough. In the 'old Europe' of the six founding member states in particular, the search for reasons for 'ever closer union' has taken the maintenance of the status quo, delimitation and exclusion to new heights. These take on quite concrete forms, particularly in relation to migration, both the internal migration of workers and the immigration of asylum-seekers. They focus primarily, however, on two larger interrelated issues: the protection of the so-called European social model and Europe's distinction from the USA. The ever more intense discussion of the EU's borders reinforces the impression of a union which sees itself no longer as an association which can be open because it looks to a bright future but instead as a rather apprehensive and rigid protectionist organisation clinging to the past.

Before we examine more closely the forces at work here and, above all, consider ways to move towards an open Europe, we first need to correct the picture painted so far. Not everything that the EU has done over recent decades has led intentionally or unintentionally to greater delimitation and closure.[5] This deficit can be offset firstly by the single greatest achievement of the EU to date, the single market.

The German term *Binnenmarkt* falls short of the far-reaching implications of the path from common market to single market. In a political culture as distant from economic questions as Germany's, the four freedoms of the single market – the free movement of people, goods, services and capital – are underestimated and sometimes described as a mere free-trade area. In fact they represent the creation of a large open economic space, and therewith one of the two linchpins of the 'Free World', the other being political democracy. Both require the rule of law. Moreover, the single market has a strong inherent tendency to expand beyond its own borders, i.e. to remain open to a world single market under the rules of the World Trade Organisation (WTO).

We can therefore place the enlargement of the EU itself on the credit side of an open Europe. It has never been entirely easy, as the British example shows in particular. But it has always led to a deepening of cooperation. In a way enlargement is deepening. The enormous potential for growth which the EU has unleashed in its new member states itself justifies a process of European scope. It is, therefore, pitiful when the old members of the EU suffer cold feet following the latest enlargement and try after all to cut themselves off a little by negotiating longer transition periods, correcting guidelines aimed at promoting competition, cutting budgets and treating new members with condescension. It is not only pitiful, but also inefficient.

Which brings us to the question of borders and how far enlargement may, can, should proceed. The plea for an open Europe proposed here does not seek to establish definitive borders as mapped out in some geography textbook. The borders are as they are drawn in individual cases, but ever wider rather than narrower. I therefore see no reason why a country, which is part of Europe when it comes to UEFA football and the Eurovision song contest, the Human Rights Convention of the Council of Europe and membership of NATO, should be debarred from the EU. Openness also means the inclusion of Turkey.

This is particularly true since June 1993, when the European Council in Copenhagen decided on political and economic criteria for all new member states. The document, just three pages long and easy to read, is one of the most important resolutions ever adopted by the EU. What is more, it is written in clear, comprehensible language. Here is an example of the political criteria:

They are democracy, the rule of law, human rights and respect for minorities. It is expected of countries wishing to become members of the EU that they not only recognise the principles of democracy and the rule of law but also practice these in daily life. They must also ensure the stability of various institutions, place the authorities and the judiciary, the police and local administration in a position to function effectively and thereby the consolidation of democracy.[6]

Moreover, these criteria are explicitly linked to the European Convention on Human Rights and the Council of Europe – another sign of openness not always characteristic of the EU.

For some, a list of indicators of an open Europe would also include the resolutions adopted by the EU in Lisbon in 2000 to strengthen the competitiveness of the European economy. These resolutions on innovation, liberalisation, economic dynamism, employment and the environment are a model of openness for the world. But they are also an example of the failure of good intentions immanent in the EU. As Jacques Delors, President of the European Commission, presided over the move to a single market, he had at his side Commissioner Lord Cockfield, who translated the principle into more than 270 individual decisions made by the European Community. For the Lisbon agenda there was no Lord Cockfield, nor could there ever have been, since the required individual decisions lie almost entirely beyond the competence of the EU. It is therefore no surprise when, in its 'Lisbon Scorecard V', the London-based Centre for European Reform gives overall score on a scale of A–E of C, i.e. satisfactory at best.[7]

And so this is how the European balance sheet looks when it comes to the openness of the real union: expensive and moderately successful in protecting the status quo and assisting the victims of change, enjoying some successes but also failures when it comes to projects with a promising future. That would be a tolerable, albeit not entirely satisfactory, result were it not for the extraordinary pretensions of the EU. Political elites wanted to prescribe for it a constitution. In foreign policy the EU was to become a power, even a great power, to replace nation-states in important policy areas. Though the Convention was able to dissuade its president Giscard d'Estaing from using the term, it was to be something along the lines of the nucleus of the United States of Europe. The Brussels Convention has been compared with that of Philadelphia in 1776.

Why is this? Is it not enough that the EU contributes to peace and prosperity? Could we not concentrate on improving the EU's record on openness, thereby allowing other countries to enjoy just such peace and prosperity? Why the desire for an 'ever closer union' with quasi-state symbols and institutions? These are precisely the 'forbidden' questions of which Gisela Stuart spoke. Since the project to establish a European constitution has failed, we would do well to ask them anyway and to look for answers which appeal to others besides the *habitués* of things European. I want to examine two issues in particular, both of which have of late dominated the so-called philosophical discussion about Europe. The first is the question of European identity and the second that of Europe as a centre of power in a multipolar world. Both issues inevitably lead us into the difficult terrain of relations between Europe and America.

In recent years it has become difficult to overlook the literature emerging on the subject of the idea of Europe or its identity. Behind it all lies a theory – whether unspoken or explicit – which sees European unity not as a political project but as the fulfilment of a historical task. Though seldom encountered in countries inspired more by

John Locke and David Hume than by Herder and Hegel, the idea is not new. Walter Hallstein, the first of the two great presidents of the European Commission, saw European unification as 'an organic process in which an existing structural unit, long established in culture, commerce and political consciousness, is translated into a definitive political form'.[8] The second great president of the Commission, Jacques Delors, liked to speak of the search for 'the soul of Europe'.

A Reflection Group initiated by the then Commission president Romano Prodi and coordinated by Polish philosopher Krzysztof Michalski took up this idea and asked what provides European cohesion, since neither the single market nor the political institutions are sufficiently powerful. It is, they concluded, 'Europe's common culture'. Europe is a 'common cultural space' before it is ever an economic area or adopts a political constitution. It is this common culture which creates the necessary solidarity. There follows the critical statement. 'This solidarity must be stronger than the universal solidarity which binds (or should bind) all human beings together and which underlies the idea of humanitarian aid.'[9]

The cultural philosopher George Steiner puts it in his own more entertaining language when, in his lecture on the idea of Europe at the Nexus Institute, Tilburg, he calls Europe the continent of coffee houses. You find them from Lisbon to Odessa, Copenhagen to Palermo, though hardly ever in Moscow and not in England, either. And of course there are 'none in North America with the exception of the Gallic outpost New Orleans'. All of which leads Steiner to conclude: 'It is essential that Europe maintains certain convictions and bold ventures of the soul that the Americanisation of the planet, for all its boldness and achievements, has obscured.'[10]

It is only fair to add that such Gallic cultural pessimism was foreign to both Hallstein and Michalski's reflection group. Hallstein insists that European unification 'is not inaccessible, even dismissive, but open'.[11] Michalski and his group emphasise repeatedly that the European cultural space is 'in principle open'. 'Europe and its cultural identity thus depend on a constant confrontation with the new, the different, the foreign...Europe's boundaries too must always be renegotiated.'[12]

Nevertheless it seems to me a mistake to set out to trace the concrete process of European cooperation and integration back to a deeper sense of identity or a higher idea. Even attempting to describe the unique character of the European cultural space highlights features that are not limited either historically or intellectually to Europe. This is particularly true of 'Enlightenment', a term which describes, simply but clearly, the core of any definition of a community of values. In both theory and practice, the Enlightenment includes America. At the same time, a place like Europe knows enough nooks and crannies which were only partially affected by such values. At times they were not even to be found in the very heart of Europe itself. *Sonderweg* or not, the German debate initiated by the likes of Fritz Stern back in 1963 with his dissertation on 'cultural pessimism as political danger' cannot simply be forgotten when the talk is of Europe.[13]

Europe stands above all for diversity. Praise of diversity does not necessarily mean, by the way, that unity has to be created; however, unity does mean that diversity is limited. It is also relevant to emphasise diversity in the context of that apparent concretisation of European identity taking place increasingly under the banner of the European social model. Comparing and contrasting Anglo-Saxon and Continental social indicators is neither accurate nor politically meaningful. A thorough empirical study carried out by Jens Alber shows that there is an extraordinary range of social models across the EU. Some are closer to, others further from, the American model. In important questions such as high regard for independence or the acceptance of inequality, France is particularly close to the USA. With a careful choice of words and close reference to empirical data, Jens Alber concludes that 'it became apparent that the differences within Europe are mostly greater than the difference between the European Union and the United States'.[14] In the light of a study such as Alber's, we might even conclude that if the USA belonged to the EU, its social model would not mean that it was out of step with other members.

Which is not to say that there are no significant differences between Europe and America. Why do we love de Tocqueville, if not for his portrayal of such differences? And there are certainly European interests which are not shared by America, including a large part of the EU's legal and internal affairs portfolio. And in foreign affairs there are European interests which complement but do not overlap with those of the USA. And yet even with Joseph S. Nye's now so popular distinction between hard and soft power, caution is called for.[15] In important questions (such as Iran's nuclear programme and peace in the Middle East) there is no soft power without the back-up of the hard, military variety. And anyway, France and the UK are unwilling to share even a quantum of their hard power with others, and the post-Communist countries knew quite well why they first had to join NATO and only then the EU.

Such considerations lead almost of necessity to cooperation between Europe and America. In any case, the confrontation which some seek nowadays is a mistake with serious consequences. And it is illusory to consider it a stimulus to European unification. As a consequence of a multipolar conception of the world, it is a dangerous betrayal of the shared values of the enlightened world. Jürgen Habermas is too subtly and too closely associated with American thought and thinkers to advocate such a crude position. And yet the general thrust of his 'Plea for a Common Foreign Policy, Beginning in the Heart of Europe' (published in collaboration with Jacques Derrida in May 2003) can only be read as a plea for an independent, emphatically non-American identity. Both the social model and opposition to hard power, particularly in the case of Iraq, lie at its heart.[16]

In the ensuing discussion, Timothy Garton Ash and I responded (in July 2003) with a wholly different stance. We spoke of the spirit of the practical Enlightenment and called for European renewal in this spirit. Garton Ash has since pursued this idea in his book *Free World*.[17] His book is so important because it transcends the old concept of the West and makes clear that we are talking about a fundamental attitude which can be applied universally. In view of the organisations of the world in which we live at the start of the twenty-first century, I have already alluded several times to the creation of a political parallel to the OECD, the Organisation for Economic Cooperation and Development. The dissemination of all that is called by the shorthand term 'democracy', i.e. the liberal world order in the sense of the EU's Copenhagen criteria, is a foremost task. It requires a community of existing democracies and in this respect would be an OPCD, Organisation for Political Cooperation and Development.

When all is said and done, Europe only makes sense if and insofar as it contributes to the development and spread of the liberal order. And it can only do this if it is open in two senses: open to all others in the world, starting with its neighbours, but also open in the character of its politics – from service directives to agricultural policy, from the treatment of asylum seekers to the fostering of innovation.

Habermas and Derrida, as well as Garton Ash and I, have called Kant as a witness. In the 200 years since his death, Immanuel Kant has – in the way of great thinkers – been claimed as their own by all kinds of interpreters, and so we may argue over authenticity. However, Garton Ash and I saw traces rather of Rousseau in Habermas and Derrida, or at least an Arcadian portrayal of the order of human affairs about which Kant had something to say in his *The Idea for a Universal History with a Cosmopolitan Intent*. In contrast, we adopted a tougher position, one which does not rule out a change of regime as an objective of international intervention. Europe is not to be aspired to as some peaceful welfare heaven but as the anticipation and model for an order with global validity. The European imperative is therefore: Act in such a way that everything you do can be valid as the principle of a universal order. Europe's success is to be measured in terms of its contribution to freedom in the world.

Is that enough? Ulrich Beck seems to hold a similar view in his *Das kosmopolitische Europa* (co-authored with Edgar Grande). His cosmopolitanism opens up a thoroughly attractive prospect since it 'combines an appreciation of difference and otherness with efforts to imagine new democratic forms of political rule beyond the nation-state'.[18] Beck, however, holds firm to the attempt to bring a united Europe – even a 'European Empire' – into the cosmopolitan context. I feel closer to the approach of Hermann Lübbe, who sees Europe as an organised interest group in a world in which, on the one hand, mutual dependencies exist across larger areas than Europe and, on the other, smaller states and communities see an increase in their 'right to self-determination and their chance of achieving it'.[19]

Once again, is that enough? Can such a Europe move or even inspire its citizens? The Europe being proposed here is a thoroughly political Europe, which entrusts its future neither to an inner logic nor to a world spirit. Its practical cohesion is guaranteed above all by what the British social economist Andrew Shonfield, speaking in the BBC Reith Lectures in 1972, called the growing habit of cooperation.[20] This habit both provides the prerequisites for a cooperation which can serve as a model of governance in the age of globalisation and acts as its permanent method.

My title, 'Unified or open? The European alternative', postulates an opposition which many will say is unnecessary. Why should Europe not strive for ever closer union while remaining open both inwardly and outwardly? Was this not the dream of all great Europeans? My conclusion, however, is that this combination is only ever the stuff of grandiloquent speechmaking. In practice, one has to decide. The Constitutional Treaty served unity, not openness. It is a good thing to have been spared it. Enlargement bespeaks openness, even if it does not necessarily promote unity. We should pursue it courageously and so bring hope to the still rudimentary states of the Western Balkans and strengthen the forces for an open society in Turkey, Ukraine and indeed in Europe itself.

Whether all this can inspire citizens remains an open question. Perhaps it cannot. But we will get nowhere if we set Europe up as a last Utopia, something the political right used to do and which is now the fashion on the left. Such seduction comes before a fall. It is not enough to follow Ludwig Erhard's example, either. In the German parliamentary debate on the EEC Treaty on 21 March 1957, the then minister for trade and commerce pulled apart the idea of a regional economic union, which could interfere with free world trade. He was applauded for saying that a thing did not become sacrosanct just because it bore the adjective 'European'. But then he performed a volte-face in order not to thwart Chancellor Adenauer's plans, declaring that he would vote for the EEC Treaty so that Europe's youth above all might trust in a happy Europe in the making.

So the contradiction between grandiloquent pronouncements on Europe and the reality of European unification is an old one. I believe that this contradiction is one of the reasons why many citizens today are turning away from organised Europe. That some supporters of European unification pursue their goal with passion is laudable, but that is not a sufficient reason to give priority to the goal itself. For my own part, freedom is the priority. I am a rational rather than a passionate European, but I am a passionate liberal. Europe only has a place in my passions if it opens wider the path to freedom. Closer union in Europe is only desirable in an open Europe. The cosmopolitan vision of universal freedom is therefore the benchmark of all politics in Europe.

Notes

1 This chapter is based on the Werner Heisenberg Lecture given by the author in Munich on 11 July 2005. Translated by Bernadette Boyle.
2 Hallstein 1973, p. 21.
3 Ibid. p. 24.
4 Stuart 2003, p. 16.
5 Here as elsewhere reference is to the EU and its preceding organisations, the European Community and the European Economic Community.
6 European Council, Final Conclusions of the Copenhagen Summit, EU Enlargement – An historic opportunity. Available at: http://europa.eu.int/comm/enlargement/intro/criteria.htm
7 Murray and Wanlin 2005.
8 Hallstein 1973, p. 14.
9 Quoted from the Reflection Group's report 'The Spiritual and Cultural Dimension of Europe'. Available at: http://europa. eu. int/comm/research/social-sciences/links/article_3336_en. htm
10 Steiner 2004, p. 34.
11 Hallstein 1973, p. 14.
12 Michalski 2005.
13 See Stern 1974.
14 Quoted from Alber 2005.

15 See Nye 2004.
16 The Habermas–Derrida paper along with numerous commentaries and responses – including the commentary by Garton Ash and myself referred to later – are to be found in Levy *et al.* 2005.
17 Garton Ash 2004.
18 Beck and Grande 2004, p. 25.
19 Lübbe 2005, p. 35. Francis Cheneval's position is also very close to mine. See Chevenal 2003.
20 See Shonfield 1973.

References

Alber, Jens, 2005, 'Das europäische Sozialmodell und die USA'. Text of a lecture given at the Forum of the Friedrich-Ebert-Stiftung on 28. February 2005, 'Europa sozial gestalten: Grundzüge und Chancen des Europäischen Sozialmodells'. Halle.

Beck, Ulrich and Edgar Grande, 2004, *Das kosmopolitische Europa*. Frankfurt/M: Suhrkamp.

Cheneval, Francis, 2003, 'Die kosmopolitische Transgressivität der modernen Demokratie', in (Georg Kohler, and Urs Marti (eds.), *Konturen der neuen Welt(un)ordnung*. Berlin/New York: de Gruyter, pp. 102–19.

Garton Ash, Timothy, 2004, *Free World*. London: Allen Lane.

Hallstein, Walter, 1973, *Die Europäische Gemeinshaft*. Düsseldorf/Wien: Econ.

Levy, Daniel, Max Pensky and John Torpey (eds.), 2005, *Old Europe – New Europe – Core Europe: Transatlantic Relations After the Iraq War*. London: Verso.

Lübbe, Hermann, 2005, 'Interessen und Werte. Die europäische Einigung und der neue Pragmatismus der Stimmbürger', *Neue Zürcher Zeitung*, 10 June, p. 35.

Michalski, Krzysztof *et al.*, 2005, Reflection Group's report 'The Spiritual and Cultural Dimension of Europe'. Available at: http://europa.eu.int/comm/research/social-sciences/links/article_3336_en. htm

Murray, Alasdair and Aurore Wanlin, 2005, *The Lisbon Scorecard V. Can Europe Compete?* London: Centre for European Reform.

Nye Jr, Joseph S., 2004, *Soft Power. The Means to Success in World Politics*. New York: Public Affairs Books.

Shonfield, Andrew, 1973, *Europe – Journey to an Unknown Destination*. London: BBC Publications.

Steiner, George, 2004, *The Idea of Europe*. Tilburg: Nexus Institute.

Stern, Fritz, 1974, *The Politics of Cultural Despair. A Study in the Rise of the Germanic Ideology.* Berkeley, CA: University of California Press.

Stuart, Gisela, 2003, *The Making of Europe's Constitution*. London: Fabian Society.

Index